CHANGE AND HARMONIZATION
IN EUROPEAN EDUCATION

*Published with assistance from
the Roger E. Joseph Memorial Fund
for greater understanding
of public affairs, a cause in which
Roger Joseph believed*

Change
and Harmonization
in European
Education

▼▼▼▼▼▼▼▼▼▼▼▼▼▼▼▼▼▼▼▼▼▼▼▼▼▼▼▼

ROBERT H. BECK

UNIVERSITY OF MINNESOTA PRESS □ MINNEAPOLIS

Library of Congress Catalog Card Number: 75-167299

ISBN 0-8166-0623-4

for MAEVE and CARL

The purpose of this book is to invite attention to changes in European education which are part of a growing "harmonization." Harmonization is an interesting term; European educators use it quite often. (The term *integration*, perhaps because of its connotations of uniformity, is employed with considerably less frequency.) Harmonization in education means that European educators are coming to agreement on how to cope with certain common, critical issues. It also means that there is increasing agreement that training in other countries should be equivalent to that in one's own.

No magic has brought about this increased harmonization. Three factors, all well identified, have been principal: greater communication among countries, common ideological commitments, and, most influential of all, a variety of economic challenges.

Perhaps the most effective promotion of harmonization through communication has been unintentional. Certainly the Comparative Education Society in Europe did not intend harmonization, but nevertheless it has provided a forum for the discussion of issues critical in most European countries. Some of these common challenges have been ideological in the main; others have been pretty much economic.

The ideological commitments should be perfectly understandable on this side of the Atlantic for we too have taken seriously the maximization and equalization of educational opportunity. Discrimination on the basis of race and ethnic identification may not be as familiar to Europeans as they are to citizens of the United States, but on both sides of the ocean there is reason to regret discrimination on the basis of wealth, sex, and the geographical residence of one's family. And Europeans, just like Americans, have been committed to winning more years of formal education for more and more young people. In a sense communication and ideological commitments have spanned the ocean, becoming important parts of a true Atlantic Community.

What applies to communication and ideology holds for the economic facts of life. Actually, economic forces have entered into much of the communication on educational issues and have reinforced the common commitments in ideology. Such ideologically inspired reforms as adding to compulsory schooling and transforming vocational education have found support in the practical demands for more and more highly trained manpower. The Organisation for Economic Co-operation and Development and the European Community have been particularly effective in broadcasting the educational implications of economic facts.

Significant changes in education have appeared on the European scene in the process of moving toward harmonization. Awareness of academic-vocational guidance — or at the least of guidance orientation wedged between the end of elementary schooling and the beginning of the upper levels of secondary school — is only one example. We already have mentioned maximization and equalization in educational opportunity and the addition of another year, or even two or three, to the conventional requirements of compulsory education. Even more striking has been the demand for more places in upper secondary and higher education. In addition there has been a cry for what the British call "parity of esteem" between general, academic education and vocational training. The German *bildung* (education) and *erzieung* (training) have moved closer together. But at the same time there has been a struggle to upgrade the status of vocational training, and in Eastern as well as in Western Europe vocational training increasingly has been reconstructed into technical education.

Educational reformers have pressed for such changes and have gained support for their proposals through the process of communication. We shall note the communication of professional educators gathered in such an institution as the College of Europe in Bruges, Belgium, and in such organizations as the European Teachers Association and the Comparative Education Society in Europe. An even more potent influence has been exerted directly by the Council of Cultural Co-operation of the Council of

Europe and indirectly by meetings of the Western European ministers of education.

The reader then will find that there have been many potent factors promoting simultaneous change and harmonization in European education. Considered as a package these changes and the process of harmonization have been powerful enough to transcend the philosophic, political, and economic boundaries which divide the USSR and the people's republics of Central and Eastern Europe from the countries of the West.

Only a romantic optimist, of course, would see a steady march toward reconstruction, especially toward harmonization, in the educational systems of Europe. To dream such a dream would indeed show one's self to be *traumverloren* and most naïve. Nevertheless, the nations of Europe are clearly moving along similar lines in the recasting of education and in the achievement of harmonization.

Finally, a brief word about usage. A work of this nature must of necessity use many terms from many languages, some of which have become familiar to readers of English and others not. For the sake of consistency therefore I have, after the first mention, treated the names of the various kinds of French, German, and Swedish schools and some other terms as though they were English-American words. For reasons of convenience too the German Democratic Republic and the Federal Republic of Germany are referred to throughout as East Germany and West Germany respectively.

Minneapolis, 1971   R. H. B.

ACKNOWLEDGMENTS

The generosity of the Hill Family Foundation of St. Paul, Minnesota, and the Office of International Programs of the University of Minnesota made it possible for the author to visit educators in many countries of Europe. Three men gave unsparingly of their time in advancing my study: H. Brugmans, College of Europe, Bruges; G. Connell, Directorate of Education and of Cultural and Scientific Affairs, Council of Europe, Strasbourg; and D. Kallen, Directorate of Scientific Affairs, OECD. The information freely provided by other educators, who are far too numerous to mention individually, is recognized with deep feelings of appreciation. The author wishes to note the indispensable aid given by Mrs. Jean Belden Taber, research assistant, without whom the project could not have been done.

I wish to acknowledge the unstinting aid given by personnel of the Education Library, Reference Service Department, and Map Division of the University of Minnesota Library. Special thanks are due to the administration of the College of Education, which has supported this project handsomely, and to Mrs. Barbara Krumm, Miss Trinidad Montero, Miss Jo-Ann Moody, Miss Mary Raymond, Miss Jeanne Schleh, and Miss Deborah Vigness, who shepherded the manuscript through its preparation. Miss Anne Marie Nelson and Miss Sandra Robin typed the final version of the manuscript; I am especially grateful to them. During this preparation Miss Josephine Zimmar made available the indispensable facilities of the Faculty Secretarial Office of the College of Education. The author's colleague, Emma Birkmaier, read the manuscript and offered invaluable suggestions. Finally, I wish to express gratitude to the Graduate School of the University which underwrote research assistance.

CONTENTS

TABLES

CHANGE AND HARMONIZATION
IN EUROPEAN EDUCATION

CHAPTER ONE

Communication and Coordination Part One

Cooperation and coordination increasingly characterize Europe and European education. There are several components of this new movement toward unity. One is the creation of formal organizations composed of ministers of education and other government officials from the West European nations. Such alliances as the Council of Europe are active and constructive.

A second element contributing to unity is the greater sharing of languages, especially English, French, and German, throughout Europe. Important in this respect are the special "European Schools," which enroll students from many countries and stress the exchange of languages and cultures. A third factor to be noted is the desire of many European countries to have their school systems correspond more closely to those of their neighbors. Many systems, for example, are adapting the "new mathematics" and the instrumentalist approach to the teaching of mathematics. Along similar lines "freedom of establishment" — that is, a student's ability to transfer his secondary-school academic credit from one country to another — is being urged for all Western Europe. So too is the standardization of the secondary-school leaving examination and its conversion into a European Baccalaureate, although, as we shall see, many uncertainties envelop the future of the leaving exam.

In the fourth place, the revision of geography, history, civics, and literature textbooks undoubtedly enhances harmonization, for the revised books present Europe as an interdependent community. Finally, the work of the European Association of Teachers in promoting European federation is an important force toward unity. In this chapter I will discuss all these supports for harmonization. In the next, I will highlight other steps toward integration, but will also delineate the handicaps to Europeanization — especially, of course, the tensions between Eastern and Western Europe.

The Council of Europe

Since 1945 Western European countries have joined together in various alliances in order to effect a harmonization of the European community. Two formal organizations which have made outstanding contributions to the ideal of unity in European education are the Organization for Economic Co-operation and Development (OECD) and the Council of Europe with its Council for Cultural Co-operation (CCC). The OECD, a consultative and coordinating organization, was formed in 1960. As its name implies, it is concerned primarily with matters of education insofar as they relate to economic development — the training of technical manpower, for example, or the costs of expanding a nation's school system. Certain projects of the OECD and some of its concerns with secondary education will be discussed in later chapters.

The Council of Europe, because of its important work in the coordination of activities and communication among European countries deserves more lengthy examination. Established in 1949 and now made up of almost twenty members, the council is distinguished by its political-cultural emphasis.[1] Working through the ministers of education of member countries (and their staffs), it grapples with common cultural, scientific, legal, and administrative issues. In order to focus on cultural issues, the ministers created the Council for Cultural Co-operation in 1962. The CCC deals with such diverse enterprises as the promotion of a European civics, the dissemination of films on the cultural life of Europe, the preservation of cathedrals and other cultural monuments, and the exchange of persons and materials among different countries.

The CCC has been given particular responsibility for increasing the dissemination of new ideas and techniques. For example, it has investigated teaching aids and the methodology of instruction. Today's teaching techniques include audio-visual aids such as films,[2] educational television, electronic language laboratories, and tape recorders. More important, beginning in 1963 the Council of Europe has organized an annual

Conference of (Western) European Ministers of Education. This group reviews the legislative and pedagogical prospects of employing research findings in classrooms and school systems. (There is no comparable agency in the United States or Canada.) The sixth conference of education ministers, held at Paris in May 1969, was attended by official representatives from twenty countries as well as by observers from the OECD and UNESCO. The conference's theme was "Education for All," a phrase which had proved to be the most magnetic topic for European educationists during the 1960's.[3]

Besides bringing together the ministers of education, the Council of Europe has cooperated in publishing an annual journal, *Paedagogica Europaea*, which has stimulated creation of adequate research components in European institutes for education. The council has helped to start documentation centers for education in Western Europe. (Such centers are also found in East European countries where the council has not been at work.)

The promotion of lifelong education (*l'éducation permanente*) has been another move toward harmonization. This idea is one shaped by the CCC and by the educator Laurent Capdecomme. Capdecomme writes: "The universities have become fully aware of the fundamental role that they have to play in keeping men and women abreast of the times in a period of increasingly rapid scientific and technical progress. In this work may be found the antidote to the disturbingly over-loaded curricula which tend to be imposed upon young people. It should enable pupils and students to have a choice of subjects; schools and faculties should be able to train minds rather than to cram knowledge. Many, although still somewhat sporadic, attempts have been made in engineering faculties and schools, by special courses and evening classes, to provide refresher courses for technicians and engineers, to bring their knowledge up to date. These give opportunities for further study and possibly for readaptation. The success of such measures depends largely on the relations between the universities and industry: these are becoming closer and mutual trust is growing, and in 1961 in connection with each University Council there was formed a committee for technical training and social advancement, including representatives of the university and of the economic sector. The problem of life-long education is regarded as so important that provision was made for the creation at the beginning of the 1962 session of a National Institute of Adult Education at Nancy University, as a development of the University Centre for Economic and Social Co-operation (C.U.C.E.S.), which has already fully established its worth on a regional level." [4]

Modern Language Teaching

For many years the European ministers of education have taken an interest in language studies as a means of harmonization. As early as their second and third conferences (Hamburg, 1961, and Rome, 1962), the ministers acted to increase support for modern language teaching. The CCC published *Modern Languages and the World of Today* (1967),[5] and at the end of the 1960's it recommended a highly intensified teaching program. Its recommendations embraced five areas:

1. Primary and secondary schools: the teaching of at least one widely spoken European language, beginning with pupils at about the age of ten; experimentation with the possibility of introducing instruction at the earliest practicable stage to younger children; the development of language courses using the most modern methods and technical facilities.

2. Institutions of higher education and other forms of post-secondary schooling: modernization of courses of study to ensure proficiency in the use of modern languages and a knowledge of the civilization of the countries concerned; the use of modern equipment for practicing languages and the arrangement of study visits abroad.

3. Adult education: the creation of facilities to enable all European adults to learn efficiently a language or languages of their choice.

4. Initial and in-service training of modern language teachers: the organization of courses on new teaching methods, on relevant findings in linguistic science, and on the effective use of modern teaching apparatus; the promotion of regular interchanges or study visits abroad; the provision of special training for teachers of adult classes.

5. Research: investigation into the factors affecting language learning and teaching for all ages and categories of learners; into the development of the most suitable materials and methods for teaching; into techniques of testing and evaluating language learning.[6]

The proposals of the CCC have not as yet been translated into actual practice. Most countries, however, are reaching for these goals. Certainly more and more nations are sharing common languages. In an article on language teaching in British schools (London *Daily Telegraph*, May 4, 1967), John Audric commented: "In the past five years the teaching of foreign languages in schools has had a sudden and sustained impetus . . . partly due to the belief that, sooner or later, Britain will enter the European Common Market and that a knowledge of languages will be necessary if we are to play an effective part." Audric felt that Britain would not be at a disadvantage in the Common Market, partly because so many teachers were graduates in modern languages. Audric gave the following figures: "all science subjects, 13,129; English, 12,386; Modern Language, 11,223; History, 9,824; Mathematics, 7,947; Geography, 5,775."

The cooperation on language programs between Germany and France, those traditional enemies, is also heartening. In 1968 Edgar Faure, French minister of education, met at Munich with Dr. Goppel, the minister plenipotentiary for cultural matters in the Federal Republic of Germany. The ministers noted that as a result of reforms then in progress German was being taught in French schools more widely than formerly, and that in Germany consideration was being given to strengthening the position of French as the first foreign language. Three practical programs were proposed at the ministerial meeting. One was an exchange between the two countries of twenty kindergarten teachers, with the aim of introducing young children to the language of another country. A second proposal related to the then-current German effort to present additional foreign language courses on television; it was suggested that representatives from both French and German broadcasting and from adult education programs should take part in the next conference.

In a third recommendation the ministers gave high priority to the establishment of Franco-German grammar schools. They agreed on the "introduction of bilingual features into existing schools," where concurrently with normal instruction there would "also be instruction given by exchange teachers in French in German schools and in German in French schools." There was "complete agreement between both parties on the introduction in these schools of a Franco-German Abitur [secondary-school leaving examination] which will be recognized in both countries." [7] These conversations and cooperative actions between France and Germany are supplemented by an effective agency, the Office Franco-Allemand pour la Jeunesse, whose German counterpart is the Deutsch-Französisches Jugendwerk. [8]

The harmonization of Europe, then, is being substantially aided through the teaching of languages other than the native one. At the end

7

of the 1960's, language exchanges, sponsored by formal agencies and especially by the Council of Europe, were common.

Special European Schools

Language exchanges, an obvious and vital stride toward Europeanization, are fostered by such schools as the so-called "European Schools," established for children whose parents are associated with the European Economic Community (or Common Market) and the European Atomic Energy Community. These schools have made the modern languages of Western Europe central in their curriculum. Though the European Schools (*Schola Europaea*) were originally established in 1957 to provide education for the children of EEC officials, and though they were founded in the six member states of West Germany, Belgium, France, Italy, Luxembourg, and the Netherlands, they are now open to students from throughout Europe. In 1969–70 the schools enrolled 7,500 pupils of many different nationalities.[9]

The objective of the European Schools has been to promote Europeanness and at the same time to avoid the eroding of patriotism.[10] The effort at communion in Europe need not assume disloyalty to one's country, nor necessitate being a European without a preference for the traditions of a motherland. On the other hand, nationalism need not prevent enjoyment of and profit from a culture common to all of Western Europe. The European Schools consciously work to balance mastery of the mother tongue with fluency in other European languages and in English (which is obligatory beginning with the third year of secondary school and continues for four years) and with mastery of a working language (either French or German).[11] Europeanists wonder when Russian will be added as a working language.

The primacy of the pupil's mother tongue is assured by dividing the primary school into four language groups — German, French, Italian, and Dutch. Three times as many hours are spent learning the native language as learning the working language if it is not native. An article in *Forward in Europe*, a publication of the Council of Europe, explains: "Each child entering the school at the age of six has to choose a 'mother-tongue.' It does not necessarily have to be German for a German boy. In fact, we have some German parents who want their children to be brought up in the French section and vice-versa. However, it must be one of these four

8

sections, even for those children who are not German, French, Italian, or Dutch.

"One completely new feature is that, from the very first day, the children have to learn a foreign language. Even though they do not yet know how to read and write their own tongue, they nevertheless learn German or French, the two most important languages of the Community. The Germans have to learn French, the French and Belgians have to learn German, and the Italians and Dutch have a choice."

Six hours a week are *heures européennes* (European hours), which the European School officials believe are indispensable to their philosophy of education. Working languages are used during these European hours, which are devoted to singing, drawing, gymnastics, and manual skills. The working language is also used in the teaching of history, geography, art history, and other subjects. No German boy has history lessons with a German teacher in German, but with Dutch and Italian children in French, and with a French teacher.[12]

The European Schools, we see, have pioneered in the sharing of languages which the ccc has repeatedly recommended. The ccc's resolution at a conference in May 1969, for example, stated the belief "that if full understanding is to be achieved among the countries of Europe, the language barriers between them must be removed . . . that only if the study of modern European languages becomes general will full mutual understanding and co-operation be possible in Europe." [13]

Freedom of Establishment

Besides the sharing of languages and the setting up of special European Schools, "freedom of establishment" is an additional step toward European unity.[14] Many people have urged that the secondary school systems of different nations correspond more closely to each other, so that a student can easily transfer his academic credit from one country to another and thus re-establish himself. It has been noted for example, that "owing to the high degree of abstraction in French mathematics teaching, German engineering students who have taken their preliminary diploma are *not* at present able to take part in the first year studies in a *grand école*. On the other hand, they are perfectly capable of entering on French second year studies, as at this stage applied mathematics is called for." [15]

Certainly differences between school systems exist. The English economist John Vaizey correctly observes that the "quality of education obviously varies substantially from country to country. It is one's impression that the *studentexamen* in Sweden, for example, approximates in intellectual level (although not necessarily in the contents of subjects) to the standard of two A levels in Britain." Vaizey asks: "Is it possible to develop a system of comparison of international qualifications which will enable a much closer comparison of the rate of output of qualified people in different countries to be made? People will say that education in each country is so idiosyncratic, so peculiar to that country, that these comparisons are always subject to major qualifications. Nevertheless, the fact remains that doctors, engineers and people of high professional skill are allowed to practice in foreign countries, that their qualifications are approximated, and it seems to me that more comparisons of this sort would enable valid judgements to be made." [16] Such comparisons are being made, and European nations are striving for freedom of establishment and for equivalence in subject matter.

A first and rather idealistic step toward freedom of establishment was taken by France in the Orientation of Higher Education Act of 1968. Article 2 of Title I, "The Aim of Higher Education," is exclusively devoted to "very close ties" at least with the universities of EEC member nations: "The universities and the national and regional institutions . . . are to take on, within the framework determined by the Government, the initiatives and to make the provisions necessary to organize and develop international university cooperation, particularly with universities of those countries which are members of the European Economic Community." [17]

Useful progress has been made by country-to-country agreements. Jean Murat, for example, describes work done by representative rectors of French and German universities. Since the rectors are appointed by the university faculty from their own ranks and for periods of less than five years, their conclusions are an adequate expression of faculty thought. The Germans and French felt that what Murat terms "global equivalence" had been achieved. That is, over all, French and German secondary-school leaving examinations were held to be equivalent. It was hoped that "partial equivalence" within the exams could also be achieved — that portions of a German test and a French test cover the same texts; for example, "by an additive process two *Proseminarscheine* or two *Hauptseminarscheine* might be held to give evidence equivalent to the oral tests for the certificate of *Etudes Supérieures de Philologie Allemande*." [18]

10

Problems of Franco-German equivalence were also discussed at the 1968 meeting, mentioned above, between Ministers Faure of France and Goppel of West Germany.[19] Goppel requested that Faure present to the competent authorities in France the viewpoints of Germany on the training of engineers in both countries and on the recognition of their qualifications within the EEC. Faure suggested that an expert commission should be asked to prepare a study of the training and examination procedure in both countries so that joint Franco-German action on this question would be possible.

Though the idea of freedom of establishment has been a goal of the EEC,[20] two series of publications by the CCC, "Education in Europe" and "Companion Volumes," have done the real spadework in reconstruction of curriculum which is essential for freedom of establishment. In 1968 a CCC program to increase freedom of establishment was developed for the university teaching of physics. A survey in twenty member countries of the CCC resulted in the report *The Teaching of Physics at University Level*.[21] While the council lacks the legal authority to champion officially an innovation or an especially successful project, the report publicized promising developments in physics programs which, it is to be hoped, will bring the countries with the least well-developed programs of physics up to those with higher standards. The *Information Bulletin* of the CCC expressed a wish "that the report may serve physics training in European universities, enabling particularly interesting or favorable conditions and developments in certain branches or countries to be recognized. This may also facilitate freedom of movement of academically trained physicists between the different member countries." [22] Other similar studies in the CCC's Education in Europe series are *Engineering Education* (1964), Guy Ourisson's *The Teaching of Chemistry at University Level* (1966), and Jean Leclerq's *How to Qualify as a "Biologist" in the Universities of Europe* (1967).

Some Europeans, however, recoil from the curricular homogeneity which is sponsored by the CCC and others. They fear that academic standards will be lowered. To alleviate this fear and to spur freedom of establishment, a series of European curriculum studies was inaugurated with the support of the CCC. In the first of these studies, published in 1968 and devoted to mathematics, the Oxford University Department of Education (under the direction of W. D. Halls and Doreen Humphreys)[23] analyzed the academic secondary curriculum of the CCC member countries.

Equivalence and the Study of Mathematics

The Halls and Humphreys report on mathematics covered six areas: aims, specific objectives, syllabuses, method, academic secondary leaving examinations (as distinct from vocational and technical leaving examinations), and teachers in academic secondary schools.[24] What were their findings? They write: "It [mathematics] is one of the few subjects studied in the academic secondary school by all pupils for at least the first four or five years of the course, and in many countries right up to the time of leaving school. It is also one of the few subjects for which a qualification, either at a higher or a lower level of study, is required in practically every country, before a pupil can proceed to higher education." [25]

Halls and Humphreys reported that European secondary schools, in a step toward harmonization and freedom of establishment, were rapidly adopting the "new mathematics" and were arriving at a "new conception of the unity of the subject," which entailed a good deal of syllabus revision. "Artificial division of the subject into elements such as 'algebra', 'geometry', 'calculus' etc." they wrote, "militates against the logical unity of the subject. Instead, pupils are now often presented with problems which, for example, may only be resolved by using algebra, arithmetic and trigonometry at one and the same time." [26]

The authors found a great deal of agreement on the aims of mathematics taught in the six countries' academic secondary schools, agreement that is, of course, significant for harmonization of European education. Halls and Humphreys note: "Mathematics should . . . be taught, all countries agree, from the *instrumentalist* viewpoint. By this is meant not only the use of mathematics in the day-to-day business of life, but also the use of the subject in other academic fields of knowledge, particularly science, technology, sociology and economics." There was also accord on the untested assumption that mathematics imparts a mental training to pupils who study it. "Among the qualities which are alleged to be sharpened by mathematics are pre-eminently logic (mentioned by no less than five countries), imagination and creativity (mentioned by three countries), and qualities of precision, clarity, resourcefulness and judgment." All countries stressed the "value of mathematics as a means of developing the powers of expression," for, after all, mathematics is precise.[27]

Despite the general agreement on theoretical aims, there was little uniformity in the mathematics topics actually taught in academic secondary schools. A sampling survey of fifteen nations indicated that a surprisingly small number of 180 concrete topics listed in a checklist were studied in most of the countries. "This lack of consensus between countries is all the more surprising when one considers that it is normally from the most socialised mathematics sections in the secondary school that are drawn the specialist university students in mathematics." [28] Harmonization has obviously not yet occurred on the practical level.

Information gathered from the countries studied enables us to predict the syllabus of the near future. Modern mathematics is increasingly characterized by a "concentration upon set theory and vectors. Some countries are also beginning to introduce probability theory and statistics." [29] The technique used by teachers of mathematics is also changing. As French educators put it: "The active method is important — the retention of a certain number of ideas and facts which have not always been fully understood does not contribute to the pupil's intellectual training. Every pupil must participate effectively in the [mathematics] lesson. Much of the activity of the pupil should be devoted to the study and search for the solution of problems. . . . In this way the ability of each pupil to apply what he has learned can be effectively followed; the development of this ability should be one of the main objectives of a 'cultural education.' " [30]

What generalizations can be made about European progress toward equivalence and harmonization in the field of mathematics? Our first observation is that what Halls and Humphreys found in Western Europe can also be observed in Eastern and Central Europe. In all countries of advanced technology, mathematics is — and will be — in great demand in the labor market; occupations calling for skill in mathematics will pay well. Students in the social sciences will find that there is an increasing demand for knowledge of at least some statistical theory and of the techniques of both design of experiment and analysis of results. It is safe to predict that the new mathematics and the activity method will continue to gain ground.

The obstacles blocking equivalence and freedom of establishment are not great. Where there are national differences in educational patterns, the problems often are manageable through consultation. An example of such communication is the November 1968 conference in Bad Godesberg, Germany, of the Joint Committee of the French Grandes Ecoles and the German Institutes of Technology. At this meeting conferees made comparisons of courses of study and proposed exchanges in the subjects of structural engineering, electrotechnics, machine construction, agriculture, chemistry, physics, and mathematics.[31]

The Secondary-School Leaving Examination

Equivalence of school course work can be achieved in still another way. The European Schools, mentioned previously because of their stress on modern foreign languages, are the first to have a *European* secondary-school leaving examination, the famous European Baccalaureate. The Regulations of the European Baccalaureate (part of the agreements giving the European Schools their legal status) explicitly require that graduates of the schools prepare for a European baccalaureate acceptable in each country that signed the agreement.[32] The equivalence of secondary-school leaving examinations is, of course, closely related to freedom of establishment. Many enthusiastic internationalists have looked beyond the European baccalaureate to an international baccalaureate. It was logical that the two should develop under the same aegis, as indeed they have done.[33]

The International Baccalaureate Office (IBO), which has its headquarters in Geneva, has recently evolved a secondary-school leaving examination which is accepted by virtually all the universities in England and Wales, by all the Swedish universities, by the Standing Conference of German Ministers of Education (which means acceptance by the West German universities), and in Switzerland by the universities of Geneva, Lausanne, and Zurich, and the Institute of Economic and Social Sciences of Saint Gall. In France, however, each case is considered individually, and the International Baccalaureate does not apply to French students unless their parents have lived abroad "for a period." [34]

The International Baccalaureate, a pilot project presently conducted in about fifteen schools, should be regarded as an experiment.[35] W. D. Halls of Oxford University has directed the research effort,[36] which began in 1962 with a preliminary experiment financed by UNESCO to secure the harmonization of history syllabuses in international schools. An IBO bulletin describes the progress: "The first Trial Examinations began in 1964 with volunteer candidates who were at the same time sitting for a national examination — examinations on this basis will continue in 1969. The first full official examinations will take place in 1970 at the

14

end of a two-year course which began in the . . . academic year 1968–
69. . . . The experiment will continue until June 1976, by which time
it should be possible to assess results. . . . Meanwhile, with the cooperation of Governments and Universities in several leading countries, provisional agreements have been reached which will enable holders of the
International Baccalaureate to secure places in institutions of higher education on the same basis as the holders of national diplomas." [37]

The success and acceptance of the International Baccalaureate has
complemented the support for the European Baccalaureate. In both cases
national boundaries of secondary-school education have been transcended. In working for the same goal, those associated with the International
Baccalaureate and the European Baccalaureate have enjoyed the support
of the CCC and the aid of the Research Centre at Oxford University.

In all European nations the secondary-school leaving examinations
have traditionally been highly valued, for a pupil's score on them is presumed to indicate his degree of mastery of secondary education and may
give entrance to all faculties of a university (as in Germany, Austria,
Switzerland, and Spain) or to particular faculties (the German *Fakultats-
reife*).[38] As a supposed indicator of academic readiness for the university,
the score has been heavily relied upon by admission directors. Recently,
however, a number of criticisms of the test have been heard throughout
Europe.[39] Some educators claim that the rating cannot predict a student's
future academic success and that it is only a certification of knowledge
attained in secondary school and a demonstration of the quality of the
pupil's rhetorical expression. Science faculties too have begun to acknowledge the imprecision of the leaving exam and are supporting separate
examinations for admission to the university.

The French *baccalauréat* has been called an "obsession des candidats,"
"terreur des familles . . . générateur des scènes de ménage," but, above
all, an unfair examination that a number of presumably select candidates
fail.[40] It is divided into two parts, the first given in the sixth year when
students generally are seventeen years old, the second in the terminal
seventh year when most students are eighteen. In the decade 1950–60
an incredible 44 percent of the candidates failed Part I and 35 percent
failed Part II.[41] The number of successful students has increased in the
past decade; in the latter half of the sixties the usual percentage of those
passing ranged between 60 and 65, but these figures are not completely
trustworthy for France frequently modifies the test.

In various ways the power of the leaving examination is being attacked or reduced. Centers for psychological and pedagogical research offer other techniques for predicting success in the university. With Aldo Agazzi's excellent description of how to select and classify pupils who apply for admission to universities,[42] European educators no longer need to rely totally on the leaving examination scores. Some universities have adopted admission policies which include their own examinations; such a plan is now practiced at Oxford and Cambridge.

The leaving exam, then, may be disappearing. If it is supplanted by a fairer European or International Baccalaureate, harmonization and freedom of establishment will be enhanced. On the other hand, the leaving exam may give way to a more specialized examination which is administered by each country. The long-range effects on the unification of European education are difficult to ascertain, for the test itself is being altered. Among nineteen countries, eleven are contemplating an immediate reform in the examinations, six foresee reform in the next four or five years, and only two do not have tests under study.[43]

Textbook Revision

Although the future of the leaving examination is uncertain, revision of textbooks can be recognized as a most positive addition to Europeanization. The CCC has again led the way with its sustained efforts since World War II to reduce national bias in geography and history textbooks and in the maps of Europe.

In geography texts, for instance, distortion is apt to lie in a patterning by national boundaries and in a failure to reveal the common problems, opportunities, and resources of the European community. To correct this distortion, in the mid-sixties the European Economic Community asked I. B. F. Kormoss of the College of Europe at Bruges, Belgium, to prepare maps showing administrative regions and units, population density, land utilization and main crops, livestock and fishing, energy and steel, and aspects of industry, transportation, and external trade for the Common Market countries. By 1967 more than a quarter million of the completed maps had been requested by European schools. The pupils and teachers who use Kormoss's *The European Community in Maps* are encouraged to think beyond a single nation to a region and to a larger, interdependent community – if only the community of the six. The maps show, for example, that coal which is mined in one country is not only consumed by

16

individuals and industries in that country but is also bought by another country in order to produce, say, steel. The finished product may then be shipped back to the first country. With such a demonstration, the pupil sees how a coal and steel "community" develops because of the interdependence of countries.

Distortions in geography are also being attacked in conferences. An illustration is the monograph and maps reported as *La Première Conférence sur la Révision des Manuels de Géographie: Résultats et Pérspectives,* published in 1962, and the *Conférence des Régions de l'Europe du Nord-Ouest* held three years later.[44] The proceedings of these two conferences were published in French, German, and Dutch-Flemish; the information flows, we see, across national and linguistic boundaries.

In 1968 the CCC complemented Kormoss's pioneering work with the publication of E. C. Marchant's *Geography Teaching and the Revision of Geography Textbooks and Atlases.*[45] After reviewing some of the types of maps needed for the most effective study of European geography, Marchant pinpoints the standard errors in textbooks and atlases which take a narrowly national view of resources and the uses made of them. Such nationalistic interpretation is now recalled bitterly as a cause of European wars, for example, the conflicts of France and Germany over the Saar's coal resources. (The location of the Council of Europe in Strasbourg has been a continuous reminder that Strasbourg, now a French city, was once a part of Germany.)

The revision of history textbooks has also been a challenge to the CCC. A giant step was taken in 1960 when the CCC oversaw the publication of Edouard Bruley's and E. H. Dance's *A History of Europe?* [46] This work demonstrates how the idea of Europe can be made central in a history text without either belittling any one nation — thus undermining patriotism — or, on the other hand, denigrating the rest of the world.[47]

UNESCO has likewise attacked provincialism in textbooks of history and geography. By financing educational planning and organizations such as the International Universities Bureau, UNESCO has helped to widen the horizons of youth and adults so that they can see the community of all mankind. UNESCO's aim is to impart an international spirit of brotherhood.

This international spirit is surely growing, as Bruley and Dance have pointed out.[48] The same pan-European outlook also permeated six conferences which, with the backing of the Council of Europe, were held

17

between 1953 and 1959 on the theme of European history.[49] Sections of these conferences transcended European history and examined every historian's largely unconscious and national bias. These breaks with and criticisms of conventional historical categorizations, we predict, will continue. Though discussed first by professional historians, the new interpretations have already become practically available for teachers in textbooks (probably too numerous to be screened by professional historians) and in model lessons, which have been prepared for and circulated by the Council of Europe.[50]

The revision of history and geography textbooks has had a long history. In 1949 Georg Eckert led the German resumption of an international textbook review which had been interrupted in 1933. On Easter 1951 the first Anglo-German history teachers' conference was held at the Kant-Hochschule in Brunswick, and the conferees created the Institute for International Textbook Revision. In 1953 the Ministry of Culture of Lower Saxony adopted responsibility for the institute, which has been the national center of all attempts to revise textbooks, particularly history books, in West Germany.[51]

More and more such national centers for the revision of geography and history textbooks are being formed. For example, in September 1965 a resolution adopted by the CCC called for the creation of national information and documentation centers in all countries in order to improve history and geography textbooks.[52] The CCC also adopted a resolution in 1965 expressing the opinion that these centers should be coordinated and that the institute at Brunswick, "which has had long experience and is unanimously appreciated, is particularly well placed to act as the coordinating body." [53] Such an international body will take years to form but several impressive national centers have already been created. Otto-Ernst Schüddekopf, one of the deans of textbook revision, provides a list of them: "In Switzerland there are the excellent institutions of the former League of Nations in Geneva, which are not, however, of national character. In Antwerp, Malines, Belgium, L. Th. Maes has been developing the *Centre Pédagogique d'Histoire Actuelle Internationale* (*Pedagogisch Centrum van Actuele Internationale Geschiedenis*) that has been devoted to the educational aspects of history since 1914. Textbook libraries exist, of course, in many countries, but it is part of their character not to concern themselves with current problems of textbook revision. It should, however, be one of the future tasks of the European

Textbook Centre to encourage contacts between these separate institutions in order to gain an overall impression on what older textbook collections exist in Europe." [54]

But textbook revision, though vastly important, is not sufficient in itself for the harmonization of education in Europe. Problems exist. Indeed, as Schüddekopf has pointed out, there should be "better textbooks instead of textbook revision." [55] There are few geography and history books in Europe, in his opinion, containing "judgments that deliberately do harm to other nations." But this is not all that could be desired. Ideally there should be a way to review history textbooks before printing and a way to correct mistakes after publication — yet publishers and authors often resist such corrections.[56] And textbook revision, though aimed at harmonization, is still sometimes defeated by nationalistically inspired doubt: "Even today," Schüddekopf reports, "fear of an unsuitable uniformity and the anxiety that the special features of national history might be lost altogether make many historians and history teachers reluctant to write and teach history from a European point of view. Nevertheless we do feel that we have proceeded a little further than the situation of the interwar years. There are signs today of a European approach to history that often simply occurs by force of circumstances. . . . We constantly talk about overcoming nationalist thinking in history books but far too little has been done hitherto in this direction. If one goes right back to the tradition of the European tribes, who by joining up in different national States formed the Europe of today but were then overtaken by exaggerated centralist tendencies — and this applies to all the European national States — and if one then links this up with the future, namely with a United Europe, we should find a way of making good the mistakes of the recent past and freeing the so urgently needed constructive force." [57]

Yet another stumbling block to textbook revision is the resistance of Eastern Europe. Although East European nations have sent representatives to a number of the more than one hundred conferences that have been held in Europe on textbook revision, the socialist camp has hurled criticism. Schüddekopf writes that such criticism "is largely of a political nature and is therefore liable to fluctuate sharply according to the political climate prevailing. To a great extent these States fail to recognize the real facts of textbook revision . . . and they apply the rigid hierarchy of their own educational system to Western Europe, arriving at misjudgements like the following: 'the West German International Textbook Institute manipulates the contents of textbooks.'[58] . . . these States . . . suspect the attempts to rectify textbooks in Western Europe of being part of an anti-Communist aggressive ideology led by the Institute in Brunswick."[59] Thus the harmonization of Western and Eastern textbooks is now only a dream.

Yet harmonization toward civics, at least in Western Europe, is a reality. In civics textbooks, as in geography and history textbooks, the European community is being stressed. Indeed, the ministers of the Council of Europe formally adopted a resolution in 1964 which stated that the imperative duty of secondary schools was to implant an understanding of European facts and problems.[60] Two years later a book by René Jotterand, *Introducing Europe to Senior Pupils*, was ready for distribution to European teachers.[61] The book was one of several responses to the belief of Pierre Duclos that "Europe will only come into being when it exists in the hearts and consciousness of men."[62] Jotterand, secretary general of the Department of Education of the Canton of Geneva, presented a practical approach to European cultural education by giving teachers illustrative materials for instruction. Even a critic of Jotterand's formal class approach acknowledges that "those who work in a less systematic framework [than Jotterand's formal class instruction] should, nevertheless, derive great benefit" from the book and its concomitant materials.[63]

Jotterand knew there could not be a totally European civics "since no homogeneous European society as yet exists as a basis for study comparable to the national civics traditionally taught in many countries." But in the "temporary absence" of a European citizenship he used the term *European civics* "to signify an awareness of being a member of a larger unit than one's own country and the duties and responsibilities devolving from this."[64] Jotterand's text obviously will have to be taken as propaganda for the integration of Western Europe, for it demonstrates a conviction that there can be one Europe, albeit Western, without a loss of patriotism. Jotterand's book, then, is the analogue of the ideal textbook on European history which was sketched by Bruley and Dance. Jotterand requests students to think of their allegiance in terms of concentric circles: "In a mounting progression from municipality to county or province, and then to country, the scope of syllabuses and textbooks should also extend to Europe and the world which form, as it were, the fourth and fifth concentric circles."[65]

There may be more steps between Western Europe and the world than

Jotterand envisaged. If there are, that would not make Jotterand's book useless, but would only show how dynamic the subject of civics really is and how close it is to the core of education in modern Europe and certainly to the schooling of young men and women on the verge of citizenship.

The importance of civics was highlighted in a lecture presented at the College of Europe in 1966, during a three-day conference on the theme "Europe Tomorrow and Its Responsibilities." Bertrand Schwartz projected civics as an essential part of general education for all. Noting that the responsibility of his school, the Ecole des Mines de Nancy, was to prepare professional engineers, Schwartz asked the rhetorical question: Why a general education and what is the place of civics in it? Most of the particulars of Schwartz's answer must be left to his essay, but his concluding paragraph may be one of the best defenses for *civisme* in the education of the Western European: "Have I put culture into its ultimate form and is it civically oriented? Perhaps, if I have developed the autonomy of man in cultivating his depth of reflection. Perhaps, if his culture is more attached to contemporary life. Perhaps, if I have developed give and take, and thus, if man has become more communicative and simultaneously more independent; if he works more with others — more integratedly for closer rapport. Perhaps, if the nonscientific and nontechnical aspects of the scientific and technical framework have revealed man's worth." [66]

Besides the Europeanizing of textbooks in geography, history, and civics, the presentation of literature is also being altered to show a larger perspective. In 1966 the Centre International d'Etudes Pédagogiques at Sèvres held a conference devoted to the teaching of literature in the senior grades of the European secondary schools. A European style in writing, painting, and music was emphasized. Denis de Rougemont commented: "In this domain, everything is in common. Among other things we would cite: the epic, the novel, comedy . . . the ballad, sonnet, the rhymes, the strophes. . . . In painting: the use of the easel peculiarly European. . . . Analogous remarks could be made about music. . . . In brief, this basic structural similarity is not perceived simply because it is too evident." [67] New textbooks will surely reflect de Rougemont's view and he will be seen as an ideological leader in the European orientation of textbooks. The Centre International d'Etudes Pédagogiques at Sèvres, on the outskirts of metropolitan Paris, has been a major focus of this ideal, and for professional educators visiting Europe from Canada and the United

States it has been their first introduction to harmonization and Europeanization in European education.[68]

The European Association of Teachers

Although the Centre at Sèvres and the Council of Europe have made inestimable contributions to a pan-European education, teachers also deserve much credit. The European Association of Teachers (EAT) was founded in 1956.[69] Its members are elementary and secondary school teachers and administrators, as well as staff members from colleges and universities for teacher training. The EAT's four basic aims are: "(1) to create among teachers an awareness of European problems and to disseminate information which has a bearing on the realization of European federation; (2) to work by all available means towards a deeper understanding of those essential qualities which are characteristic of European civilization and to ensure their preservation; notably by increasing the number of international contacts at the personal level; (3) to develop a similar understanding among the pupils and in all other fields where the teacher may exert an influence; (4) to support all activity directed to this end and to collaborate with other organizations which have similar international objectives."

In its brochure the EAT further explains its goals: "As teachers we are concerned to bring up young people so that they will be able to become useful and happy members of their profession and their society. But the present is a time of rapid change in the world, and these changes impose upon us a double task. We must, in our teaching, take account of new developments and, further, we must endeavor, through education, to influence those developments. Perhaps the most important development of the present day is the emergence of a new harmony and the interdependence among the countries of Europe. A new community is developing and it is vitally necessary that we should equip young people to play their part in it as free men and women. This community is Europe. . . . Within Europe the way of life and the respect for freedom which have characterized its peoples must be preserved. In a wider context Europe must be able to help shape events beyond its borders. . . . But to preserve its identity and play a full role in the world the rivalries and quarrels of the past must be forgotten."

To achieve this new community of Europe, the EAT plans a number of practical activities: one-day and weekend conferences, lecture series, study groups, the publication of a national bulletin, and the organization of meetings between educators from the different member countries. Such events are obviously invaluable for increasing the spirit of the European community. These events, along with textbook revision, a possible standardization of the leaving exam, the trend toward freedom of establishment, the greater coordination of school subjects (especially mathematics), the establishment of the special European Schools, the increased teaching of modern languages, and the efforts of the Council of Europe are all roads leading to harmonization of European education.

CHAPTER TWO

Communication
and Coordination
Part Two

Other roads lead to communication and coordination. This chapter focuses first on formal studies and university courses in Western European integration and their dramatic growth in recent years. Then we shall look at the first postgraduate institution for the specialized study of European affairs, the College of Europe at Bruges, Belgium. A third and complementary force has been the work of the Comparative Education Society in Europe, which draws its membership from both East and West Europe and studies problems confronting *all* European countries. It is undeniable, however, that ideology divides the two parts of Europe, and a sober appraisal of this ideological split is essential. So too is an examination of the divisive effects of internal linguistic struggles in Ireland, Norway, Belgium, Yugoslavia, and Greece.

The spectacular interest in university courses dealing with the European community and its problems has been a vital force promoting harmonization of education. To be sure, the European Economic Community (and its Commission) have not yet been able to realize the dream of establishing a university which would concentrate on teaching and research in European integration.[1] Instead of a university, the EEC Commission in 1958 was able to create the European Community Institute for University Studies, a private organization devoted to the initiation of teaching and research on European problems and European integration. Though unfortunately the institute has never been adequately funded,[2] it has been able to publish several volumes of *University Studies on Euro-*

370.94 B388c
c. 1

pean Integration. The contents of these reports doubled in size between 1965 and 1967, a testimony to the attention which European universities were giving the studies. By 1969 there were so many university courses and activities dealing with European integration that the institute limited its publication to a report of research. Its series is now supplemented by the small monthly journal *Nouvelles Universitaires Européennes*,[3] edited by F. De Fontaine, a leader in the reconstruction of French higher education and a steady contributor to movements toward European integration. The journal provides *University Studies on European Integration* with lists of courses and seminars on European themes which occur throughout the year.

As recently as 1950 no one reported studies of European integration, if indeed there were any. The meetings and colloquiums that took place during the years 1953 to 1958 were the first formal beginnings of the studies that flourish today. It was not until the first half of the 1960's that universities developed policies for the serious study of the many, varied, and often quite new juridical, economic, and political problems that have arisen because of the European communities, the best known of which is the Common Market. By 1960 the European Community Institute for University Studies was ready both to report on and to encourage such studies. The accompanying tabulation shows the increase in courses and seminars presented in various European countries. The growth of studies in Italy, it might be noted, is truly remarkable.[4]

Country	1964–65	1965–66	1966–67
France	59	69	73
Belgium	17	26	30
Germany	32	40	45
Italy	10	21	27
Netherlands	4	10	15
Great Britain	11	32	33
Switzerland	12	17	13
Total	145	215	236

Academicians on both sides of the Atlantic have become interested in European studies. When, for example, a colloquium on industrial policy and the contribution of foreign capital in integrated Europe was held in Paris in May 1966, no one was surprised that economists and representatives of the business community from the United States were present.[5] It has often been said that some of the strongest advocates of European integration live in the United States. This thesis would be difficult to document, but it is a simple fact that universities in this country have shown

25

much interest in European problems. Specialized postgraduate institutes at Harvard, Columbia, and Michigan have been conducting extensive research into the legal, economic, and political aspects of European integration.[6] Johns Hopkins University has a Center for Advanced International Studies at Bologna, Italy, with one of the best libraries in Europe on problems of European integration, and there are a number of other important centers on the continent which study the same problems.[7]

The European Cultural Foundation, located in Amsterdam, initiated in 1968 a far-reaching collaborative project called "Plan Europe 2000" which will involve many scholars in education and the social sciences in a long-range exploration of prospects for European society. The plan calls for five years of research, studies, and conferences. According to a recent account, the design encompasses "four comprehensive 'projects' (each subdivided into numerous 'studies') and an antecedent set of sixteen 'prospective studies.' " The four major research programs are: (1) Educating Man for the Twenty-first Century; (2) Man and Industrialism of the Future; (3) Urbanization: Planning Human Environment in Europe; and (4) Rural Society in the Year 2000. Prospective studies for these projects are now under way.[8]

Despite doubts among faculties, the body of material to be studied has grown steadily since the first stirring of a European community. The economic community has certainly not atrophied. As H. Lesguillons writes: "This tendency [growth of an economic community] was naturally boosted by the success of the Messina negotiations and the ratification of the two new treaties signed at Rome in March, 1957." [9] The first academic studies soon appeared in the universities, a trickle that was to become the flow reported in *University Studies on European Integration*. Without spelling out the reasons, we will take the year 1958 as a starting point for the establishment of university institutes on juridical, economic, social, and political aspects of European integration.[10]

In the early 1960's there was a lack of institutional arrangements for dialogue between students working on European political theory and behavior and those studying contractual arrangements, licensing, and so forth. Similarly, literary and other humanistic responses to European integration were not necessarily coordinated with the responses of other faculties. Contact was informal and very much a matter of chance. Lesguillons had this in mind when he wrote: "The efforts which did finally lead to the mapping out of a consistent university policy were . . . the result of a series of private moves which were gradually all linked together." [11]

As research and teaching of European studies developed, a new opportunity was perceived and has been imaginatively exploited. *University Studies on European Integration* is concrete evidence of this exploitation. This publication, it has been pointed out, has "done much to develop contacts between research workers of the same or different nationality engaged in similar or related subjects. Such contacts have often led to the establishment of permanent links and in some cases have given rise to joint action such as the holding of colloquia. Indeed the annual list has become an essential tool for all those concerned with European activities in the universities." [12] There is vigorous research on European integration, though these studies have lacked an emphasis on the harmonization of education.

Table 1 indicates the number of theses on legal, economic, and political aspects of European affairs, either in preparation or completed, for the years 1965 and 1966. (As the term is used here, a "thesis" is approximately equivalent to a doctoral dissertation in Canada or the United States.) It will be noted that the year 1966 shows a substantial increase. In the five countries of West Germany, Belgium, France, Italy, and the Netherlands, a total of 340 theses on European integration were completed or in preparation in 1965, while the corresponding figure for 1966 was 503, an increase in one year of 26.5 percent. The four subjects which

Table 1. Number of Theses on European Affairs

Country	In Preparation		Completed		Total	
	1965	1966	1965	1966	1965	1966
Germany	150	166	22	36	172	202
Belgium	12	14	. . .	1	12	15
France	85	100	19	25	104	125
Italy	18	72	26	71	44	143
Netherlands	8	12	. . .	6	8	18
Great Britain	12	15	2	. . .	14	15
Switzerland	2	10	. . .	4	2	14
Poland	. . .	9	. . .	. . .	. . .	9
Austria	. . .	5	. . .	. . .	. . .	5
United States	14	29	3	4	17	33
Greece	. . .	5	. . .	. . .	. . .	5
Total	301	437	72	147	373	584

SOURCE: Adapted by permission from *University Studies on European Integration*, No. 3, 1966, p. xvi.

27

received the most attention from students and researchers were, in order of popularity: community versus municipal law, competition and taxation, agriculture, and the European court of justice. Studies of the political consequences of integration, while still few, are expected to increase in number. The relative lack of student emphasis on political aspects of integration reflects the fact that it is the faculties of economics and law which have displayed the greatest interest in the impact of integration on their fields.

There are several other indications of an increasing academic interest in European integration. In West Germany, where the greatest interest in European studies has occurred, at least one course per semester in European integration was taught in each university in 1966. Since 1962 France has required students to take a general course on European organizations during their third year at the university. In Paris in 1964 a Committee for the Study of the European Communities was established. Composed of the dean or a professor from each of the French law faculties, the committee communicates with all professors in the field. In Belgium three of the four universities had major centers for European studies in 1966. In Italy, where there was no professorial chair in European studies in 1961, 71 theses had been completed five years later.

Britain too has begun to focus on formal studies of European integration. As the 1966 volume of *University Studies on European Integration* explains: "A remarkable phenomenon this year has been the tremendous growth of interest in European affairs in the various British universities. The number of European courses has leaped from eleven to thirty-two. They are particularly numerous and varied at the London School of Economics and the University of Sussex, where a post-graduate centre for European research has also been established. Five other universities (Exeter, Lancaster, Leicester, Manchester and East Anglia) have instituted European study programmes, three of which constitute full degree courses in European studies and civilization: at Leicester and Reading the courses lead to Master's degrees and at Exeter to a Bachelor's degree. . . . Research into European problems is also steadily expanding, notably at the Center for Advanced European Studies of the Royal Institute of International Affairs and at the British Institute of International and Comparative Law. University teachers indicated their active interest in the study of European integration by holding two meetings in London (November 1965 and May 1966), when they discussed the organization of European teaching in British universities: the main question was at what stage in the university course European studies should be introduced." [13]

In the academic year 1967–68, according to the fifth volume (1969) of *University Studies on European Integration*, the number of theses in preparation and completed had increased again, sometimes in a very impressive fashion. In Germany, for example, the number grew from the 202 reported in 1966 to a total of 344 for 1967–68, although it should be noted that the latter figure includes research papers. A similar degree of growth can be seen in Italy, where 143 theses were reported in 1966 and a total of 262 in 1967–68. In Italy, it might be observed, a candidate cannot obtain the equivalent of the American doctorate without writing a thesis, a situation which acts to increase the number of theses reported. Without any such special incentive, however, the Netherlands have moved from 18 to 24 theses, Great Britain from 15 to 39, and Switzerland from 14 to 32.

In addition to creating the European Community Institute for University Studies, the EEC Commission has also promoted the establishment of documentation centers in institutes of law, economics, and political science, and, on occasion, it has founded academic chairs.[14] More specifically, since 1962 the EEC Commission has awarded forty-six annual scholarships to students attending universities which have a program in European studies. Preference is given to students wishing to study outside their country of nationality.

The awarding of scholarships and prizes, the prodding and help with physical arrangements for meetings to promote cooperative work, and even the encouraging of simple conversation require administrative legwork; such tasks as these have been admirably performed by the EEC Bureau d'Information des Communautés Européennes, headed by Jean Moreau. The bureau's purpose is not simply to distribute documents, but actually to promote activities which the EEC has envisaged. It has tried to initiate conferences, gatherings of students, professors, and other academic ranks — anything which will promote serious and scholarly attention to European integration and European problems. Its activities testify to the strength of the European integration movement in higher education.

The College of Europe at Bruges

The first postgraduate institute for the specialized study of European integration is the College of Europe at Bruges. It opened in 1949 under the

29

direction of a leading Europeanist, Henri Brugmans, whose *L'idée européenne, 1918–1965* has since become a classic in the literature which deals with the ideal of one Europe.[15] Students for 1968–69 came from Austria, Belgium, Czechoslovakia, Denmark, France, West Germany, Great Britain, Greece, Holland, Ireland, Israel, Italy, Luxembourg, Norway, Sweden, Switzerland, the United States, and Yugoslavia. The quarterly publication of the college, *Informations*, describes the program of general European studies as a "series of courses on the concept of Europe as an entity, contemporary European history, the development of the idea of European unity and the European organizations." Beyond this introduction to European studies, the work of the college has extended into three sections: economic, legal, and political.[16]

To the record of the harmonization of European education should be added something of the history of the College of Europe. The chronicle has woven into it, like the figures in a tapestry, the names of many distinguished ideologists of Europeanization, men and women who assisted in the creation of an institution that has grown strong because of its success in meeting real needs.

The account goes back to the first years after World War II. The college may be said to owe its establishment to the Congress of Europe held at The Hague in May 1948. With the goal of promoting European union, the congress was convened by a number of official and unofficial groups, gathered in an umbrella organization that was shortly to be renamed the European Movement.

The driving force of the Congress of Europe was the Spanish philosopher and author, Salvador de Madariaga, who was president of the congress's Cultural Commission and of its successor, the European Movement's International Cultural Division (Section Culturelle Internationale du Movement Européen).[17] In its sessions at The Hague the Cultural Commission received a report from Denis de Rougemont, one of the earliest of European federalists. De Rougemont proposed the establishment of a center or agency for cultural exchange and propaganda for Europeanization, which he visualized as a factor in the renewal of Western culture.[18] Other delegates to the congress also introduced ideas related to the promotion of Europeanization through education. Though the establishment of the College of Europe did not follow as a direct consequence of the congress at The Hague, the exchange of ideas taking place there did create a favorable climate. Such delegates as Henri Brugmans, Jean Drapier, Julius

Hoste, de Madariaga, Joseph Retinger, and Father Antoine Verleye were all to play a part in starting the college.[19]

De Madariaga was not only a well-known writer but he had also been the permanent delegate of Spain to the League of Nations. He knew what Europeanization was all about — at least cultural Europeanization — and he was especially concerned that an agency be established that was suited to the formation of specialists in European civilization. He came gradually to conceive of an "institut universitaire," an educational establishment to be composed of an "elite of 'postgraduates.' " [20] De Madariaga had taught at Oxford University and was an admirer of the English college, and he thought it would be desirable to have a similar community atmosphere at the proposed institute (and this has indeed turned out to be the case at the college).[21] In the International Cultural Division of the European Movement, of which he was president, de Madariaga had at hand a useful agency for furthering his project. Here then was one phase of the process which led to the college.

A second strand was provided by Father Antoine Verleye, a member of the Belgian delegation to the Congress of Europe and an associate of de Madariaga on the Cultural Commission.[22] Verleye had been much struck by de Rougemont's idea for a cultural center and he proposed the city of Bruges as a possible site. On his return to Belgium after the congress, Verleye pursued his idea of Bruges as the location for an institutionalized effort at Europeanization. As it turned out, de Rougemont was to open his Centre Européenne de la Culture in Switzerland in 1950; it has been independent of the College of Europe but has worked with it in efforts at Europeanization.[23] Nevertheless, the possibility of a location at Bruges had entered into the deliberations which led to the formation of the college.

In January 1949, seven months after the congress at The Hague, the European Movement's Cultural Division met in London. De Madariaga, de Rougemont, and the distinguished philosopher Etienne Gilson were present. A memorandum on a European university, embodying the ideas of de Madariaga, was submitted to the London group, which gave the project favorable consideration.[24] For years afterward the ideal of a European university continued to attract the interest of those who espoused Europeanization. It would take us too far afield to speculate on why such a university has not been initiated; suffice it to say that the establishment of an entire university was not feasible at the time and it became increasingly clear to those concerned that the proposed institution would have to be scaled down to a college.

Meanwhile the city of Bruges grew in attractiveness as the site for an educational institution, in part because of the efforts of Les Amis de Bruges, a cultural association started after World War II, and the European Union of Federalists (L'Union Européenne des Fédéralistes). The two organizations pooled their efforts and the latter was enlarged in scope because of Verleye's success in attracting the interest of Paul van Zeeland, president of the Belgian Council, and Duncan Sandys, Winston Churchill's aide and president of the European Movement's International Executive Council (Bureau Executif International du Mouvement Européen). Moreover, the location at Bruges complemented the town's plans for expanding its cultural activities.[25]

Events moved rapidly after the London meeting of January 1949. Happily, a congress of the International Council of the European Movement was called for February 25–28 in Brussels, and the proposal for a collegiate institution was presented to the membership. Meanwhile, the name Collège de Europe was introduced for the first time at Paris meetings of the Cultural Division.[26] In both Brussels and Paris the reaction was favorable, and it did not take long to frame a concrete proposal. Additional meetings of the Cultural Division were held during the spring in Bruges.[27] Both local leaders and the executive committee of the European Movement, which met at Paris in June, were enthusiastic about the College of Europe. The Communal Council of Bruges appropriated 150,000 Belgian francs to underwrite the expenses of a group which would draw up working papers and plan for the opening of a College of Europe: in the words of the college's historian, "Enfin la route était libre." [28]

Preparatory sessions ran through the fall of 1949, and those attending held discussions on pan-European topics.[29] A discussion led by M. Lindsay was titled "The Coordination of Western Education." Salvador de Madariaga, talking on a more literary theme, "L'Esprit de l'Europe," compared the literary images of Hamlet, Don Quixote, Faust, and Don Juan. There were other topics and other papers, among them one by Henri Brugmans entitled "Le Conseil de l'Europe." These preparatory sessions developed the format of the College of Europe.[30] Students from eleven countries and six areas of study attended, and there was a good deal of communal life and completely free discussion between students and professors.[31] This atmosphere was, of course, a model for the future college.

All that was needed was the official backing of the national councils of the European Movement. Fortunately a propitious time for securing approval was at hand. A Conference on European Culture (Conférence Européenne de la Culture) was meeting at Lausanne from December 8 to 12, 1949. Salvador de Madariaga presided. At the meeting Denis de Rougemont proposed three commissions to undertake specific tasks, and the proposed college at Bruges was discussed by Julius Hoste's commission on the development of specifically European institutions.[32] Many sponsors of the college were present for the meetings of Hoste's commission — such men as Henri Brugmans, Father Verleye, and others.

The Lausanne conference, recognizing that actions already taken by the government of Belgium and the city of Bruges had made the college viable, called on the other governments of Western Europe to provide the necessary funds and credits. The conference also recommended to the Cultural Division of the European Movement that it back the petitioning of these governments.[33]

The most important practical step to be taken before the start of the first academic year, scheduled to begin in the fall of 1950, was the naming of a rector. Henri Brugmans, professor of modern French literature at the University of Utrecht in Holland, and since 1947 president of the European Union of Federalists, was chosen for the post in April 1950. The buildings of the College of Europe were ready for occupancy in October 1950. The Hotel St. Georges served as lodging for staff and students while the Brangwyn Museum was converted into administrative headquarters and classrooms. The celebration of the beginning of the first regular academic year was set for October 12, 1950, 458 years after Columbus discovered America, as de Madariaga pointed out. Now Europe was to be "discovered."

Communication between East and West Europe

Up to this point we have stayed within Western Europe, except for noting the cosmopolitan ideas of those associated with the College of Europe and the Centre Européen de la Culture. Fortunately for harmonization of education, the countries of Eastern and Central Europe and those of Western Europe are being drawn closer together. One magnet is the Comparative Education Society in Europe, which studies pedagogical problems confronting all European countries (some of which will be discussed in Chapter 3). Founded in 1961 with members from both Western and Eastern Europe, the society held its first meeting at Sèvres, France, in 1963.

The society has encouraged a closer look at, and communication on, a number of common issues. It has turned its attention to the nature of general secondary education and has continued to examine issues in the controversial arena of post-secondary education. Leading problems, for example, are the organization of higher education and the provision of sufficient laboratory space, library facilities, and instructors for an ever-increasing number of students. The society is also concerned with research methods in comparative education and with the increasing enrollments and other developments in higher education. The agendas of its meetings will certainly not be hard to fill for the foreseeable future.

Thus far we have recorded some of the successes of harmonization in Western European education, though always with a feeling that Europe will have great difficulty in arriving at a cultural détente between the socialist and nonsocialist countries. It is time we dealt with this problem.

The most perplexing fact a Europeanist must acknowledge is the hegemony of the Soviet Union over the countries of Central and Eastern Europe. At the very least, the USSR is *primus inter pares*. The study of language in the satellite states is certainly an index of its influence. For example, while no one in the USSR is required to learn Rumanian, the Russian language is required in Rumanian schools. Since 1960 about a tenth of the hours devoted to the humanities (including language, history, and civics) has been required for the study of Russian. (On the other hand, Rumania's link with Western Europe is illustrated by the requirement of a Western language for only slightly less than the number of hours given over to Russian.[34])

The Russian invasion of Czechoslovakia during the summer of 1968 showed that the Soviets are nervous leaders of the Eastern bloc and jealous guardians of orthodoxy.[35] Despite this Soviet discipline, it would be wrong to exaggerate the degree to which the Soviets have controlled nationalism in countries such as Poland or Rumania. A tempting postulate is that the farther one travels from Moscow, the greater the people's feelings of independence. But we eschew that generalization for the simple and undeniable fact that in educational matters not only the countries of Eastern Europe but to some extent Russia itself interacts with the West and with the United States. The part played in European education (both Eastern and Western) by the educational practice and theory of the

United States has increased over the years with accelerated pace, as has the amount of communication on pedagogical issues. Such interests explain why the Institute of National Schools, where the educational systems of other nations are studied, is one of the large units of the USSR Academy of Pedagogical Sciences in Moscow. East-West pedagogical exchanges include the June 1969 meetings in Prague of the Comparative Education Society in Europe, devoted to the subject of curriculum development at the secondary level, and a conference on international research in education, held at Warsaw in September 1969, to which educators of the world were invited. Eastern and Western countries are united too in the search for adequate texts, a quest that has sent representatives from the Eastern bloc countries to conferences on textbook revision.[36]

Nevertheless we must recognize the ideological dependence upon the USSR of those countries which lie in its political and economic orbit. The impact of this dependence on educational matters is worth describing here in some detail. The situation in Poland, for example, has been delineated by Gusta Singer, who points out that the years "after World War II witnessed a sudden turn toward Soviet pedagogical thought. The main educational problems of this period were the relation between political ideology and science, the polytechnization of education, and the full interpretation of Pavlovism. . . . The contacts were strengthened by repeated trips of Polish educators to the Soviet Union and by the penetration of Soviet literature and pedagogical writings." At the same time, however, there was a growing opposition to Soviet educational theories, because they required the Poles to reject their own cultural and educational tradition.[37] Polish educational literature, Singer notes, was "full of condemnation of the efforts made to belittle the Polish historical past and of the moral harm which was done to the growing generations by splitting their personalities through the contradictions between the teachings of the school and the tradition of their homes." [38]

Poland, then, has struggled to maintain its own identity. It has also incorporated Western ideas about educational practice and theory. According to Singer, "there is no doubt that a deep interest in western educational theories exists among educators, and research is often based on western theories of education." [39] Strengthening such ties were the visits of Polish officials to Western Europe, Canada, and the United States after 1956.

Poland's efforts to preserve its uniqueness should not, however, encourage more than a moderate optimism about European harmonization. An examination of Soviet influence on education in Bulgaria shows a thoroughgoing concurrence with Soviet models. Peter Georgeoff, who has studied the socialization of youth in Bulgaria, describes the Soviet influence as follows: "A number of aspects of Bulgarian education . . . closely resemble the patterns in the Soviet Union, from whom the Bulgarians receive inspiration for much of their pedagogical thought as well as for their political ideology. Indeed, the two elements cannot be separated, since educational practices are an extension of the political factor and are intended to give support and continuity to communist ideology." [40] Statements by Soviet party leaders on education are often reflected in the paterns later adopted in Bulgarian schools. Educators study with care the writings of such Soviet pedagogues as N. Krupskaya and A. S. Makarenko, and Bulgarian students are frequently required to read translations of Soviet textbooks on education.[41]

Georgeoff further observes that "extracurricular activities, the program of work education, and the ideological impact upon the content of the school curriculum all include many elements from Soviet practice. Bulgarian objectives of education, which emphasize economic competence and Party and national loyalty, are like those of the Soviet Union, with the exception that an additional aim is included, that of promoting 'friendship and brotherhood with the Soviet nation and its peoples.' " [42] There are many parallels too between teaching methods in the USSR and in Bulgaria.

The result, as Georgeoff points out, is "that the educational system of Bulgaria has the task of developing a sense of national identity among the young and, at the same time, of fostering in them a spirit of gratitude and respect for the Soviet Union. Developing this dual set of loyalties is one of the most difficult problems faced by Bulgarian teachers." [43]

Bulgarian educational practice is moving closer to Soviet educational and political theories. A Soviet law connecting "schools with life," initiated by Premier Nikita Khrushchev in 1958, became in 1959 the model for the Bulgarian "Law for Closer Ties between School and Life and for the Further Development of National Education." Its purpose was to increase practical training and other aspects of polytechnical education. Writing of the decree, Georgeoff says that the "school curriculum was redesigned to conform yet more closely with theoretical Communist principles on education as they were currently interpreted." [44] In Bulgaria, as elsewhere in the socialist countries, the enemy was "bookishness" and any kind of education not directly linked with "the practical (that is, industrial and agricultural) side of life." [45] The result of the directive for the curriculum was not significantly different in Bulgaria than in other socialist lands. Georgeoff writes: "part-time work in industry, agriculture, and building construction was made mandatory for all secondary school students, and the general secondary schools were renamed General Polytechnical Secondary Schools. In this manner academic education was combined with 'socially useful labor,' making it possible for every young person graduating from secondary school to have gained skill in some trade as well as in academic subjects. It was felt that this work-study program would produce the 'new, ideal socialist man' — one who possesses a basic education, has technical or vocational competence, and is a convinced, thoroughly dedicated Marxist." [46]

The ideology of Communism, in varying degrees, clearly binds the socialist countries together. Poland and Bulgaria have been examined. Let us turn to Rumania, perhaps the most independent of the iron curtain countries. When the Communists gained control of Rumania in early January 1948, following the forced abdication of the monarch, Rumanian education was greatly altered. Randolph Braham writes: "Designed to achieve a highly centralized, uniform school system, the reform reoriented Rumania's basic educational policies away from French-German educational concepts towards those of Soviet Russia. This change was reflected in the gradual reorganization of the schools along Soviet lines, the adoption of Marxist-Leninist principles of education, and the coordination of educational policies with the basic requirements of the planned economy." [47]

The social education found in Bulgaria also characterizes Rumanian education. Braham describes "patriotic education," which "in the lower grades is pursued throughout the teaching of all subjects . . . since 1956 the high school curriculum has provided for two new required subjects: 'elements of Marxism-Leninism' and 'elements of political economy.' Both are envisioned as 'raising the theoretical level of the students' and inculcating in them a feeling of 'socialist patriotism' and 'proletarian internationalism.' " [48]

Polytechnization is one of the essentials of education in all socialist countries in Europe. Braham writes: "Communist educators trace the basic principles underlying polytechnical education to Marx, Engels, and Lenin. According to Marx, 'polytechnism,' as it is often called, is 'an education which, in the case of every child over a certain age, combined labor with instruction and physical culture, not only as means for increasing social production, but as the only way of producing fully developed beings.' In accordance with the Leninist principle of 'the unity of theory with practice,' polytechnical education forms an integral part of the Communist education of youths and aims to equip them with 'the knowledge of the scientific foundations of the principal means of production.' " [49]

It should be remembered, however, that polytechnization is not unknown in Western European education. As Braham observes: "For all practical purposes, polytechnical education is work-experience education that combines manual work and academic study. Reminiscent of John Dewey's concept of 'learning by doing,' these activities, resulting in the production of useful goods and services, are expected also to serve as a means for molding the individual's social and intellectual development." [50]

There are similarities to be observed also between Western and Eastern Europe in the area of educational planning. But in order to understand the parallels, we should first examine the planning policies of countries in the Soviet orbit. In these nations the state and party dictate planning, although interests of the individual and family have been increasing in persuasive force. This may be called *prescriptive* planning, which means that an agency such as the central USSR Ministry of Higher and Specialized Secondary Education (responsible primarily for vocational and technical training) uses the research of the USSR State Planning Committee.

The basic rationale, according to Seymour Rosen, is that both higher education and secondary technical education have as their object the production of "trained specialists within a government-planned framework, for employment by industries operated by government agencies. . . . The logistics of planning those specialties which are needed in the economy are the responsibilities of U.S.S.R. State Planning Committee (*Gosplan*) . . . education planning is considered as one segment of total manpower planning." [51]

A similar situation prevails in East Germany, where in 1965, after some two years of study and discussion, legislation was enacted to establish a "coordinated social educational system." According to a statement by Alexander Abusch, deputy chairman of the Council of Ministers, "the State Planning Commission, which has been given the central responsibility for questions of vocational training must consistently see to it that the principles of planning and directing vocational training in the entire national economy are put into effect. Above all, the content of the vocations taught must be newly defined beginning with the leading economic branches; and the manpower requirements must be pre-calculated in long-term scientific plans. The fulfillment of both these tasks is a prerequisite for the timely beginning of vocational guidance for the attendants of secondary schools and for a modern vocational training that accords with the future demands made on the skilled worker. The standards of qualification of the working people have to be planned and raised well in advance in accordance with the principal direction of the scientific and technical development and the development goals of the branches of the national economy and the individual enterprises." [52] The economic role of educational planning is manifest but, more important, it is a type that would be approved in both East and West Europe.

With variations, then, the socialist countries share the dominant Soviet model of educational planning for the development of manpower. The prescriptive character of planning may suggest that individuals are directed to advanced schooling without regard to their aspirations and wishes. This is not true now, nor has it been true for a number of years. However, there are rewards for doing what the planners recommend. Differentials in wages and housing and other material rewards show that the carrot is used more than the stick. The carrot has brought socialist educational planning closer to the kind of planning that is familiar in Western Europe.

The prescriptive planning of Eastern European states does not radically diverge from the normative planning of France or the descriptive planning of countries such as England. The career master in England who describes to a pupil the present and future prospects in the labor market is guiding that pupil by narrowing the number of choices to those which are realistic. There is certainly more guidance in France than in England, and still more in Eastern Europe. But in each country the guidance is compiled from data supplied by a planning agency or a division of the ministry of education. Whether the planning is prescriptive or descriptive, the factors playing on an individual's choice of a career are not widely different. After all, planners in Eastern Europe do not wish to have dissatisfied people — square pegs in round holes — any more than do planners in Western countries.

In other words, the grounds for harmonization in educational practice are greater if we see that planning actually lies along a continuum whose extremes are not so far apart. Without intending oversimplification, we

39

think there is evidence that by working at educational matters common to all countries, educators will continue to climb over the wall of ideological differences.

Language: A Handicap to Cultural Harmonization

We have observed that the exchange of languages can encourage harmonization. Paradoxically, there are times when one can make too much of a language. We are not referring to modern European languages but to the struggle between linguistic groups in a single country. Eire (Republic of Ireland) is a good example. In Eire the official and political backing given the Irish language in the schools appears to be a more tangible issue for the Irish people than the rather abstract ideal of pan-Europeanism.[53] Though few people today would consider Ireland an applicant for Europeanization, it is worth noting that the country has formally applied for membership in the Common Market.

Norway as well has internal linguistic conflicts. In this small country there are two languages: Bokmål (Riksmål, as it formerly was called) and Nynorsk (or Landsmål). Bokmål, which dominates the newspapers, radio, and television, developed during the period when Norway was ruled by Denmark and has for centuries been recognized as an official language. Nynorsk, on the other hand, has received official recognition more recently. In 1885 teachers and high school students were required to pass examinations in Nynorsk as well as in Bokmål. Partisans of Nynorsk claim it is the old and authentic language of the Norwegians, tracing back to dialects that antedated the Danish hegemony. Because both languages are studied in school, the language program at the secondary level is very heavy. The economic costs of teaching two languages (two sets of textbooks) is, of course, a strain on educational budgets. The controversy over Bokmål and Nynorsk illustrates how powerful — and divisive — a dual language tradition can be, particularly when it is remembered that in a language dispute a whole set of meanings are being communicated, and these meanings include values and attitudes. Such internal divisions present an obstacle to Europeanization, for the attention of Norwegians, like that of the Irish, is focused on their domestic problems in education rather than on the issue of Europeanization.

In Belgium linguistic legislation has been passed in an attempt to regulate the Flemish-Walloon controversy, but it concomitantly defines two cultural communities — the Flemish (Dutch-speaking) north and the

Walloon (French-speaking) south. Brussels and certain other localities are legally considered bilingual. In unilingual areas the language of the region is the language of instruction in the schools; in bilingual areas, the maternal language of the child (as sworn to by the head of the family) is the language in which he must receive instruction, regardless of any contrary desire of the family or of close proximity to a school in which instruction is given in the other language. The difficult linguistic situation in Belgium, where both Flemish and French are official languages, is captured by one dryly official paragraph in the bulletin *Schola Europaea*: "Dutch pupils may have supplementary tuition [teaching] in French or German from this first year onwards [of the seven-year secondary section]. Similarly, Belgian pupils whose mother tongue is French are given four hours fortnightly tuition in Dutch, in order to satisfy the basic legal requirements of their native country." [54]

Language is so much a part of education that friction which is generated in linguistic controversy directly affects the schools. The level of education in Belgium is high yet it has not really acted to reduce the tensions of the linguistic halves of one of the most civilized of the European countries. These tensions may eventually rupture the Belgian system of higher education. For instance, while the state universities offer instruction in both French and Flemish, the world-famous private University of Louvain (located in the Flemish-speaking area) is now racked by ugly disputes which have caused two totally separate faculties to be established and will most likely lead to the physical removal of the French-speaking faculty ten miles away to the French linguistic area. On a purely economic basis, this is a waste of resources and money which the country can ill afford.

Language questions are a plague not only in capitalist countries; political ideology cannot seem to prevent linguistically defined splits within the socialist countries. One of the problems for Russian specialists in the psychology of learning language is that of teaching Russian as the first language to all people in the Soviet Union, where there are 120 registered languages. Furthermore, intranational differences in language are increasingly more evident in Yugoslavia. A manifesto issued there in 1967 by seventeen Croatian cultural associations (including the Writers' Association and the Academy of Sciences) charged that the federal organs of Yugoslavia were using a version of the Serbo-Croatian language that was more Serbian than Croatian. The complexity of the issue is suggested by a 1969 news dispatch from Belgrade: "Under the Yugoslav constitutions all six republics — Serbia, Croatia, Bosnia-Herzogovina, Macedonia, Slovenia and Montenegro — have equal status. The languages of Macedonia and Slovenia, though related to Serbo-Croatian, have been established as distinct tongues, and Federal documents must be published separately in them. . . . Traditionally the Croatians, as well as the Slovenians and Macedonians, have resented the domination of Yugoslavia by Serbian Belgrade." It was later reported that "at least ten Croatian writers and professors have been expelled from the Yugoslav Communist party in a political dispute that threatens to disrupt national unity." [55]

In Greece too language conflicts exist. In that country the problem at first glance appears to be similar to the language debate of Norway. Demotic, like Bokmål, has become the familiar tongue and is used by many internationally known Greek writers. But the proponents of Katharevusa (a term which connotes purity) make a claim for authenticity that seems similar to that of the proponents of Nynorsk. The stalemate in Norway between advocates of Bokmål and Nynorsk has been expensive, but the struggle over demotic and Katharevusa has been far more costly, though not, as in Norway, in terms of textbooks that must be published in two languages, nor of the precious hours of school time absorbed.

Katharevusa is the official language for state documents, which ties the lawyers to it. Religious texts and services are in Katharevusa, which binds the clergy to it. Both secular and sacred law are in Katharevusa because it presumably is the language of the ancient Greeks. Of course, no one knows what the oral language of the ancient Greeks was, but that is a point for philologists. Our concern here is with the effects of the "rhetorical tradition," as one Greek educator put it, the hold of classical humanism on modern Greece.

In a recent report on education in Greece, William Tudhope writes that while there have recently been substantial modifications in school curriculums, "The fact remains that boys of 15 in the third year of the gymnasium, many of them future scientists and engineers, will still spend 10 hours a week out of a total 32 on modern and ancient Greek with only 3 for a foreign language, 4 for mathematics, and 3 for science. The same boys three years later in the lyceum will be spending out of a total of 29 hours 8 hours on Greek and the same time as before on the other subjects. One can hardly refrain from asking whether a foreign language . . .

can be acquired as an effective means of communication with such a time allowance, especially with large classes and few teaching aids. Can sufficient groundwork be laid with this allowance of time for mathematics and science?" [56] Tudhope further observes that the emphasis on the classics — which is intimately related to the arguments for Katharevusa — precludes the adequate study of modern foreign languages which are indispensable to European cultural integration. Thus, the price of the language dispute in Greece is not only a neglect of technology and natural and social sciences, but also a barrier to the possibility of European cultural integration.

Examples of linguistic dispute can be found in many more countries. The problems that such controversies raise are not exotic subjects for the airy disputes of scholars in etymology; they involve serious educational and political issues. If only language was concerned, there is a good chance that the differences could be settled. But language has always been the center of a culture and it is vitally linked with religion, historical records (which we know vary from group to group), and even mythology or more refined forms of literature. Calling the conflicts that result "linguistic" is only a strategy of convenience, and a frank recognition of the situation is necessary if we are to be realistic about the chances of harmonization in European education.

It would be dishonest to ignore the ideological handicaps to Eastern and Western European cooperation and the internal linguistic conflicts within individual countries. Nevertheless these problems must be balanced against remarkable strides toward harmonization which have been produced by the new formal studies of the European community, by the establishment of the College of Europe at Bruges, by the dialogues carried on in the Comparative Education Society in Europe, and by the recognition of common desires (like efficient planning and polytechnization) shared by Eastern and Western European educators.

CHAPTER THREE

The Demand
for Secondary Schooling

H aving traced in the first two chapters the movements toward harmonization, we turn now to the scrutiny of some specific issues in secondary and higher education, issues that are common to all the nations of Europe. Of these pan-European problems, none perhaps presents more difficulties for educators and political leaders than the increasing demand for schooling, particularly at the secondary level. To give only a few examples, secondary-school enrollments have doubled in the Netherlands, more than doubled in Spain and Italy, and tripled in France, Yugoslavia, and Portugal. Before exploring this topic in more detail, however, a few words of definition are in order.

Among European educational systems there is a good deal of variation in the length of schooling at the various levels. In England, for instance, the primary level is designed for children from the ages of five to eleven, but in Scotland pupils do not begin primary school until the age of six. In England, at least, the school which enrolls children aged five to seven (or, in some areas, eight) is called an infant school. The infant school may be housed separately from the junior school, which carries on until the child is eleven. Occasionally, however, as in Oxfordshire, infant and junior schools are in the same building.[1]

But in the USSR and Sweden primary school does not begin until the child is seven years old, and it is difficult to say just when the primary grades end and the secondary ones begin. Drawing a line of demarcation poses a special difficulty in East European countries, where there are forms of the comprehensive school in which upper primary and lower secondary grades tend to run together. The best one can say is that primary education lasts for four to six years and ends when children are ten or eleven.

The definition of secondary schooling is just as hazy. The safest course is to define secondary education as schooling which involves those in the age group between ten or eleven and eighteen or nineteen. (This definition actually places the upper stage (grades five to eight) of the Yugoslavian primary school in secondary education, as well as grades seven to nine of the Swedish comprehensive school.) Such a loose categorizing means that in Turkey a pupil is ready for higher education after eleven years of primary and secondary school, in Germany and Italy after thirteen preparatory years, and in the majority of the European nations after twelve years.

To relieve this confusion, European educators, like those in Canada and the United States, increasingly divide secondary education into two parts — junior and senior, lower and upper, first and second cycle, or incomplete secondary and complete secondary. This kind of division makes a useful distinction between compulsory general education for all children up to the age of fourteen or fifteen and the subsequent schooling (usually for three years) in which curriculums are "specialized" or "differentiated." *Specialization* is a term associated with the upper division of a comprehensive school, while *differentiation* is associated with the selective or multilateral organization.

Some discrepancies in the age group served by secondary schooling may exist among European countries, but they are united in facing an unprecedented demand for such schooling. Before examining the statistics of this demand, though, let us review the targets for European education in 1970 which were formulated by the 1961 conference of the Organization for Economic Co-operation and Development. The main topics brought forth at this meeting summarize the themes which we will encounter in this chapter and in the following ones.

Targets for Education in Europe in 1970

In 1961 the OECD sponsored a policy conference at Washington, D. C., on economic growth and investment in education. The conclusions of the conference were reported in five volumes, the second of which was called *Targets for Education in Europe in 1970*.[2] The proposals of the conferees serve to highlight the common objectives in educational development of many European countries as they entered the 1960's.[3]

A first target defined by the conference was the "generalization of secondary education," i.e., ensuring the entrance of more young people into the upper levels of secondary education in order to provide highly qualified manpower for the job market.[4] At the same time legitimate fears were expressed that the growing number of pupils might lessen the quality of education and that expansion might come too fast: "with the provision of school places outrunning the supply of teachers not only in the secondary but also in the primary schools . . . the trend towards the study of sciences and technology is gaining such impetus that, with limited resources for expenditure on education, the great heritage of European literary tradition may to some extent be neglected." [5] It was suggested, however, that with a rise in the gross national product, the "rate of expenditure on education normally increases faster than the rate of economic growth [so that] the problem largely reduces itself to one of a wise assignment of priorities within the educational budget, taking full account of the need for teachers as well as the cultural and economic factors." [6]

As we shall see later, the quantitative expansion of education has not been the only problem attendant on the expansion of educational opportunity; there is also the issue of the structure of the school system. The OECD report suggests: "There are people who think that if, in a universalized secondary education system, the schools for the academically abler young people are not kept separate from the rest, there will inevitably be a lowering of quality in the education of the abler students. This is an assumption, and those who hold it take it to be obvious. But it has by no means been proven." [7] The issue actually is a choice between the *comprehensive* and the *multilateral* school systems. Indeed, during the 1960's Europeans debated intensely over the advantages and disadvantages of multilateral schools, where students are separated by their presumed abilities and career expectations, and comprehensive schools, where students of all levels of ability and future plans are collected. We will return to this issue in Chapter 5.

Another principal emphasis of the OECD conferees was that of increasing the educational chances of all young people of ability. The authors of the report wrote primarily of Western Europe, but their remarks are applicable to Eastern Europe as well: "One thing that can be said with some confidence . . . is that there is certainly a much larger 'reservoir of ability' than has yet been tapped. Even in the United States qualified observers would hesitate to say that the large section of each age group that goes to college is approximately co-extensive with those that ought to go in terms of ability. In almost all European countries the reservoir of untapped talent is much larger than in the United States. Even where, as in the United Kingdom, access to the university is now reasonably 'democratic' for those who have stayed at secondary school till the age of eighteen, there is a serious loss for the simple reason that large numbers of potentially suitable entrants to the university leave school well before they are eighteen. . . . Because of the steady shift of manpower from the unskilled to the more skilled, from the primary producer to the distributor and administrator, the need is increasingly for the higher quality and more expensive kinds of education, both technical and general." [8]

The last major concern of the conference was to persuade those involved with European education that general education should extend over not six, but at least nine, years, and that it should not be sacrificed to specialization before the age of fifteen or sixteen. The report emphasized that general education is necessary to help young people maintain flexibility in a world of constantly changing technology, and that highly qualified technologists require a broad basis of knowledge applicable to a wide range of problems. Neither the authors of the report nor the conference members disapproved of students in England who wish to have less than the required specialization for the "A" level Certificate of Education (the advanced certificate needed for university entrance). No one was to quarrel with East and West German and French students who want to present fewer subjects for the secondary-school leaving examination and to draw them from the two large categories of science and the humanities. The report explained that a majority of these students wanted a "broad education up to the end of the secondary school, including some subjects from the sciences and some from the humanities. So many careers nowadays call for familiarity with both these modes of thinking that it would be folly not to provide such an education for an increasing number of young people, leaving as late as possible commitment to either the sciences or the humanities." [9]

The economic effects of extending education were, of course, explored, but the report concluded with a humanistic perspective: "Investment and productivity are after all not ends in themselves, but means to a better and fuller life. If education has not been too narrowly 'economic,' the generations educated and trained to meet the needs of a growing economy will have developed tastes and interests which will in due course be reflected in a further demand for education both for themselves and for their children." [10]

The problem with extending general education, however, is mainly financial — the allocation to education of sufficient resources to accomplish the agreed-upon ends. The conferees included a section on the allocation of resources to education, acknowledging that an "increase of expenditure on education can . . . only be obtained at the expense of other types of consumption or investment," assuming that manpower and other factors are fully utilized.[11] Certainly expenditures for higher education in Europe have increased in the 1960's, as we will note in Chapter 4.

Although the OECD policy conference did not suggest increased empirical research on pedagogical questions as a target, it did attend to educational planning,[12] which has been universally adopted in Europe. We do not know how successful educational planning has been, but its popularity would suggest that European countries find it both effective and satisfactory. Furthermore, the European planning agencies appear to have what the conference described as an advanced pattern, "characterized by close co-operation between government, institutional research, experts from various fields, and representatives of social groups." [13]

The conference report delineated the usual types of planning for educational development and economic growth in Europe. France has come to rely on planning consistent with its centralized administration, and such planning is hampered only by the recent and relative autonomy of French universities. By 1960 the French had entrusted most educational planning to the Commission de l'Equipement Scolaire, Universitaire et Sportif, an integral part of the French Commissariat Général au Plan. The commissariat has representatives from higher education, municipal government, trade unions, employers' associations, and other groups.

In Great Britain the Ministry of Education is responsible for forecasting and planning, and a number of groups, such as the Statistical Branch of the ministry, provide data for the well-known permanent and ad hoc advisory committees. Two other countries make use of specialized educational forecasting and planning agencies, described in the conference report as follows: "In Sweden a forecasting unit with a large research staff has been established within the Labour Market Board. It investigates long-term trends in the demand for various types of education and training. Special planning problems, such as the extension to nine years of compulsory schooling to include occupational education and training, are delegated to Royal Commissions. A special unit in the Department of Education co-ordinates all planning activities. . . . In the Netherlands the Research Department of the Ministry of Education, Arts, and Sciences is concerned with the regular forecasting of the number of pupils in primary education and the corresponding demand for teachers. Other planning work, e.g., on higher education, is carried out by advisory bodies such as the Commission for the Development of Higher Education." [14]

By contrast, West Germany relies on ad hoc commissions. Education is controlled by the länder, with a degree of national harmonization assured by the Permanent Conference of Ministers of Education (Ständige Konferenz der Kultusminister).

As we have mentioned in Chapter 2, Gosplan, the state planning commission in the USSR, is a model for education in Eastern Europe. [15] Although its economic decentralization and its exclusive concern with long-range goals have lessened the responsibility of Gosplan, it is still the most comprehensive planning agency in the world. All plans by ministries and state committees of the Council of Ministers are reported to it. The role of Gosplan in educational planning is evident, because its principal branch is devoted to cultural and public health. As Herbert Rudman explains: "This branch department has its counterpart in republican gosplans and within local planning commissions. Soviet industry and agriculture need trained specialists, whose training is not left to chance and personal choice but is an integral part of national economic planning. The number of specialists needed during a given period of time is related directly to proposed expansion in the economy. Quotas and priorities are established among educational institutions to ensure the training of needed specialists. . . . Admission patterns in educational institutions are directly affected by state plans; student stipends are increased or decreased depending upon the specialty needed; laboratory and classroom facilities are added or denied; personnel are increased in one department and frozen in another depending upon the priorities established during a given planning period." [16]

The final pattern of educational planning for economic development is that of the Mediterranean countries (Greece, Italy, Spain, Turkey, and Yugoslavia) and Portugal, who collaborate with the OECD to establish national planning teams which relate educational expansion to economic growth. [17] The Mediterranean Regional Project (MRP), which will be discussed in Chapter 8, cannot be judged as an unqualified success, but the idea of regional planning, calling on the facilities of pan-European agencies such as OECD, has proved very worthwhile.

These targets of educational planning, extending general education, increasing educational opportunities for all young people of ability, and enrolling more students in the upper levels of secondary education are all emphases of the OECD conference and of European education in general in the 1960's and 1970's. A brief look at statistics will illustrate them.

The Education Explosion

The demand for secondary and higher education is the most common and serious problem facing politicians and educators in Europe. Canada and the United States can also be included, for they are responding to social and economic forces similar to Europe's, and they are listed in some of the following tables which indicate the dimensions of the demand. Among the socialist countries, Yugoslavia has data comparable with those of many Western nations. Turkey's inclusion in the tables is consistent with the recommendation of Bruley and Dance that, historically, Turkey be thought of as part of Europe. Data on the supply of education will not be given because the ability to respond varies with resources; it is not a pure measure of the desire to meet the demand.

Table 2, showing the sharp rise in secondary school enrollment for a fifteen-year period beginning in 1950, indicates as well the increase in the relevant age groups for both secondary and higher education. In the absence of a depression, a war, or some other crisis that would slacken the uniformly high demand, pressure on political and educational leaders for more secondary schools, especially classes in the upper grades, can be expected to continue. From 1950 to 1965, with the exception of Austria and West Germany, there was a total increase in enrollment of almost 90 percent. Table 3 summarizes the zooming nature of the demand in a more dramatic way. Secondary enrollment tripled in countries like Yugoslavia, Turkey, and Portugal, and doubled in Spain and Italy; all these countries had low enrollment ratios in 1950.

The reality of *l'explosion scolaire* can be readily documented throughout the length and breadth of Europe. In part its causes lie in the increased birthrates during the years after World War II. Rosier observes that the birthrate in Europe, which had declined between 1900 and 1950, rose "in a more permanent fashion than simply a resurgence of births following the war." The impact on secondary education can be judged from

The Demand for Secondary Schooling

Table 2. Secondary-School Enrollments and Growth Indexes
for OECD Countries, 1950–55 (1955=100)[a]

Country	1950–51	1955–56	1960–61	1965–66
Austria				
Actual number[b]	563,269	611,843	600,361	600,648
Index	92	100	98	98
Belgium				
Actual number	361,895	390,863	525,431	620,475
Index	93	100	134	159
Canada				
Actual number	394,000	608,683	882,247	1,263,725
Index	65	100	145	208
Denmark				
Actual number[c]	98,171	134,861	139,193	158,931
Index	73	100	103	118
Finland				
Actual number	173,685	226,635	343,198	425,875
Index	77	100	151	188
France				
Actual number (full-time)	1,055,648	1,476,000	2,010,448	3,060,861
Index	72	100	136	207
Actual number (full- and part-time)	. . .	1,613,900	2,173,648	3,110,661
Index		100	135	193
Germany (FR)				
Actual number (upper primary and part-time included)	. . .	5,610,353	5,246,239	5,571,753
Index		100	94	99
Actual number (upper primary and part-time excluded)	981,047	1,371,479	1,438,882	1,679,625
Index	72	100	105	122
Greece				
Actual number	. . .	209,802	327,779	377,205
Index		100	156	180
Ireland				
Actual number	73,225	86,835	111,197	145,828
Index	84	100	128	168
Italy				
Actual number	1,220,566	1,507,968	2,184,046	3,014,478
Index	81	100	145	200
Luxembourg				
Actual number	7,325	8,009	10,508	11,253
Index	91	100	131	141
Netherlands				
Actual number	582,372	740,340	1,050,430	1,130,274
Index	79	100	142	153
Norway				
Actual number	84,771	100,646	143,420	179,734
Index	84	100	143	179
Portugal				
Actual number	89,402	125,074	220,782	291,000
Index	71	100	177	233

Table 2 – continued

Country	1950–51	1955–56	1960–61	1965–66
Spain				
Actual number	386,723	506,183	714,349	1,121,750
Index	76	100	141	222
Sweden				
Actual number	174,684	205,819	285,147	275,165
Index	85	100	139	134
Switzerland				
Actual number[c]	90,866	124,839	138,450	. . .
Index	73	100	111	
Turkey				
Actual number	146,900	242,900	467,500	721,500
Index	61	100	193	297
United Kingdom (England and Wales)				
Actual number	. . .	1,914,814	2,723,158	2,829,747
Index		100	142	148
United States				
Actual number[d]	9,363,000	11,760,000	14,354,000	18,200,000
Index	80	100	122	155
Yugoslavia				
Actual number (with upper primary)	513,203	632,618	1,410,374	1,895,157
Index	81	100	223	300
Actual number (without upper primary)	234,237	265,318	350,147	566,346
Index	88	100	132	213

SOURCE: Adapted from *Development of Secondary Education* (Paris: OECD, 1969), Table 2, pp. 24–25.

[a] For certain countries data for the years selected were not obtainable; therefore the nearest year available was used. Instead of 1950–51: 1951–52 for Austria, Canada, Denmark, Italy, Norway, and Switzerland; 1952–53 for Belgium, Sweden, and Yugoslavia. Instead of 1955–56: 1956–57 for Denmark and Switzerland; 1954–55 for France. Instead of 1960–61: 1961–62 for Denmark; 1959–60 for France and Germany; 1964–65 for Switzerland. Instead of 1965–66: 1964–65 for Belgium, Canada, France, Netherlands, Portugal, Spain, Sweden, United Kingdom, and Yugoslavia; 1963–64 for Greece; 1962–63 for Luxembourg.

[b] Including part-time berufsschulen (vocational schools).

[c] General education only.

[d] Public education only.

Rosier's estimate that the 9–15 age group has increased from 35 percent of the total population to 44 percent since World War II. [18]

Other demographic factors have been at work too. In France, for example, about a third of the increase in total population since the war has been due to immigration (a percentage somewhat smaller than in other European nations). Migrant workers and transplanted residents from former French colonies affect the population base which French planners

The Demand for Secondary Schooling

Table 3. Summary of Changes in Total Enrollments
in Secondary Education in OECD Countries, 1950–65

Trebled	More Than Doubled	Doubled	Increased by Three Quarters	Increased Less Than Half
Canada	Finland	Norway	Denmark	Germany (FR)
France	Spain	Netherlands	Sweden	Austria
Yugoslavia	Italy	United States	Belgium	
Turkey		Ireland	Luxembourg	
Portugal			England and Wales	

SOURCE: Adapted from *Development of Secondary Education* (Paris: OECD, 1969), Table 2, p. 26.

must consider when projecting educational needs. In general there has been a flow of workers, sometimes accompanied by their families, from the rural, agricultural, and less industrialized countries of southern Europe to the nations of northern Europe such as France, Germany, Sweden, and Switzerland. For the host countries there is an obvious population increase and, if the workers remain, estimates of projected enrollments must also increase. On the other hand, the return of large numbers of migrant workers and their families to their original country will affect enrollment projections there.[19]

Table 4 shows the increasing number of young people of secondary-school age in OECD member countries in 1950 and 1965 and projections for 1980. Because Europe does not have a strong tradition of attendance in senior secondary-school grades by children from lower and lower-middle class backgrounds, the number of 10 to 14 year olds have been tabulated separately from the 15–19 age group. Canada and the United States are included for purposes of comparison. Countries where the 10–14 age group increased more than 50 percent between 1950 and 1965 are Canada, France, Iceland, Turkey, and the United States. In the same period there was a slight decrease in this 10–14 age group in Austria, West Germany, Greece, and Italy. Greece and Yugoslavia showed a slight decrease in the 15–19 age group during those years. Projections for the future indicate that Austria and West Germany will experience an increase of 20 percent or more in the 10–14 age group by 1980. The countries of Austria, West Germany, Canada, and Iceland will have an anticipated increase of more than 25 percent in the 15–19 age group. After 1980, if the projections hold, there will be little difference among European nations, and the changes altogether will be less impressive.

53

Table 4. Size of Secondary-School Age Groups in OECD Countries, 1950–80

Country	1950	1965	1980 (projected)	Percentage Change 1950–65	Percentage Change 1965–80
10–14 Age Group					
Austria	548,900	477,446	649,647	−13.0	36.1
Belgium	570,800	721,800	860,000	26.5	19.1
Canada	1,143,500	2,040,100	2,468,300[a]	78.4	21.0
Denmark	315,700	372,200	421,800	17.9	13.3
Finland	327,400[d]	442,065	. . .	35.0	
France	2,741,000	4,115,900	4,122,200	50.2	0.2
Germany (FR) ...	4,248,100	3,893,300	4,672,000	− 8.4	20.0
Greece	765,691	709,964	740,795	− 7.3	4.3
Iceland	11,448	20,304	. . .	77.4	
Ireland	260,900	285,000	341,000[b]	9.2	19.7
Italy	4,189,000	3,981,000	4,633,000	− 5.0	16.4
Luxembourg	. . .	. . .	. . .		
Netherlands	824,500	1,105,400	1,340,600	34.1	21.3
Norway	211,000	302,100[c]	326,800	43.2	8.2
Portugal	799,700	846,300[c]	1,019,200	5.8	20.4
Spain	2,326,800	2,672,978	2,949,974	14.9	10.4
Sweden	451,200	541,602	628,902	20.0	16.1
Switzerland	306,500	399,800	432,900	30.4	8.3
Turkey	2,354,700	3,848,864	. . .	63.5	
United Kingdom ..	2,835,000	3,812,000	4,939,000	34.5	29.6
United States	11,351,000	18,853,000	21,495,000	66.1	14.0
Yugoslavia	1,717,200	. . .	. . .		
15–19 Age Group					
Austria	441,900	490,943	624,910	11.1	27.3
Belgium	623,000	715,500	780,000	14.8	9.0
Canada	1,108,300	1,775,600	2,293,800[a]	60.2	29.2
Denmark	292,300	422,200	377,500	44.4	−10.6
Finland	317,500[d]	488,616	381,940[a]	53.9	−21.8
France	3,112,000	3,994,000	4,069,900	28.3	1.9
Germany (FR) ...	3,436,600	3,490,000	4,786,000	1.6	37.1
Greece	789,398	729,956	734,888	− 7.5	0.7
Iceland	12,183	17,806	23,312	46.2	31.0
Ireland	241,200	263,000	310,000[b]	9.0	17.9
Italy	4,053,000	4,198,000	4,452,000	3.6	6.1
Luxembourg	. . .	21,880	. . .		
Netherlands	810,800	1,167,300	1,203,000	44.0	3.0
Norway	204,000	316,500[c]	299,500	55.1	− 5.7
Portugal	811,000	835,500[c]	961,300	3.0	15.1
Spain	. . .	2,570,964	2,912,421		13.3
Sweden	416,300	631,630	535,330	51.7	−15.2
Switzerland	327,800	417,300	421,500	27.3	1.0
Turkey	2,388,000	2,918,806	. . .	22.2	
United Kingdom ..	2,736,000	4,300,000	4,736,000	57.2	10.1
United States	10,663,000	16,924,000	20,525,000	58.7	21.3
Yugoslavia	1,771,100	1,627,765[a]	1,706,430[a]	− 8.1	4.8

SOURCE: Adapted from *Development of Secondary Education* (Paris: OECD, 1969), Table 3, p. 27.
[a] Estimated.   [b] 1981.   [c] 1966.   [d] 1949.

54

The demand for further education at the secondary level can be explained too by the lengthening of the period for compulsory education. In fact, the extension of obligatory schooling in many countries makes it difficult to see exactly how much enrollments have actually increased. Since 1945 nearly all European countries have advanced the school-leaving age and now require a total of eight to nine years of education. This figure varies from country to country, ranging from the age of 14 in Holland and Denmark to 16 in France.

Table 5. Number of Years of Compulsory Schooling
in OECD Countries[a]

Country	1955	1965	1975 (projected)
Austria	8	9	. . .
Belgium	8	8	. . .
Canada	7–9	7–9	. . .
Denmark	7	7	. . .
France	8	8	10
Germany (FR)	8(+3)[b]	8–9(+3)[b]	9(+3)[b]
Greece	6	6–9	9[c]
Ireland	8	8	9–10
Italy	8	8	. . .
Luxembourg	. . .	9	. . .
Netherlands	8	8	. . .
Norway	7	7–9	9
Portugal	4	4	6
Spain	6	8	8
Sweden	8	9	9
Switzerland	8–9	8–9	. . .
Turkey	5	5	8[c]
United Kingdom	10	10	11
United States	8–9	8–12	. . .
Yugoslavia	7	8	8

SOURCE: Adapted from *Development of Secondary Education* (Paris: OECD, 1969), Table 54, p. 98.

[a] Many parts of Germany and Switzerland already have a school leaving age of 15. Since 1959 the leaving age in France has been 16. Compulsory schooling ends at 14 in the other countries, except Portugal and Turkey. At the end of the 1960's, Norway, Sweden, the United Kingdom, and most parts of the United States will have compulsory schooling until age 16. The school leaving age will be 15 in at least seven more: Austria, West Germany, Ireland, Italy, Spain, Yugoslavia, and most Canadian provinces.

[b] Three years of part-time schooling in the berufsschulen are compulsory. By 1990 it is planned to have ten years of compulsory schooling.

[c] Planned, but decision not yet taken.

What is the trend in compulsory education? Table 5 shows that in most countries obligatory attendance will require that a boy or girl of 15 or 16 be in school and receive some upper secondary education.

In order not to unfairly lump together all countries, rich and poor, it should be kept in mind that such countries as Spain, Portugal, and Turkey are relatively poor and have a high proportion of workers in agriculture. In economists' terminology, the agriculture of these countries consists of relatively small family-run farms using a minimum of machinery, modern weed or pest control, and chemical fertilizers. Obviously all hands are needed on the farm. Europeans have said that accessibility affects attendance at school. Poor roads and/or the need to travel long distances discourage attendance, and this condition partly accounts for children who first report to school a year or two after they have reached the age of compulsory schooling. Despite such inaccessibility, however, there are countries with large agricultural areas which have succeeded in increasing attendance at school.

Tables 2 and 3 show that in the Mediterranean countries, including the less well-developed regions of Yugoslavia, school attendance increased sharply within a few years. An increase in enrollment from about 50 percent to 80 or even 90 percent places a heavy burden on the economy. As a result, the demand for primary school has outrun the provision in some countries. Portugal in 1967 did not have enough schools for the 6–12 age group because the system was geared to taking care of those in the 6–10 group.

Another explanation of the demand for further schooling at the secondary level is the increase of participation in schooling. (The OECD uses the term *participation* to mean the years spent in education.) That is, the more years a youngster has been in school, the more likely it is that he will continue his education. In other words, the more education a person has, the more that is desired. Related to this cumulative desire for education is an increase in literacy, which contributes to the ability to use schooling.

Table 6 indicates voluntary enrollment — the number of young people who are staying on in school even when they are not compelled by law to do so — in the early and middle 1960's. Since pupils must stay in school until 14 years of age, the crucial figures for patterns of future enrollment are those for the 15 to 18 year olds. It is expected that the increase in voluntary enrollment of the past decade will be sustained at least until

The Demand for Secondary Schooling

Table 6. Percentage of Young People Enrolled in Full-time Secondary
School in Selected Countries

Country	Age 14	Age 15	Age 16	Age 17	Age 18
Denmark (1960–62 average)..	87.0%	70.0%	46.6%	10.0%	8.0%
United States (1960)	95.3	92.9	86.3	75.6	50.6
Netherlands (1961)	85.0	66.7	53.8	44.7	34.0
Sweden (1963)	55.1	32.2	26.6	15.2[a]	
Portugal (1963)	22.1	20.4	19.3	15.6	13.3
Germany (1965)	78.3	47.8	26.5	16.9	11.2
Austria (1965)	67.0	59.0	53.1	35.8	17.0
Belgium (1964)	84.0	69.7	55.1	42.2	30.7
France (1964)	71.9	57.8	50.0	36.7	24.4
England and Wales (1965) ...	100.0	62.5	25.7	13.7	4.8
Italy (1964)	40.0	28.8	24.5	19.0	13.8

SOURCE: Adapted from *Development of Secondary Education* (Paris: OECD,
1969), Table 8, p. 32.
[a] Percentage enrolled in the combined 17–18 age group.

1975. The latest available forecasts indicate that by 1980 all northwestern European countries and Yugoslavia will enroll between 60 and 90 percent of the 15 to 18 year olds in full-time education.[20] Even in a relatively poor country such as Greece, 50 per cent participation is forecast. A participation figure of 30 percent in Turkey and Portugal may seem low to an American, but this fraction nevertheless represents a very large economic cost.[21]

What might be called the increasing attractiveness of education is illustrated by statistics compiled for Austria, where compulsory schooling ends at 15 and there is a low rate of transfers between work-oriented and pre-university curriculums. In effect, youngsters are discouraged from transferring to curriculums that lead to higher education, and thus the percentage of 16 and 17 year olds in Austrian schools is particularly noteworthy. Table 7 shows that the percentage has been increasing and can be expected to continue to do so.

Table 7. Percentage of Austrian Young People Enrolled in Full-time
Secondary School, 1955–75

Year	Age 14	Age 15	Age 16	Age 17	Age 18
1955	57.5	47.8	43.0	26.7	15.5
1965	67.0	59.0	53.1	35.8	17.0
1975 (projected) ..	87.5	65.5	60.2	54.4	38.0

SOURCE: Adapted from *Development of Secondary Education* (Paris: OECD, 1969), Table 9, p. 33.

57

By 1976 it is expected that 12,750 pupils (11.4 percent of Austria's total projected population of 18 year olds) will take the secondary-school leaving examination (*Maturenten*). Ten years earlier 7,490 pupils (7.1 percent of the 18 year olds) sat for the examination, a figure which was almost double the 4.0 percent of 1955. This increase of almost 300 percent in twenty years is due largely to an increase in the "survival rate." As Table 8 demonstrates, in 1950 one out of three entrants to secondary school, aged 12, survived (that is, remained in school); twenty years later, eight of ten were expected to survive.

In England, pupils who drop out of school as soon as it is legally pos-

Table 8. Survival Rates in Secondary Schools in Austria, the Netherlands, and West Germany

Year	Percentage Entering Secondary School at Ages 12–13[a]	Percentage Remaining in School to Ages 17–19[b]	Survival Rate
Austria			
1950	9.7	2.91	30.0
1955	13.9	7.25	52.0
1960	12.4	8.95	72.0
1965	14.12	11.33	80.0
1970[c]	15.34	13.25	85.0
The Netherlands			
1950	9.7	6.6	68.0
1952	10.9	7.4	68.0
1956	14.3	18.7	62.0
1958	18.9	8.5	57.0
West Germany			
1951	12.3	4.7	38.0
1952	13.4	4.8	36.0
1953	14.4	5.1	35.0
1964	15.5	5.5	36.0
1965	17.1	6.1	36.0
1966	18.2	6.8	37.0

SOURCE: Adapted from *Development of Secondary Education* (Paris: OECD, 1969). Austrian figures are from Table 64, p. 138; Dutch from Table 66, p. 139; West German from Table 65, p. 139.

[a] Austrians enter general secondary school at the age of 12; the Dutch enter general secondary education at 12 to 13; West Germans enter the gymnasium at 12.

[b] Austrians leave at 17, but the English at 18 and the Dutch at 17 to 19; West Germans obtain the abitur usually at 19 but sometimes at 18.

[c] Projected.

sible are figured in the "wastage rate," a phrase popular in Europe because it pinpoints the economic costs of "early-leaving," to use another British expression.[22] A survival rate is much like a wastage rate but the name is less pejorative.[23] A careful study of comparative survival rates has been made between England, Wales, and Austria, on the one hand, and Germany and Holland on the other. In the first three countries a growing proportion of those admitted to secondary education survived to take the leaving examination, whereas in Holland and Germany the survival rate has not changed in recent years.[24]

In England the increasing survival rate of 17 and 18 year olds (see Table 9) is probably due to demographic factors (e.g., residence near schools) and to the pupils' decisions to stay in school beyond the years of compulsory attendance. According to Little and Kallen, very little change has taken place in the percentage of children entering grammar school, the state school that gives access to the universities: in 1953 the percentage of 13 year olds in grammar school was 16.4; in 1955, 16.5; in 1959, 16.0; in 1962, 15.7.[25] Thus survival rates in England have gone up even though there has been little change in the percentage of the age group attending grammar school.

England, Wales, and Austria stand in real contrast to Germany and the Netherlands, where survival rates are not high. In the fifteen-year span covered by Table 8, enrollment in the upper stage of German secondary education increased about 50 percent. This, of course, increased the number of graduates, but the survival rate remained constant. In 1951 the survival rate was 38 percent, expressed as the percentage graduating six years later. In 1966 this percentage was 37. Similarly in the Netherlands the number of secondary-school graduates increased between 1950 and 1958, but the survival rate fell from 68 percent to 57 percent. A growth in the actual number of students enrolled in higher education

Table 9. Percentage of Students Who Continue in Grammar Schools in England and Wales, 1953–61, by Year of Entrance

Age of Students	1953	1955	1957	1959	1961
13.............	100.0%	100.0%	100.0%	100.0%	100.0%
16.............	56.0	60.4	69.0	68.6	72.7
17.............	31.8	36.2	43.8	45.5	48.7
18.............	13.1	14.1	16.8	17.2	...

SOURCE: Adapted from *Development of Secondary Education* (Paris: OECD, 1969), Table 63, p. 138.

can be expected in Holland because the size of the age group has grown, but due to the low survival rate, the percentage eligible for higher education will not increase correspondingly.

In a sense the demand for education is an individual one made by consumers of education. Their demand is realistic enough when judged by the ability of the product — the graduates of secondary and higher education — to find better employment. For this reason politicians in Europe are justified in providing maximum educational opportunity for all. The social benefit of well-qualified manpower, as well as reasonably sophisticated citizens, can be secured without excessive cost to those who previously have had a near monopoly of upper secondary preparatory and higher education.

West Germany is one country which is making definite plans for the projected increases in enrollment, even at the most advanced grades of secondary school. An enlarged enrollment at all levels of schooling has been built into the 1970 Structural Plan for the Educational System.[26] For example, it is hoped that by 1980 75 percent of all 3 and 4 year olds will attend preschool, an increase of some 40 percent over 1970. By 1990 this percentage is expected to be virtually 100. Even more dramatic is the proposed dropping of the age for entry into public education from 6 years to 5 by 1980. By 1975 a tenth year of schooling will be universally available, although it is expected to take another five years before all children can be required to complete ten years of schooling. The authors of the West German program are at pains to point out that theirs are "realistic target notions . . . it is intended to meet the double purpose of offering each individual the greatest possible chance of learning and of keeping the Federal Republic competitive in relation to comparable industrial nations." [27] In the same spirit enrollment in the upper secondary grades (Secondary Stage II for 16–19 year olds) will be encouraged. By 1980 it is hoped that about half the full-time pupils will be in the first and second year of the three-year Secondary Stage II and that from 25 to 35 percent of the older pupils will enroll in the third year.

The preparation of the long-range plans necessary to meet future demands in education is at best a difficult task, if for no other reason than the unreliability of enrollment projections. In 1966 the OECD report *Modernizing Our Schools* commented on the uncertainty of projections: "enrollments in secondary and higher education in the European OECD countries have doubled in the past 15–20 years and can be expected to double

again before 1970. In nearly all countries this rate of increase has sur-
passed even the boldest forecasts. In France, for example, the 1962–63
enrollments in higher education were 14 percent higher than had been
foreseen a few years earlier; the figure foreseen for 1970, which had until
recently been considered extravagant, will be attained by 1966–67." [28]

The growth in population, the extension of compulsory education, the
greater desire to remain in school, and the rising survival rate have coa-
lesced to create an enormous demand for secondary schooling. Planning
commissions in all European countries are attempting to predict and meet
this demand. Because the magnitude and direction of changes within an
educational system are not foreseeable in a precise way, planning should
probably be continuous, along the lines of the Swedish "rolling reform,"
which we shall examine in Chapter 8.

CHAPTER FOUR

Higher Education
Demand and Reconstruction

Higher education, like secondary schooling, has undergone a dramatic growth in the post–World War II period. This numerical expansion and its social significance deserve our attention. In considering the growth of higher education, we must also look at some recent qualitative changes, especially the rising participation of students in the making of academic policy; the increase in "relevant" technical courses; the attempts to keep students in school by shortening their programs and encouraging closer student-faculty rapport; and the decentralizing of education and the offering of extension and correspondence courses.

The European continent has no college structure comparable to that in the United States. Even the word "college" has different meanings. For instance, the *collège* of France is a secondary school equivalent to the *lycée*, and differs from it only in having more support and control from local sources than from the central government. The comparatively new *Kolleg* of Germany is also a secondary school. The college in Great Britain is a three-year institution that has a limited resemblance to the college of the United States. As with the continental European university, it is assumed that general education has been completed prior to entrance. The first two years of the American college program include a good deal of what Europe considers as secondary preparation.

In further distinction to the United States, there are in Europe (including the United Kingdom and Eire) real social differences between higher education of the university type and that of the non-university type. In West Germany, for example, a *Technische Hochschule* may enjoy a high status, and its graduates may be recognized as having had excellent training, but the university has always held a superior place, and university faculty and students have been accorded unique regard. The same thing has been true for other European countries. As Frank Bowles has observed: "If only 5% of the relevant age group enrolls in Europe's higher education, one of the reasons has been that higher education in Europe, on and off the continent, has been a concept with a very restricted connotation." [1] But such restriction is rapidly changing.

At the present time a large percentage of pupils and their families look to secondary and higher education for job preparation. Parents of lower-class background have come to view higher education as a realistic goal for their children, who have been encouraged to go into curriculums that traditionally were not considered appropriate for them. More curriculums have become preparatory rather than terminal, and higher education has come to include a greater variety of advanced studies.

Assuming that a steady increase in enrollment over a fifteen-year period strongly suggests other things such as continued economic growth, it is useful to look at statistics for higher education between 1950 and 1965. Table 10 shows the gains in enrollment during the 1950's and early 1960's. All signs, including the increase of secondary schooling, point to a further increase. Nor should we forget that many more girls will apply for higher education during the 1970's than in 1950 or 1960.[2] Fabio Cavazza reports that between the years 1938–39 and 1955–56 the percentages of females at all levels of school increased from 19.5 to 27.5 percent in Italy, from 30.5 to 36.2 percent in France, and from 12.2 to 17.8 percent in Germany.[3] Cavazza notes also the increase in the total student population: "In Germany in the last fifty years, the number of students per 100,000 inhabitants has trebled, in the Netherlands it has quadrupled, and in France and Italy it has quintupled." [4]

Z. Ratuszniak, writing as director of planning for the Polish Ministry of Higher Education, cites enrollment trends in higher education in Poland: "The number of institutions of higher education . . . increased from 27 in the academic year 1938–39, to 76 in 1960–61. The number of students increased proportionately: more than 170,000 in 1961 as compared with approximately 50,000 in 1938. This increase is even more appreciable when the number of students per 10,000 inhabitants is considered: 14.4 in 1938 and 56.6 in 1961." [5] But figures alone do not tell the complete story of educational accomplishment. Ratuszniak writes that World War II "wiped out nearly 42 per cent of the national resources and

Table 10. Growth Indexes for Enrollments in Higher Education
(1955–56 = 100)[a]

Country	1950–51	1955–56	1960–61	1965–66
Austria	108	100	201	256
Belgium	91	100	135	197
Denmark	87	100	146	221
France [b]	96	100	141	241
Germany (FR)[b]	78	100	135	178
Netherlands [b]	100	100	137	197
Norway [b]	125	100	171	351
Portugal	86	100	128	154
Spain	89	100	125	184
Sweden	75	100	163	263
Switzerland	92	100	138	195
United Kingdom (England and Wales)	...	100	143	...
Yugoslavia	77	100	163	200

SOURCE: Adapted from *Development of Secondary Education* (Paris: OECD, 1969), Table 58, p. 129.

[a] For certain countries enrollments for the years selected were not obtainable; therefore the nearest year available was used. Instead of 1950–51: 1951–52 for Austria, Denmark, and Norway; 1952–53 for Belgium and Yugoslavia. Instead of 1955–56: 1956–57 for Denmark; 1954–55 for France. Instead of 1960–61: 1961–62 for Denmark; 1959–60 for Germany (FR) and France. Instead of 1965–66: 1964–65 for Belgium, France, Netherlands, Portugal, Spain, Sweden, and Switzerland.

[b] University education only.

the Nazi occupiers systematically destroyed all cultural property." [6] Polish authorities look with pride on the growth both of enrollment in and facilities for higher education in their country. Indeed increased enrollments in advanced education, especially (one presumes) in technical education, are actively sought by authorities under a twenty-year plan (1961–80) which attempts to relate higher education to the national economy. In Poland, and probably in other Eastern European countries, the extension of facilities in higher education has been carefully programmed, along with efforts to make advanced secondary and higher schooling attractive. Technical schooling especially is being pushed.

Meeting the Demand for Higher Education

The high birthrate during the 1950's alerted European educators to the acute need for more facilities. The Danish experience is typical. By the early 1960's the increase in the number of students in higher education during the previous decade made it necessary to consider an extension of

64

the capacity of the universities in Denmark: "With a view to this, a committee was appointed by the Ministry of Education in 1961 to work out a building schedule for the Universities of Copenhagen and Arhus in the period 1961–71. As a basis for its work the committee used a forecast of the expected number of undergraduates up to 1960. According to this forecast the number of undergraduates was expected to be double during the decade; viz. from about 9,000 to 18–20,000 in 1970, made up by at least 14–15,000 at the University of Copenhagen and 5,000 at Arhus." [7] The Danish Ministry of Education made a further provisional forecast of 60,000 students in all the institutions of higher education by 1980, more than a sixfold increase from 1950.

The French experience is also noteworthy. The French have done exceedingly able planning for meeting the rising expectations in educational demand and have attempted to overcome geographical and social-economic barriers which limit access to higher education. Between 1948 and 1961 the number of students increased 73 percent. The French Committee for School, University, and Sports Requirements,[8] working under the Office of the General Commissioner for Planning, has forecast even greater expansion up to 1970: "The total number of students will exceed 500,000 in 1970; that is to say, it will be more than doubled in ten years." [9]

A report on higher education in West Germany estimated that the student population in the universities of Western Europe would double between 1960 and 1970 and that in the Federal Republic it would nearly double again between 1970 and 1980. The report noted that two sets of estimates had been prepared for anticipated student populations up to 1980: "The high alternative sets the figure at 380,000 students in 1980, as compared to 284,000 in 1964. . . . More recent surveys by the Conference of Ministers of Education about the actual and prospective attendance at secondary schools . . . indicate that this high alternative can no longer be taken as improbable, because of increasing attendance at general and technical secondary schools." [10]

In all European countries the increase of enrollment in higher education and how to cope with it are major headaches. An Italian commentator explains: "The first problem of the Italian universities, as in many European countries, is a problem of size. The universities, founded to train and educate an elite destined to enter and perpetuate the governing classes, have suddenly had to take in large numbers of students for whom

65

teaching staff, buildings and equipment are lacking. . . . Student numbers have risen enormously, with the result that the universities cannot continue to be havens of pure research and centres of advanced learning for the few. Their rigid and inadequate structure has at the same time prevented them from becoming the centres for the professional and technical training sought by the majority of the students. In fact, a crisis in the universities has been proclaimed both by those who regard them first and foremost as centres of research and learning, and by those who want them to be primarily a means of training young people for the professions, industry, commerce, the civil service and management. The former hold that the special mission of a university is to further scientific research . . . and to meet the desire of young people to acquire . . . knowledge for their own personal and social development. . . . The others — industrial and commercial circles, the civil service and management — complain that the universities continue to regard themselves as centres of disinterested research with purely theoretical aims as the guardians of juridical and humanist traditions, and do not lay sufficient emphasis on the practical training of the personnel needed for industry, the civil service and the professions . . . To this is added another stricture, that the Italian universities emphasize branches of learning which might well have answered the needs of the past but which no longer match the present requirements of the country, which are above all for technicians, economists and scientists." [11]

The countries of Eastern and Central Europe face the same problem of accommodating a rising enrollment in upper secondary and higher education and have the same reasons for encouraging the rising tide of expectations. As we have pointed out, there is no ideological difference between East and West Europe on the right of the individual to have all the schooling he can use. With Europe's rapid industrialization, manpower needs for middle-level as well as highly qualified technicians are urgent in both agricultural and industrialized countries. The phrase "scientific agriculture" is a reminder that rural manpower requires technical and scientific skills as much as urban manpower.

In the Soviet Union 80 to 90 percent of those who graduate from a ten-year school expect to continue their formal education.[12] By 1970 such schools should be available everywhere in the Soviet Union but in the past, as Yanowitch and Dodge have reported, "there must have been considerable frustration of educational expectations among these students. In 4 of the 5 areas for which such data were available, less than one-half of the graduates were successful in gaining admittance to full-time study in a *VUZ* or *tekhnikum*. Many more, therefore, were at work (two-fifths to two-thirds of the graduates, depending on the area) than had anticipated this fate some months earlier." [13]

Even though Soviet legislation may castigate education as too bookish — a customary criticism by those who wish to increase the prestige and attractiveness of farm, office, and factory work — all socialist countries boast of the rapidity with which they are expanding their institutions of higher learning. Again, the pressures of science and technology for highly qualified manpower explain this expansion, which has not yet equaled the increased demand. [14]

In other East European nations the press for facilities is just as great. Poland has a shortage of facilities not only in higher education but in secondary education as well. Although there is no appropriate formula to determine how long an economy can keep up with the rising demand for upper-secondary and higher education, it is obvious that a society can have jobs available for medium and highly qualified manpower without having nearly enough educational facilities. Despite the educational planning of Poland, in the year 1956–57, 24,000 youngsters lacked secondary schools in which to continue their studies, and by 1960–61, 42,000 youngsters were without schools. [15] Gusta Singer writes: "Taking into account those who drop without graduating from primary school, and the percentage of youngsters admitted to secondary schools every year, in relation to their total age group, the numbers decrease rather than increase. In 1955–56 the relation was 56 per cent, in 1960–61 it will be 39 per cent and in 1965–66 it will be 38 per cent." Singer concluded with the gloomy prophecy which these figures warranted: "These predictions are serious warning that growing numbers of youngsters will not be able to find room in secondary schools in the nearest future." [16]

The pressure for admission to higher education in Poland and other nations of Eastern Europe is even greater than that for secondary school. The following explanation by Singer for enrollment pressures (as well as the effects of the two forces we have already noted, the habit of education and the social need for highly qualified manpower) can be applied to almost every country: "The tremendous pressure on the universities, schools of engineering, medical academies, and all other institutions of higher learning can be explained by the fact that higher education, often

67

including board and lodging, is actually free of charge. It seems to be obvious that young people not only believe that education is the most important means for bettering their society, but also realize that knowledge opens up for them new horizons and new practical possibilities for better and higher paying jobs. Academic degrees, considered to be a sign of intellectual interests, are highly appreciated by the public and are instrumental in assuring social status." [17]

The demand for higher education and for more facilities can be explained in yet another way. Little and Kallen note that new criteria for admission have been introduced in Belgium and Yugoslavia. In 1964, they point out, Belgium permitted graduates of secondary technical education to enter the university, which had hitherto been barred to them. This indicates a change in the philosophy of education in Western and Eastern Europe. The 1964 Belgian regulation (Le nouveau régime d'access aux études universitaires) almost doubled the number of students eligible for entrance to higher education (12,000 graduates of technical secondary curriculums and 21,000 graduates of secondary general or academic curriculums). The applied sciences are evidently growing in acceptability and popularity.

Preparatory schools other than the traditional secondary ones are also growing in acceptability. Little and Kallen write that in England and Wales, where the minimum entry qualification for admission to the university is two passes at Advanced Level, between 1955 and 1960 the "percentage of the age group obtaining such a qualification increased from 4.6% to 6.5%, the majority taking their examinations in traditional grammar schools. However, on top of this, 0.2% of the age group in 1955–56 and 0.4% in 1960–61 obtained this qualification in so-called further educational institutions, or in other words outside the traditional selective school system. In Germany similar sorts of facilities are provided by the 'Abendgymnasium' [evening secondary school] and the 'Kolleg' [a relatively new type of advanced secondary school], where pupils who did not enter the gymnasium at the normal age or who left before taking the 'Abitur,' can take the examination, Abiturientenprüfung and gain entry to higher education." [18] German statistics suggest that these types of facilities are going to increase dramatically: "in 1960, 916 people graduated from either the 'Kolleg' or the 'Abendgymnasium'; in 1965 the authorities anticipate 1,836 graduates and in 1970, 2,300. This still represents a small percentage of the number obtaining the 'Abitur' (58,000 is the projected number of graduates from the traditional gymnasium in 1970) but changes like these do serve to increase the possible avenues for entry to higher education and thereby stimulate the expansion in student numbers." [19] The gain in enrollment in West Germany that Little and Kallen have described is due to the famous *Zweiter Bildungsweg* (sometimes written as *2-Bildungsweg*), an alternate route to higher education, with evening gymnasiums for those who do not take the secondary-school leaving examination. [20]

Social Equality in Higher Education

Even in such special schools for the Zweiter Bildungsweg as the one at Erlangen, West Germany, it appears (from a study by Robinsohn and Thomas) that children of unskilled and semiskilled workers were as underrepresented as they were in the universities. But the study did make clear that the school had given children of skilled workers and independent craftsmen an opportunity which they would otherwise have lacked and that many of the pupils looked forward to further education in which they were better represented. On pressing further, however, the investigators learned that lower-class parents did not motivate their children sufficiently to make mechanisms such as Zweiter Bildungsweg useful. [21] In West Germany as a whole, too little use has been made of the Zweiter Bildungsweg, [22] but in the European context this is understandable and even to be expected. Many children from lower- or lower-middle-class homes go to work after completing a vocational course. It is asking a good deal to expect them also to attend night school and prepare for examinations that would allow them to enter higher education. Only the highly motivated are likely to continue with this evening plan.

Robinsohn and Thomas also studied the grounds for selection of pupils for the gymnasium, the school for general, not vocational, study, and found the basis was not primarily academic but social. [23] Middle-class parents help motivate their children, but lower-class German families are unable to supply this kind of incentive. As experience with other West European countries and the United States has shown, lower-class parents have usually been uninformed about educational opportunity, are "socially" foreign to the world of higher education, underestimate their children's ability, and generally lack interest in advanced study for their children because of indecisiveness and want of self-confidence. [24] Even in England, which has had the highest percentage in Western Europe of students from working-class backgrounds in higher education, only 25 percent of the university population represents a proletarian background.[25] In the first years of the 1960's, senior secondary grades and higher education have apparently not been realistic options for laboring and peasant youth, who are unable to forgo the wages they would otherwise earn. Furthermore, there are either not enough facilities for them or they live too far from the existing facilities. But if lower-class family attitudes shift and begin to favor continued instruction, then enrollment in upper secondary and higher education will be increased even more.

Austria has in theory at least moved to reach lower-class students and to expand higher education. Entry requirements were broadened by the 1962 Education Act, which allows pupils to transfer into the general secondary school from other types of schools. Although the transfer can take place only during the early years of secondary school, this change in admission policy has radically affected the multilateral system and has fixed the entrance age for the general secondary school at 10 or 11. In addition Austrian educational authorities, acting on the assumption that geographical access to education makes a difference in enrollments, have provided facilities that make it possible for both graduates of rural grammar schools and those who hold jobs to enter higher education. Austria has also given graduates of various specialized secondary schools, such as teacher-training colleges, business academies, and secondary technical schools, the right to enter higher education.

Little and Kallen report that in 1964–65, 7,785 Austrian students were new enrollees in higher education, though in the preceding year only 6,591 pupils graduated from the general grammar schools. They conclude: "The difference between the two figures may give some indication of the possible magnitude of influence of the alternative methods of obtaining university entry." [26]

Increasing the availability of higher education to more students (as Austria is doing) raises such questions as who is going to make up the "power elite." Traditionally this elite has been the class or group who made the laws [27] and possessed the lion's share of status, power, and wealth. Ralf Dahrendorf has described recent changes in the social class structure, especially in the distribution of power, income, and status. In a sense the abilities of lower-class boys and girls have been recognized only in the past half century,[28] and this recognition has implications for all levels of education. The presence of a large percentage of girls and women

70

in preparatory secondary and higher education likewise has social implications. The existence of a full range of abilities in women of lower-class origin has been accepted, mostly because of the extension of suffrage to them.

In summary, writes Dahrendorf, class (and power) relationships in Europe are "no longer a matter of the antagonism of a small group of all-powerful rulers and a large mass of powerless subjects." [29] Indeed, Europe can no longer be described as a fairly rigid class society. Dahrendorf has observed a shift in power away from a small aristocratic group to the middle class. [30] Although this middle class is predominantly *haute bourgeoise*, with the *petite bourgeoisie* and particularly the lower class underrepresented in the power structure, educators can expect an increase of recruits from the lower class. [31]

Germany has begun to recognize problems of educational inequality and make attempts to remedy them. A 1965 report on the social background of German students, using the father's educational attainment as indicator, contained the following observations: "During the Winter semester of 1962/63 about 32 per cent of male students [in higher education] had a father who was a civil servant, and this was true of 37 per cent of the female students. Another 30 per cent of male and 27 per cent of female students were children of salaried employees. No less than two-thirds of both male and female students thus come from families of civil servants or salaried employees. The next largest group — 14 per cent of male and female students — have fathers who are independent businessmen or tradesmen. About an equal share have fathers in the professions; for instance, doctors, lawyers, taxation consultants, etc. This group includes about 11 per cent of the fathers of male students, and about 16 per cent of female students. Only 6 per cent of the male and 3 per cent of the female students come from working class homes; and only 4 per cent of both are children of independent farmers." [32]

Germany is now, however, attempting to right this imbalance. The Germans write of "equality of chances," and the Structural Plan for the Educational System proposed in April 1970 by the German Educational Council pays careful attention to the findings of Robinsohn and Thomas on differentiation in secondary education as well as to other studies on the link between social class and educational opportunity. Among other things, the plan not only recommends extending compulsory schooling to ten years but proposes that all technical-professional (advanced vocational) training be virtually insured higher status. Teacher training, for example, is spotlighted as a program that should be made highly visible and attractive. On the specific matter of "equality of chances" the plan says: "Equality of chances should not be aimed at by a levelling of requirements. Instead the task is far rather to balance out the differences of chances of the children at an early stage and later to differentiate the educational choice in such a way that the pupils are encouraged according to their learning interests and learning capabilities and are offered corresponding ranges of further education. . . . The improvement of educational chances is mainly regarded under the aspect that disadvantages as a result of regional, social and individual prior conditions must be eliminated." [33]

As we shall see in Chapter 8, the plan is similar to the most recent French reconstruction of education in that it provides a steady increase of curricular options for major work or specialization as the student leaves primary education and moves into secondary schooling. Authors of the plan feel that this increase in options is one way to allow for individual differences among pupils.

Nothing has been more typical of, and central to, Western European education than the extension of educational opportunity. Equally, nothing is more intimately related to the harmonization of education than the persistent effort to increase access to upper secondary, technical, and higher education. Not until 1962 did the literature of educational research and related topics give any indication that the USSR would admit to the existence of barriers to educational opportunity in that country.[34] While it is on Soviet literature that we shall draw for examples, Poland has been in the vanguard of socialist countries which are studying what we choose to call social class influences on education.[35] This attention to the relation between social class and education indicates that both East and West Europe are facing a common reality.[36]

We know that a highly developed scientific, industrial, and agricultural economy needs both medium and highly trained manpower. In recent years the Soviet Union has increasingly experienced this need. The Communist party has permitted this problem to be openly studied because Marxist-Leninist ideology favors equality of opportunity. Inequities can be allowed to surface, for they are seen as "obstacles to the efficient implementation of state policies." [37]

However, since "failures" call attention to particular and personal responsibility, which is apparently not thought desirable, Soviet literature has treated the issue as a general problem — the "considerable gap between the anticipated work careers of secondary school graduates and the types of jobs actually available to most of them." [38] Unfortunately the writers who reviewed the basic Soviet data reported only on the urban population, and the research was done by sociologists at only three centers: Sverdlovsk, Nizhnyi Tagil, and Novosibirsk. These limitations impose severe restraints on generalization and interpretation of the reports.

Eight years of compulsory education became the norm for the USSR by the mid–1960's. There are four paths open to Soviet youth following the completion of the eighth grade, according to Yanowitch and Dodge: "(1) admission to the 9th grade of a . . . [10-year] general education secondary school, the path traditionally chosen by those aspiring to a higher education; (2) admission to a specialized secondary school (*tekhnikum*) providing up to 4 years of training leading to semi-professional occupational status (technician, accountant, nurse); (3) attendance at a lower-level vocational school (*proftekhuchilishch*), preparing students for semi-skilled and skilled workers' occupations; (4) full-time employment, combined with part-time study, if desired, at evening secondary schools (*shkola rabochei molodezh*)." [39]

In the school year 1965–66, almost two-thirds of those completing the eighth grade enrolled either in the two-year upper secondary level of the general education school (the "complete secondary school" as it is called in the Soviet Union) or in one of the specialized secondary schools which train for semi-professional jobs. Studies indicated that in 1965, 20 to 30 percent of eighth-grade pupils planned to begin work, or were undecided, or thought they would attend a vocational school which trained for workers' occupations. [40]

The studies definitely confirmed that the social class to which students' families belonged affected their educational aspirations and actual use of advanced education. From the cities of Nizhnyi Tagil and Sverdlovsk came the following reports: "The educational plans of children whose parents were classified as specialists (individuals who held jobs requiring a higher or secondary specialized education) [upper class] were distinctly more ambitious than the plans of workers' [lower-class] and non-specialist employees' [middle-class] children. Fully 90 per cent of specialists' children in Nizhnyi Tagil expected to continue their secondary education (or general or specialized) upon completing the 8th grade. Among employ-

73

ees' and workers' children the comparable figures were on the order of 70–75 per cent. A roughly similar picture emerged in Sverdlovsk (with 86 per cent of specialists' children opting for continued secondary education compared to 65 per cent for workers' and employees' children). But the more striking difference between these groups lay in the type of secondary school which they expected to attend. Among specialists' children approximately 60 per cent planned to enter the 9th grade of a general-education school, the normal path taken by those aspiring to enter a higher education institution (*VUZ*).[41] Among workers' and employees' children the goal of higher education apparently seemed less attainable, with only some 30–39 per cent of this group expecting to continue their education in the 9th grade. For the children of workers and employees the *tekhnikum*, with its promise of future semi-professional status, was about as popular a choice as the 9th grade, while for specialists' children it was decidedly less appealing." [42]

Yanowitch and Dodge draw the obvious conclusion about career plans: "by the time children from specialists' families reach the 8th grade, most are already oriented toward ultimate admission to a *VUZ*. While a considerable number of workers' children also have these aspirations, approximately one-half see themselves in the future as semi-professional or skilled workers." [43]

In explaining the data, Soviet sociologists state that the homes of specialists have a superior "cultural level" and that these families more frequently and traditionally have pursued a higher education.[44] Further interpretation of the findings shows the effect of income, that is, families with more disposable income can better afford to invest in the higher education of their children. Another possible generalization is that the families of specialists will probably have higher incomes and will have children who become specialists. A similar cycle can be described for the worker, his income, and his children's careers.

The picture, of course, is not as neatly differentiated as this, but the tendency seems clear. Yanowitch and Dodge comment on a study of the educational and work plans of eighth-grade pupils based on the educational level of their parents in Sverdlovsk in 1965: "The children of *intelligentsia* [people with a higher education] typically plan to follow an educational path which will permit them to duplicate (in broad terms) the occupational status of their parents. The children of relatively unskilled workers and lower-level office employees (undoubtedly this would include most of those with an educational attainment of no more than the 7th grade) seek to transcend their parents' occupational status, but expect to do so by moving up one or two notches, i.e., to the status of semi-professional technicians or skilled workers. Relatively few expect to attain *intelligentsia* status. The latter course is aimed for, however, by a large proportion of youth whose parents are skilled workers, higher-level office employees, or semi-professional technicians (parents with an educational attainment level ranging from 8th grade through secondary specialized school)." [45]

That the Soviet Union has been seriously studying its manpower issue, without an attempt to deny the existence of problems, is a significant and unique breakthrough. Usually the socialist countries emphasize the exploitation of farm and factory workers in Western countries and contrast such exploitation with their own equalitarian paradise. Soviet sociologists — and certainly scholars in other neighboring countries will follow suit — have been at work on the same manpower-and-education problems as those studied by Western European social scientists.

The Soviet inquiry into the career plans of young people has not stopped with eighth-grade pupils but has gone on to examine the expectations of pupils in the senior class of the complete secondary school (grades 1 to 10). Using Sverdlovsk as the locus of the inquiry, and assuming it to be a typical Soviet city, the authors found that 39 percent of the class was made up of young people from the homes of workers. In the eighth grade these youngsters had made up about 60 percent of the class.[46] If a vocational school census had been taken, the composition would have been reversed. That is, a statistical overrepresentation of children from the homes of workers as compared to the percentage of workers in the general population would have been found in vocational school classes. In Sverdlovsk, for example, workers' children constituted 71.5 percent of the student body in vocational schools; the children of "peasants" made up 11 percent; but children of employees and "others" together formed only 17.5 percent.[47]

The Soviet decree to make ten-year education "universal" by 1970 will wipe out the problem of career plans by eighth-grade students, but it only shifts the issue to the tenth grade. Will there be a change in the educational and work plans of these students? It would seem so. In the countries of Western Europe when pupils are kept or lured into higher secondary education, an impressive percentage of them plan to enter higher education.

The conclusion is obvious. The political leaders of the USSR wish to strengthen their country by enlarging its pool of highly qualified manpower; therefore they must find ways to reduce the social class differential by increasing the educational appetite of adolescents from lower-class homes. This is, of course, the manner in which the social issue would be posed in a country such as England, and there is no reason for using radically different terms when the USSR is under review.

The Career Plans of Youth, a study prepared at the Urals State University in Sverdlovsk, recognizes the presence of distinct inequalities in both the aspirations and the educational attainments of Soviet young people, depending on their social class origin: "The social class composition of the student body varies markedly among the various types of educational institutions, with the share of intelligentsia children increasing and that of workers' children declining as students move from lower to higher grades of secondary school. Workers' children seem to predominate in vocational schools training students for workers' occupations, while intelligentsia children represent a disproportionately high share of pupils in the upper grades of general education schools that provide applicants for higher education. The social class composition of students receiving a higher education clearly differs from that of the population as a whole, with a particularly small representation of rural youth." [48]

Besides the underrepresentation of the lower class, Soviet leaders seem equally disturbed by the overly ambitious plans of the children of intelligentsia. The economy of the USSR needs a great many skilled craftsmen and well but not highly qualified manpower, such as engineers. The concern about too-high aspirations complements the criticism expressed by Premier Khrushchev in 1958, when he told members of the Young Communist League that 60 percent of the students in Moscow's institutions of higher learning were sons and daughters of high party officials, industrial managers, and high-ranking officers of the armed forces. [49]

No doubt there is a discrepancy between the aspiration of individual young people and the economic needs of the USSR as interpreted by the Communist party leadership. Khrushchev and other leaders have been unalterably opposed to a young person's making a career selection without being guided by the economic needs of the country (as interpreted by the party). Obviously, the Communist party ideologists and others professionally concerned with developing morality hope that the "good" Soviet man or woman will identify his or her personal career interests with the needs of the economy (or society). This attitude has been a more potent factor in career selection in Eastern than in Western Europe. However, as Murray Yanowitch writes, the "career expectations of Soviet youth are very much more 'ambitious' than the existing occupational structure or its short-run prospects can justify. The clearest expression of this discrepancy between individual aspirations and social requirements is the predominant orientation of secondary school graduates toward higher education at a time when only 20–25% of them can expect to continue full-time schooling. It is also revealed in the obvious unpopularity of production training for workers' trades in the general education schools, as well as the near-universal disdain for a work career in agriculture among rural youth with relatively high levels of schooling." [50]

In the USSR, then, familiar social problems surround the drive or lack of drive for education. Middle- and upper-class students dominate Soviet higher education, but for several reasons this dominance is changing. Furthermore, the Soviets now require ten years of compulsory education, and such a tactic will predictably increase desire for higher education. And the Soviets continue to study the social discrepancies within the makeup of their student bodies. All of these activities should make educational opportunity more equal.

Russia, Austria, and Germany, as we have seen, are moving toward the equalization of educational possibilities. Can the same be said for other countries? Michel Debeauvais and his collaborators would give an affirmative answer to the question of whether the French lower classes have increased their representation in higher education.[51] But F. L. Cavazza cites a study made in France which shows that 85 to 90 percent of small farmers, artisans, and low income self-employed workers did not feel that their children needed a full secondary education.[52]

Cavazza's finding cannot be extended to representative parental attitudes in Greece, or in either of the Germanies. In Greece, for example, even villagers in the remotest towns hope that their children, and certainly the boys, will find their way to higher education. It is not uncommon in Greece to find village girls and boys who have taken up temporary residence in towns which have secondary schools. More and fuller multi-national measures of attitudes are needed to determine the range of Cavazza's remarks.

Cavazza, in an optative mood, notes that reconstruction in education makes it increasingly more likely that children from lower-class families will seek full secondary education and even schooling beyond the secondary. Extension of obligatory education has given students more time in which to choose between early employment and continued schooling. The trend is away from the election of the short, terminal course of study followed by employment. Cavazza writes: "In Italy for example, up until 1963 the young people, after four years of elementary school had to make a choice between enrolling in the *scuola media* or in the *scuola di avia-mento professionale*. The latter usually precludes entrance into the university; it is thus a 'dead-end street,' chosen only by those who know they cannot aspire to the longer and more expensive pre-university schools." [53]

Although comparative statistics on the middle schools in more than one country and over a number of years are lacking, Mario Reguzzoni, a leading authority on educational trends (at least among the Common Market nations), feels that the creation in 1940 of the *scuola media*, the forerunner of the contemporary model, has been of importance.[54] In his book *La Réforme de l'Enseignement dans la Communauté Economique Européenne*, Reguzzoni devotes much of a chapter to the background and creation of what he calls the "école moyenne unique" (the middle school) in Italy.[55] What this middle school might mean is suggested by the term "participation." Indeed, if participation is an important determinant of continuing in education, at least to the next higher stage, the Italian middle school has served the purpose of keeping in school many young people who otherwise might have settled for a terminal vocational education.

Social inequalities in European higher education, as we see, do exist. Within countries like Austria, Russia, France, Greece, West Germany, and Italy are movements to solve such inequalities. The extension of compulsory education, the broadening of admissions requirements to the universities, and the various attempts to make education appealing to the lower classes help to alleviate the problems and to insure that the lower classes are well represented in the great clamor for higher education.

Patterns of Reconstruction

To answer the demands for a higher education, many European countries have adopted reforms. An example is the comprehensive scheme presented to the Italian Parliament in 1959 after eight years of planning: "Total expenditure for a period of ten years was estimated at about 1,400 thousand million lire, over and above the funds normally allocated for State education." (Allocations described as "substantial" were made.)

"Despite this substantial increase in expenditure, there is still a large gap to be filled, in both political and university circles there are insistent demands for further and larger grants. It is estimated, on the basis of reliable demographic data for the last fifteen years, that towards 1975 there will be no fewer than 400,000 students. . . . Six times as many . . . lecturing staff will be needed . . . and an even greater increase will be required in the number of assistants. University premises must be more than doubled, and above all there must be a very substantial increase in grants for scientific research." [56]

A similar report could be made by any one of the European countries, east or west. The case of West Germany is typical. Since the number of students in higher education in Germany may well increase from some 284,000 in 1964 to 380,000 in 1980, one can understand why their report includes "plans for expansion of existing and the founding of new universities" which will provide that "300,000 places will be available at universities. By 1970 there should in addition, be some 60,000 places at colleges of education and similar teacher training centres for which university entrance level is a requirement. There also should be some 100,-000 places at advanced technical colleges immediately below university level, and at the colleges of engineering." [57] Yet it is not quantitative but qualitative change that is most striking in European higher education.

STUDENT PARTICIPATION AND RELEVANCE

The most visible, if not the most important, new trend in European higher education is the move toward a greater degree of student involvement in the formation of academic policy. We believe that a large majority of European and American students press for such participation in order to increase the relevance of university training for careers in the modern world. Of course, modernization in education leads to modernization in agriculture, business, and industry. With the organization of such left-wing political action groups as the Students for a Democratic Society in the United States, the Socialist German Students League, the Situationists of France, and the Democratic Student Syndicate of Spain, higher education has been under continuous pressure to give students a larger share in both governing and policy decisions. In France, where the student riots in the spring of 1968 and again in 1970 were particularly violent, the government took immediate steps to increase the role of students in decision making.[58] As a result of the Orientation of Higher Education Act, passed by the French Assembly in November 1968,[59] students are now represented on all levels of the higher education organization in France: the National Board of Higher Education and Research, regional boards, and the several universities and research institutions.[60]

There are other signs that at least in Western Europe "student power" is increasing. According to Kneucker, Austria, which may be said to have a system of higher education where students possess minimal power, has a *Hochschülerschaft*, which is the "official representative of the student body: It must be heard before draft bills are sent to Parliament or rules of the Ministry of Education are issued; it participates in the administration of all scholarship programmes and disciplinary procedures. It has, however, no part in the decision-making processes of faculties (universities)." [61] But, adds Kneucker: "As in Italy and in the United States, there have been discussions as to whether or not the student body should participate in the appointment process of professors." [62] Actually, the *Österreichische Hochschülerschaft* is far more a service organization — as is a good deal of "student government" in the United States — than a body sharing with the faculty in the formulation of policy. "The *Hochschülerschaft* provides for student advisory, information, lecture, and tutor programmes, text books and study materials, sometimes even for libraries; it runs theatres, a health and insurance service, and provides for medical help, part-time jobs, student housing and cafeterias; it cooperates with foreign student groups." [63]

In Denmark there is a lively debate about whether students should take part in the administrative organizations of the universities. Under discussion in 1966 was a proposal that "for each branch of study an advisory board should be established, having about as many students as teachers on it. These advisory boards should deal with questions of syllabus and examinations, and the relationships between teachers and students. Such boards have already been set up in several institutions. . . . Further, the universities have proposed that students should have seats — without right of vote — on Faculty Boards and the Administrative Councils assisting the Vice-Chancellor of each university." [64] The Danish plan is very much concerned with the issue of relevance.

A similar philosophy of student participation prevails in West Germany, Italy, and the United Kingdom. In Germany, for example, the state of Hesse has blazed the trail, as it has often done in educational affairs. The University Reform Bill (*Referenten-Entwurf eines Universitätsge-*

setzes) [65] provides for representatives of the student-elected parliament to be members of the university *Konzilien* [66] and *Senate*, which, to oversimplify, have most to do with setting standards for the curriculum of higher education. Other German states have roughly similar legislation under review, and in Italy the Parliament has received the law *Provvedimenti Urgenti per l'Università Disegno di legge.*[67]

The British attitude is summarized in a joint statement issued on behalf of the British academic community by the vice-chancellors and principals (the equivalent of university presidents in the United States) and the National Union of Students. The statement opens with a recognition that the "social situation has been changing rapidly in recent years, and that men and women of student age are expected to bear the full responsibilities of adult life much earlier than would have been thought reasonable a generation ago. We therefore believe it to be right and proper that the form of the academic community and the role of students within it should be correspondingly modified and modernised." [68] The modernization should allow "student participation in university decision-making."

Although it is difficult to compare exactly the French, West German, Italian, and British conceptions of student participation (as reflected in their legal codes), the request of the British National Union of Students bears quoting because it touches on many of the desires which European university students have voiced. Admittedly the British statement is restrained, hardly corresponding in its tone to the militant student demands heard in many quarters of Europe. But its message is typical: "The National Union of Students seeks effective student presence on all relevant committees. Our discussions identified three broad areas of operation of such committees: (a) the whole field of student welfare — for example, health services, catering facilities and the provision of accommodation — where there should in our view be varying degrees of participation of students in the decision-making process. Apart from this, there is the area which covers, for example, the operation of student unions and the management of a wide range of extra-curricular activities, in which most university student organisations rightly have long had complete responsibility, (b) that relating for example to curriculum and courses, teaching methods, major organisational matters, and issues concerning the planning and development of the university — where the ultimate decision must be that of the statutorily responsible body. In this area, we would regard it as essential that students' views should be properly taken into account, and (c) that involving for example decisions on appointment, promotions and other matters affecting the personal position of members of staff, the admissions of individuals and their academic assessment — where student presence would be inappropriate. Students should, however, have opportunities to discuss the general principles involved in such decisions and have their views properly considered." [69]

The British statement also stressed course content and teaching methods; examinations; discipline; "the age of majority," which the students wished to be lowered from 21 to 18; career advice; and freedom of speech — but there was almost no mention of irrelevance. On the topics of course content and teaching methods, linked with freedom of speech, the statement endorsed the right of any student to be heard, however unorthodox his views might be; the reciprocal right of instructors to teach without interference, even from students, was also admitted. The statement went on to say that while the teacher must not be subject to pressure, the "relevance of the subject to the contemporary situation and to contemporary problems should be made explicit . . ." This was as close as the statement came to the issue of relevance.

"Relevant" programs have been available both in East and Central Europe and in North America, but what is the relevance that students in higher education in Western Europe desire? [70] The term is used here to mean the applied sciences and technical knowledge of business and industrial management which complement "pure" economics, computer technology which similarly complements "pure" mathematics and logic, and so on. For a long time Europe has had institutes of technical higher education, but their graduates have lacked the high social status of university graduates in humanistic studies or in the humanistically oriented professions like law and theology. Medicine, because of historical accident, is the one technical field not classified as within technology.

Premier Khrushchev's 1958 charge of irrelevance in education was the basis for reform in East European countries.[71] In response, many of these nations passed legislation on both secondary and higher education which attempted to increase education's relevance to the workaday world.

In Western Europe the upgrading of the social status of applied science graduates has resulted in additional enrollment in those fields,[72] and the trend in the curriculums of higher education has been plain even to the man in the street. As a matter of fact, the shift toward scientific studies has been on the increase since 1950. Laurent Capdecomme made specific note of this in 1966, when he wrote: "the following is the prospect: ⅖ of the students might be expected to follow scientific courses, the same number would study arts, law, administration and economics, and ⅕ would turn to medical and pharmaceutical studies. Hence the Faculties of Science, Medicine and Pharmacy must be prepared to double their numbers in the seven years from 1963 to 1970. . . . From the estimates made by the Committee on University Requirements in connection with the present plan, it appears that the schools responsible to the Directorate of Higher Education will be called upon as from 1970 to train 5,500 engineers — that is to say, about 4,000 more than in 1961, which, according to the Committee, will account for almost half of the total number of engineers receiving diplomas in France at that date." [73]

This has been exactly the trend in higher education throughout the other nonsocialist countries. In a report on higher education in Ireland prepared in 1966, a single sentence tells the story: "There has in recent years been a dramatic increase in the number of science students, from 601 in 1952–53 to 1,832 in 1964–65." [74]

In France's Orientation of Higher Education Act (1968) a brief paragraph on the student reads: "Concerning students, the universities must make every effort to insure them the means of their orientation [development] and of the best choice of the professional field to which they intend to dedicate themselves and, towards this end, to give them not only the necessary knowledge but the fundamentals of a training." [75]

The "fundamentals of a training" often turn out to be more the study of, than practice in, one or another technology. On the other hand, a paper on the reform of higher education in Italy makes this statement: "Regarding the structure of the university, faculty reform has long been in view, covering both degree syllabuses, planning of courses and so on and the need to bring the faculties into line with various academic, professional and administrative trends, according to the present needs of national life. It has already been decided to reorganize certain faculties such as that of *Ingegneria* and certain degree courses in mathematics, physics and other subjects." [76] The direction of change is toward practicality as well as up-to-date generalizations. Relevance is being achieved. But yet another problem faces European educators: the drop-outs from the university.

In Germany an effort has been made to increase the holding power of the university — the ability and/or success in keeping students in school — by shortening the time a student must attend to complete his program. In Italy, where almost half the students who enroll in the universities do not complete their studies, the approach has been imaginatively diversified. The following statement on reforms in university studies in that country is quoted at length because it itemizes many of the same points which one hears in the discussions of higher education all over Europe. The program calls for "a progressive increase in the numbers of teaching staff and assistants to allow closer contact with the students; easing and lengthening the number of syllabuses of study courses which are generally overcrowded as a result of the multiplicity of subjects and teaching methods; tightening of university discipline by making it compulsory to attend lectures regularly and to participate in seminars, written work, research teams and so on. . . . Another proposal bearing indirectly on this problem, and which would also meet the needs often expressed by industry and commerce at congresses of representatives of the universities and industry . . . is to institute intermediary diplomas or certificates before the doctorate degree. The idea is that those who want only a shorter course of study, or who are unable to complete the studies they have started, should be able to obtain intermediate diplomas and certificates, which would still require a solid academic and methodological basic training, over at least two or three years of study." A twofold advantage is claimed for this kind of diploma: "In the first place, it would enable students who were unable or who did not wish to follow a complete university course to develop and improve upon their secondary education in a serious and constructive manner without wasting their university years. In the second place, it would train people for executive jobs or for 'middle-level' careers who were up to the requirements of industry and commerce." [77]

The only other new approach of which we know is referred to by German educators as "measures to reduce the duration of studies." Though they may not appear as such, these measures are a way of coping with the university drop-out. A recent report on the reconstruction of higher education in West Germany acknowledges a serious "gap between the official minimum length of studies and their average duration," a gap particularly serious in what is called the philosophical faculty and in the natural sciences and technical subjects. To illustrate, the following statistics are reported for the philosophical faculty: "the average length of study now extends to between 13 and 14 semesters. . . . In the natural science subjects required for a teaching post in secondary schools the average time of study had, from 1960 to 1963 alone, risen by a full semester (from 10.7 to 11.8 semesters)." [78]

The question of "length of stay" has been taken up by a variety of German authorities, e.g., the state parliaments, the Conference of Länder Premiers, the Standing Conference of Ministers of Education, the Bundestag, the West German Conference of University Rectors, and the German National Union of Students. Both the West German Conference of University Rectors and the Conference of Ministers of Education are agreed on the urgency of at least reducing the amount of factual subject matter required of students "in favour of a concentration on the systematic structure of the subject, the methodology of scientific thought, and of a training in fundamentals." [79] The university rectors and education ministers further suggested that counseling services be improved so that students could make the best use of their time. They also recommended an appeal to industry and business to eliminate their demand for graduate degrees when required "solely for reasons of prestige." [80]

DECENTRALIZING HIGHER EDUCATION

In addition to the drop-out problem, the issue of decentralizing higher education is a universal one. In every country of Europe political leaders join with economists, ideologists of social democracy, and educators in desiring greater access to higher education for students who live far away from major cities. Why has legislation not yet forced decentralization? The answer is partly financial. It costs a great deal to duplicate the laboratories and libraries that are needed for a first-rate modern education. A further consideration is the fact that staff and students wish to be where entertainment and cultural events are plentiful. Perhaps France has done better than other countries with this problem.

The decision to increase enrollment in French higher education is economically wise — the benefits for individuals and for French society justify that enlargement. It is also wise to multiply higher education in cities other than the capital [81] (where 130,000 students are enrolled at the University of Paris). A proposal under serious study would create perhaps nine branches of the university, each to be placed in and around Paris. A university already has been built in Vincennes, on the outskirts of Paris.

The USSR also has attempted to make higher education widely available through correspondence study or part-time programs, which usually have permitted a technician to leave his work and be supported for the time which his study requires him to be at a university.

Denmark and Sweden, as well, have undertaken vigorous programs of decentralizing higher education. In addition to establishing a new university at Umeå, the Swedish universities of Uppsala, Lund, Göteborg, and Stockholm opened branches in 1967–68 at Orebro, Växjö, Karlstad, and Linköping, respectively. Norway may begin a university north of the Arctic Circle in Tromsö. If the ideal of educational opportunity for all is taken seriously, there must be an increase both in numbers and in access to higher education. Certainly citizens of the United States find this a familiar drive.[82]

From a practical viewpoint, providing more opportunities for higher education usually means establishing facilities in rural areas and thereby making the small cities and towns much more attractive to young people than they would otherwise be. Such decentralization reinforces the basic economic argument that most European countries cannot afford to squander their potential of highly qualified manpower.

Decentralization, taking measures to keep students in the university, making programs relevant, and allowing more student participation in academic policy-making are all activities which promise to reform European higher education. Changes in the social makeup of university student bodies is also taking place, thanks to some countries' efforts to realize egalitarianism. With various tactics the lower-class student is being wooed to enter higher education. His greater representation will have social impact, of course. The European countries, we see, share the press for higher education, and they are encouraging it in significant ways which will eventually reform higher education.

CHAPTER FIVE

The Extent
of Abilities

As we saw in Chapter 4, European countries have developed various strategies for attracting larger numbers of lower-class students into higher education. Residence outside the city where a university is located is no longer a major handicap for most rural youngsters. Easing admission policies, changing and positively reinforcing parental attitudes toward university training, creating more night school and correspondence courses all help the underprivileged student to continue his education (though, of course, these opportunities are not yet consistently pervasive). Yet professional educators' philosophical presuppositions may also block his entrance.

Platonic and Aristotelian Myths about Ability

Many educators still believe that only a small percentage of the population is able enough to enter the senior grades of the secondary school and then the university. They claim that only about 10 percent of pupils aged eleven to eighteen compose the academic elite. This elite, the argument continues, should be enrolled in a school whose curriculum suits the range of abilities found in the academic chosen few. It is interesting to consider the source of such a figure as 10 percent. No European research literature has contributed this fraction; instead, an estimate of 10 percent — and more often 5 percent — has been held as commonsensical by people for many generations. When the Swedish psychologist and educator T. Husén told an OECD study group that European nations could not afford to segregate 3, 5, or even 10 percent of pupils in the university preparatory schools of

87

their multilateral (selective) system,[1] he was challenging the venerable mythology that only a small fraction of the population is educable and that the remainder are suited by nature only for "training." Husén went on to say that a modern technological society needs at least 25 percent of its adolescents in programs which lead to higher education.

Linked to this belief in the limited extent of academic ability is the distinction drawn between education and training. Education is the study of languages (their grammar, literature, and so on), history, mathematics, and theoretical science (physical laws and the formulas with which theoretical science usually has been associated). Training, on the other hand, is preparation for a specific job or craft. For those who appear to have the talents for handicraft, there is apprenticeship in skilled trades such as cabinet making. But most often, of course, training is directed toward those who are regarded as lacking in talent. Their specific instruction lasts from one to three years. (Chapter 7 describes the present trend in vocational preparation toward longer periods of technical training and away from short-term courses whose graduates are prepared for specific jobs that may become obsolete in a modern economy.) The basic assumption has been that only a precious few have the requisite ability to become leaders of men, whether in political, social, or economic life. This assumption rests on a biological distribution of ability in the general population. But the biological argument has been combined with traditional Aristotelian and Platonic views on mankind, education, and training. Such a Platonic philosophy of education, incorporating ideas attributed to Aristotle,[2] dominated European philosophy of education until 1920 and has remained powerful up to the present.

In essence, this tradition equates ability with intelligence and intelligence with what Husén has called the "theoretical" as distinguished from the "practical." [3] Theoretical studies are found in the academic curriculums, while practical studies have been seen as developing the manual skills necessary for menial, not learned, occupations. This economic division was a natural outcome of the Platonic and Aristotelian philosophy, though over the centuries a change has evolved that was not implicit in the original agreement. Plato and Aristotle took for granted a landed aristocracy which illustrated its intellectuality in political activity and in maintenance of the right order. With the development of a much more complex economy, an occupational hierarchy became identified with an elite order.

But however the hierarchy was determined, the rich or wellborn always had access to the best education.

For centuries the fitness of this order had been esteemed as natural. Aristotle's *Politics* was used to demonstrate its rightness, which presumably had been demonstrated originally for the West by Plato. The Platonic typology was triangular; the apex of the triangle was occupied by a very small elite whose chief responsibility was to govern in accordance with rules based on the moral and physical order of nature. In *The Republic* Plato drew the apex of the triangle to such a fine point that but a single person stood at the top, the "philosopher-king." [4] Plato regretted that Athenians would not accept the notion of a philosopher-king, and he assured his friend Glaucon: "Until philosophers are kings, or the kings and princes of this world have the spirit and power of philosophy, and political greatness and wisdom meet in one, and those commoner natures who pursue to either the exclusion of the other are compelled to stand aside, cities will never have rest from their evils, — no, nor the human race, as I believe, — and then only will this our State have a possibility of life and behold the light of day." [5] Plato designated as "golden" those people whose natural qualities fitted them to rule. The education appropriate to the golden ones was an education preparatory for rule. Filling in the remainder of the triangle were men whose nature Plato described with successively less noble metallurgical images. These men were the hands of society, the workers. The base of the triangle, the largest area of it, was occupied by those whose nature was of a common sort — like iron. The educational implication of the Platonic typology was that the golden nature went along with the ability to do theoretical studies, such as studies of the laws of the physical sciences or of the rules in grammar. (Today we describe this education as that which teaches pupils to manipulate symbols — especially words.) In contrast, most men, according to Plato's diagram, did best with the information and skills which (even recently in Europe) have been thought of as appropriate for short-term vocational training during early adolescence. Those who were governed — those who worked with their hands rather than their heads — obviously needed little theoretical or academic study before embarking on vocational training preparatory to work at the age of fifteen.

Aristotle, too, thought of wisdom as intelligence, and intelligence as exercised by theoretical studies rather than by vocational training. The latter was for those who must labor and not for those who must rule. These traditional views about theoretical education and practical training are alive today, as Husén points out: "It is evident that aptitudes are moulded by the cultural and social factors influencing the society within which the school is operating. Thus, the dichotomy 'theoretical' and 'practical' can be regarded as a reflection on the occupational stratification: professions demanding some type of academic training on the one hand and manual occupations on the other. In the former types of occupation a high demand on the ability to operate complex symbols is put upon the incumbents. Those who are proficient in one way or another in manipulating symbols — scientists, lawyers, engineers, etc. — are the rulers and masters of modern society. Most of our so-called intelligence tests are validated against criteria which measure some sort of verbal ability. A certain level of verbal intelligence is a necessary prerequisite for a successful career in general education, which in its turn is a necessary prerequisite of obtaining a high-quality specialised education." [6]

We have cursorily traced the history of the categories "theoretical" and "practical." What has been their effect on European education? Can the academically able be distinguished at an early age?

The Measurement of Ability

Husén believes that differentiation of pupils on the basis of presumed differences in ability ought to be postponed at least until the age of fifteen, and he has criticized the assertion that academic aptitude can be assessed accurately enough at the age of ten or eleven. (Many European school systems differentiate pupils at this early age.) He explains: "This assertion . . . needs the qualification that, *within our present social system*, one can determine the actual scholastic ability of a child and predict its academic achievements with a fairly high degree of accuracy for a period of a few years." [7] His was a very charitable estimate of the understanding educators have had of theoretical ability and of the instruments, such as teachers' grading marks, that have measured it. Nevertheless, because most executive, professional, and other careers demanding highly qualified manpower require higher education (often at the university), pupils enrolled in vocational training have their careers effectively determined at age ten or eleven.

Research performed in Swedish schools has pointed toward the conclusion that if theoretical ability could be assessed at a relatively early age, *practical ability* could not. Therefore, Husén concluded, it was erroneous to transfer a majority of pupils into practical (terminal vocational) curriculums because these pupils did not score well on intelligence quotient tests and/or did not have high grades in their primary school classes. Husén argued that pupils were being transferred to practical curriculums not on the basis of a known practical bent, but because of their supposed deficiency in the intelligence needed for theoretical studies preparatory for elite occupations. European and American educators have come to realize that lower-class homes by and large accept the idea that "education is not for the likes of us." This attitude can easily be mistaken for a confession of academic inability. Husén has documented the greater lack of interest in further education among pupils from homes of lower social class origin than among those from homes of upper-class standing. This tended to be the case especially when students were differentiated at the ages of ten to thirteen. Twice as many youngsters with average marks were apt to come from lower-class homes as from upper-class homes. Even pupils with great promise for theoretical studies tended not to continue their schooling beyond the obligatory years if they came from homes of the lower class.[8]

In conclusion Husén emphasized the fact that, "according to the criteria adopted by the school itself, a fairly high number of academically talented pupils from middle or lower class homes do not even apply for admission to schools providing academic education, in a situation where transfer on a selective basis takes place at a fairly early age. We therefore arrive at the tentative conclusion that, when selection in a double stream system is made at an early age, a large amount of talent is 'lost.' A reasonable hypothesis is that if 'creaming-off' of the academically talented is postponed to a later age or if they are taken care of within a more flexible comprehensive system, they are more likely to commit themselves to a longer and more promising school career." [9] By way of illustration, Husén noted that in the Swedish rural districts where the nine-year comprehensive school (students not segregated according to "ability" or social class) had been introduced and "where roughly 25 to 30 per cent of the age groups have been provided with the equivalent of the *Realskola* education (lower section of the pre-university school), the Gymnasium enrollment has been twice that of comparable districts where there is no provision beyond a seven-year elementary school." [10]

Jean Floud has referred to social class inequities by recalling the French phrase *la famille éducogène*, which means families "providing for their children an educative environment including, in particular, supporting social and intellectual pressures in the same direction as those exerted by the schools.[11] For obvious reasons, such families are proportionally more numerous at the top of the social scale. At any given level, 'la famille éducogène' as so far identified by investigators, need not be more prosperous, though it tends to be smaller than average; it is likely that the parents will have had some education beyond the compulsory minimum; the mother before marriage may have followed an occupation superior to that of the father; and the climate of opinion in the home will be educationally favorable by such elementary criteria as willingness to visit the school and talk with teachers; and a knowledgeable approach to educational facilities. The children of such families will tend to be more successful on the average, both as regards competition for entry to selected schools and universities, and as regards propensity to stay in the course once admitted." [12]

Theoretical and practical abilities, then, are hard to measure and often depend on the student's social background. Too often a student is discouraged because of a traditional and faulty view that he is one from the unacademic masses or because of a low test score which illustrates his social class more than his inherent capabilities.

The Effects of Social Class on Educational Opportunity[13]

The Robbins report on higher education in Britain spotlights the lower social class — the working class — as the major reserve of untapped ability.[14] Floud reported in 1961 that while the proportion of British working-class boys in preparatory secondary schools had increased by 50 percent since 1945 the figure was "still very low — rather less than one in six as compared with nearly one in two of children from non-manual homes. At the university level, the chances of working-class boys are virtually unchanged, although those of boys from other families have more than doubled. Only one working-class boy in fifty proceeded to the universities in the post-war period, as compared with one in five boys from other families." [15]

Europe has had few people better qualified to speak of the influence of social class than Floud, who writes of it as a "prime source of . . . 'unnatural' inequalities which do not rest on differences of endowment." Many would agree with Floud that social class is related more closely to educational inequality than to any other factor. She writes that social class has interfered with the balance of educational opportunity and performance in several ways: "at any given level of ability, it is both cause and consequence of inequalities of educational opportunity, in the sense of unequal chances of access to educational institutions or facilities; or, again at a given level of ability, it may influence the volume and direction of pupils' energies and, hence, their educational output; or, finally and more radically, it may affect the very structure of ability itself." [16]

Before 1945 the influence of social class on education was perceived as "snobbery in education — with invidious social differences in school or overt social bias in selection procedures," according to Floud. Until 1945, "roughly speaking, the problem of social class in education was seen . . . primarily as a *barrier to opportunity*. The problem was an institutional one: how to secure equality of access for children of comparable ability, regardless of their social origins, to institutions of secondary and higher education designed for, and still used in the main by the offspring of the superior social classes." [17]

The political response to the problems of class structure was inevitably to reduce material disadvantages stemming from poverty. But more than full employment and relative affluence are required. There is a "need to formulate the problem more subtly and to see social class as a profound influence on the educability of children." [18] In other words, differences in social classes produce many long-range handicaps which are not often articulated.

For example, although demand for further education persists at all levels, there is some question about the effectiveness of this demand. Floud observes that the "rising demand from working-class families for a selective and extended education for their children, their success in competition for places in the grammar schools in which this demand can be met, and the upthrust of advanced courses in the secondary modern schools catering overwhelmingly for working-class children, are commonplaces of the English education scene." Yet, as she points out, the "fact remains that there is quite severe class-based wastage and early-leaving from these grammar schools." [19] Some 59 percent of the children from families of professional, managerial, clerical, or other nonmanual backgrounds can be found among those in a sample of pupils who leave school at age seventeen or eighteen, but only 7 percent are offspring of unskilled or semiskilled manual workers. [20]

Social class is likewise related to failures on examinations. A greater percentage of lower-class children fail than do pupils from the upper classes. Husén reports that in 1940 the Swedish School Committee followed up some 11,000 pupils in the lower section of the pre-university school: "Only half the pupils reached the leaving examination or were transferred to the Gymnasium within the normal number of years. A fifth of the pupils repeated at least one grade." Husén held that the same situation prevailed in Germany, "where the overwhelming majority of pupils admitted to the Gymnasium at the age of ten do not reach *Abitur* at all." [21]

The message is that a significantly higher percentage of pupils from homes rated "lower class" leave school early or fail than do pupils from homes in the upper order of society. Husén concluded: "The high failure rates in secondary academic schools in many countries imply a considerable loss of talent. A system in which at least a quarter of the pupils carefully selected for the lower section of the academic school drop out, while another 10 to 25 per cent repeat grades, must be judged to have failed in meeting its own objective of educating the high-quality pupils." [22]

It will be difficult, Husén maintains, to reduce the failure and drop-out rates by means of contemporary forms of screening. "Screening is an important element in European education, and applies both to transfers from one level to another, and to the pursuit of studies within a given level. In Western Germany, selection for the *Gymnasium* takes place at the age of ten, but in most provinces (*Länder*), less than one fourth of those admitted take the final examination (*Abitur*), in spite of severe competitive selection from the beginning. In France, between 40 and 50 per cent fail in the corresponding examination (*baccalauréat*), for all the screening that has occurred up to and during the lycée stage. In England a committee appointed by the Ministry of Education to look into grammar-school failures notes that more than one third of the students never got as far as a final certificate, in spite of their having been screened on admission by means of the 11-plus examinations." [23]

Lower-class students, then, encounter many subtle difficulties in entering and surviving in school. But is there proof that reserves of ability do exist in the lower classes? Research in Europe during the last twenty years confirms the hypothesis that the lower classes are as well endowed as any other class with a full range of abilities. Halsey has concluded that innate capacities are randomly distributed between social classes, a conclusion based on the "polygenetic character of innate intelligence and a consideration of the type and volume of social mobility which has occurred in the history of the present industrial societies." [24]

94

A further comment by Halsey on the distribution of ability tells a good deal about educational trends in Europe: "whatever the underlying genetic realities, social class differences in tests of intelligence or attainment distort rather than reflect them.[25] . . . What is of special relevance in this context, is that the distribution of high measured intelligence in typical class structure is such that the largest reserves are among the lower strata, the decreasing proportion of highly intelligent individuals in each lower stratus being insufficient to balance the increase in total numbers." [26]

The effect of social class differences is not absent in the United States, as Dael Wolfle, an internationally known student of manpower, pointed out at a conference in Kungälv, Sweden, held under the auspices of the OECD. In 1960, Wolfle noted, the National Merit Scholarship Corporation awarded university scholarships to 831 secondary school students judged to be the best of 550,000 who took the first qualifying examination. The students were presumably selected without regard to their social origins or to other possible handicaps such as sex, ethnic origin, or rural location. Yet in 1960 only 25 percent of the fathers of the winners were "in manual service, and lower clerical occupations" — farmers, machine operators, truck drivers, postal clerks, and so on.[27] Wolfle's conclusion is instructive because it shows how much the United States and Europe have in common: "The relatively large group of manual workers, farmers, minor clerks, and men employed in service occupations contributed only one fourth of these highly selected scholarship winners, while the smaller group of fathers in the professions, business management, and other 'higher' occupations contributed three fourths of the scholarship winners. . . . certainly, the intelligence difference [between these two large occupational groupings] is not as large as the difference in the number of scholarship winners. . . . Even in as open and socially mobile a society as that of the United States, family background exercises a large influence on the educational achievement and motivation of the child. The corollary is that even in such a society there is a substantial reserve of potential intellectual talent that is not developed." [28]

The Robbins report on higher education discusses the "pool of ability" in the lower classes and admits that while all estimates of potentially able students in British higher education are in danger of being confounded by the speed of change, the "evidence up to this point demonstrates that, in terms of ability, 'more' need not mean 'worse.' " [29] In looking ahead to the 1980's, the authors foresaw no shortage of young people with the potential ability to profit from higher education. The report says: "If there is to be talk of a pool of ability, it must be of a pool which surpasses the widow's purse in the New Testament, in that when more is taken for higher education in one generation more will tend to be available in the next." [30]

Two experts on manpower, de Wolff and Härnqvist, have carried the subject beyond the concept of a pool of ability. Rejecting the idea of measuring ability for a given type of education with only one variable such as the intelligence quotient, they have urged that a whole complex of personality traits (perseverance, motivation, interest) be considered.[31]

All these emphases on the difficulty of measuring intelligence; on the incomplete definitions of intelligence; on the dangers of screening students and dividing the academic sheep from the vocational goats; on the unsubstantiated Platonic myth of an academic elite; on the profound influence which social class has on the student's performance have produced or are producing a climate for educational reform. That reform has already taken place in Sweden.

Multilateral and Comprehensive Schools

Prior to 1950, when Sweden legislated a single type of school for each pupil (as in Russia and the United States), the conventional educational arrangements in Sweden provided one system of schools for lower-class children and another for upper-class children. Sometimes children of mixed social classes attended the same four- or five-year primary school, but more often there was a separate primary school for the lower-class child oriented toward a short secondary course of vocational training. Upper-class youngsters often attended a primary school which was associated with an academic secondary school. Whether lower-class children attended the same primary school as upper-class pupils or were in separate and class-bound primary schools, the largest fraction of pupils in the multilateral system usually went on to a vocational secondary school. The majority of upper-class young people, on the other hand, went on to a secondary school which prepared them for the university.

Between 1950 and 1968, the "period of implementation," Sweden shifted from a multilateral to a comprehensive school system. "Even in a country with a social and ethnic homogeneity like Sweden, the changeover from a selective to a comprehensive system is quite an educational revolution," as Husén has said.[32] It is a triumph for both social democratic ideology and educational psychology. Instead of differentiating pupils at an early age, the comprehensive plan postpones occupational choice until the eighth grade, when the adolescent is fifteen or sixteen. More important, the comprehensive plan has kept more students in school. Between 1950 and 1970 Sweden experienced a fivefold increase in the number of students entering higher education. The new comprehensive schools have allowed for great flexibility in course selections as well, because Swedish educators have questioned the validity of strict categories like "theoretical" and "practical." The comprehensive system (to be discussed more fully in Chapter 8) obviously provides greater educational opportunities for all. Lower-class students are not segregated at an early age, nor does unfair screening cut short a candidate's dreams of a higher education. The comprehensive system and its success in Sweden is a hopeful sign for all of European education.[33]

Certainly Sweden's tapping of intellectual reserves is impressive. Great Britain, which has likewise operated on a selective, multilateral system, is experimenting with comprehensive schools. But many British educators have worried that the mixing of all students would result in a deterioration of educational quality. In the multilateral system students in Britain take the 11-plus examination at the end of the primary school. Those with scores in roughly the upper 15 percent have traditionally been eligible for the grammar school, the academic, preparatory school that has been the preferred type in Great Britain. Pupils with lower scores are eligible for the secondary modern school.

In the comprehensive system all pupils would be admitted to secondary school at the end of their primary grades. Would these students then do better on the two secondary-school leaving examinations which come at the end of secondary schooling? The first examination is known as the General Certificate of Education or GCE "O" (ordinary) level and the second is the GCE "A" (advanced) level.

A report in 1967 described what happened at the Wandsworth Comprehensive School in London as a result of abolishing the 11-plus examination and admitting pupils with varying intelligence quotient scores to a comprehensive form of secondary education: "There is no question but that the exam results support those who want to abolish the 11-plus. Between 1955, the last year of the grammar school, and 1965, after ten years of comprehensive organization, the number of GCE 'O' levels passed went up 700 per cent, and 'A' levels went up 300 per cent. In 1955 ten boys went to university, in 1964, twenty-four. . . . 'The increase in success is entirely due to the boys who would have been 11 plus failure,' according to the headmaster. 'The absolute number of grammar-school standard pupils went down after 1955.' " [34]

Other Steps toward Educational Equality

The comprehensive school, we see, recognizes and encourages the development of more of a student's abilities. Certainly Sweden is the leader of such education in Western Europe and as such is the cynosure. Yet other countries, although they still employ a multilateral or modified multilateral structure, are also making efforts to encourage lower-class students and those who do not at first seem academically promising. In Britain there has been a moderate growth of lower-class students in higher education. John Vaizey, the British economist, reported in 1961 that the working class remained underrepresented in British higher education. And two years later the Robbins report noted that "the proportion of young people who enter fulltime higher education is 45 per cent for those whose fathers are in the 'higher professional' group, compared with only 4 per cent, for those whose fathers are in skilled manual occupations. The underlying reasons for this are complex, but differences of income and of parents' educational level and attitudes are certainly among them. The link is even more marked for girls than for boys." [35]

Nevertheless, the Robbins committee found that between 1954 and 1961 the "proportion of the age group achieving university entrance qualification rose from 4.3 per cent to 6.9 per cent — an average addition of nearly 0.4 per cent a year. In other words, the proportion grew by over half in this period of seven years." At this rate, 10 percent of the age group would achieve university entry qualification in 1970 and 14 percent in 1980. [36] An increase of this sort, though modest, would be abhorred by latter-day Platonists. The Robbins report concluded by recommending that 344,000 students be accommodated in British higher education in 1970 (there were 122,000 places in 1954–55), and the projection for 1980–81 was for 558,000 places, about two and one-half times the number available in 1962–63. [37]

Poland demonstrates dramatic progress in education. The Polish educator Z. Ratuszniak writes that in 1937–38 the children of "industrial workers" constituted 8.9 percent of the university students, whereas by 1961–62 this percentage had increased to 26.3. A somewhat lesser magnitude of change characterized the "peasant" group, where the representation was 8.0 percent in 1937–38 and 19.0 percent in 1961–62. The representation of "intellectuals" and "artisans" declined during those years from 57.5 to 53.8 percent.[38] Ratuszniak reports that 60 percent of the students in higher education were housed in government hostels. It is clear that the Polish government is encouraging young peasants, as well as the sons and daughters of industrial workers, to go on to higher education. Convenient accommodations, scholarships (half the Polish students in higher education received scholarships), and canteens and medical services attract the poor and rural student.[39]

The concern with the influence of social class on education is common to the North Atlantic community as well as to Europe. Europeans frequently refer to investigations of social class in Canada or in the United States. Of the two, the United States has been consistently cited as the home of the comprehensive school and as a country which has maximum upward social mobility. The extensive research on American barriers of social class to educational opportunity has been closely studied by European researchers.

In France too, according to a recent report, the lower classes have increased their representation in higher education.[40] The upward shift is particularly noticeable for tradesmen and craftsmen. The latter have tripled their representation, which is a "better" showing than that made by either white-collar workers or civil servants.[41]

But to claim concrete improvements in the French educational scene is very risky. Debeauvais warns that though there is a good deal of French literature on the democratization of higher education, "there has been little research into the subject, so that at many points there is a dearth of statistical information." He observes, however, that " factory workers and agricultural labourers are less well represented in higher education than in the secondary cycle. The children of agricultural workers represent a declining percentage of the total enrollment at the different levels; they constitute 9 per cent of the total from the sixth to the fourth class, 5.8 per cent from the third class to the second part of the *baccalauréat*, and 4.8 per cent in non-agricultural higher education. In higher agricultural education, however, they provide 33.8 per cent of the enrolment." [42]

The Debeauvais report presents an ideological stand that probably characterizes all of Great Britain and Western Europe: "Public opinion in

France is very sensitive on the question of establishing social democracy at the university level, so that any disparity between the size of a particular social category and its representation in higher education is almost universally regarded as a defeat which should be remedied." [43] Perhaps this social view was a causative agent in the French educational reforms of 1959. The heart of these reforms consisted of compulsory education (after 1967) to the age of sixteen, and orientation or guidance to help students enter an appropriate secondary school curriculum. There is no evidence available as yet, but probably as more and more lower- and lower-middle-class families show confidence in the schools, there will be more requests for university preparatory programs and for more places in higher education. Debeauvais speculates that the net effect of the law will undoubtedly be "to bring into secondary education a considerable number of children hitherto prevented by social traditions, or by the fact that they lived in remote places, from going on beyond the primary cycle." [44] The law, then, will eventually help change the present attitude of many older members of the lower class. "The majority of low income self-employed workers, especially small farmers (89 per cent) and commercial artisans (85 per cent) [up to now] declare that they do not desire for their children an education much higher than their own." [45]

In Ireland it is still the case that rural and lower-class children have markedly less chance for extended education. Increased participation in education cannot be gained solely by increasing the number of scholarships, because middle- and upper-class families are more motivated to apply for them.[46]

Parts of Europe, then, are marked by an encouraging desire to realize a student's full academic abilities, regardless of his social class or rural residence. Much important work is being done too in educating the emotionally, mentally, and physically handicapped. Adult education also deserves at least passing mention; such education is being extensively studied by the Italian educator Mario Reguzzoni.[47] Furthermore, the reports of Pierre Laderrière on the efforts of France to achieve greater equality in the educational experience and the reports of the Westergaard-Little study of the English scene are samples of the solid research which justify optimism for the future of European education.[48] The Westergaard-Little report significantly warns that unless a society becomes less rigid in its social stratification, it cannot achieve equality in upper secondary and higher education.[49] This research and the sometimes modest and sometimes breathtaking progress in educational equality in European countries (especially the comprehensive school) are encouraging. Certainly no European country can economically afford to neglect abilities. Certainly no country can ignore social science research and its proof of the human waste which results from the exclusion of the lower class from higher education.

CHAPTER SIX

Secondary Education Differentiation, Guidance, and Curriculum

The first part of this chapter raises two questions which have become central in European discussions of education and are doubtless familiar to the reader by now: Is it feasible to differentiate students into separate tracks or curriculums before adolescence? Or should differentiation take place on the basis not of primary-school performance, but of performance in the first four years of secondary school? We shall see how various countries have attacked this problem.

Guidance in the secondary school is discussed next because of its relationship to the differential treatment of pupils and of their routing into distinct academic or vocational curriculums. Academic guidance has not been highly developed in Europe, though France leads the rest of Europe in research. To be straightforward about it, most European guidance at the present time suits the multilateral school system, which is rapidly losing ground to the comprehensive system.

The final part of the chapter turns to other aspects of secondary education, particularly new trends in curriculum and in pedagogical research and innovation. No school can hold itself aloof from changes in the economy and society. That the curriculum has responded to the impact of science and technology, even in the economically underdeveloped countries, is not surprising, but the pattern of response may be.

102

Differentiation, Guidance, and Curriculum

Organization and Change in Differentiation

Europe is on the verge of a new era in secondary education. Currently there is a great debate between the proponents of a total comprehensive school organization and those who advocate a comprehensive lower school followed by various types of specialized secondary schools (humanistic, vocational, or technological). This new era is the result of four factors, all of which can be related to the technological revolution, which has shaken European secondary education to its very foundations. First, technology has been transforming agriculture, industry, commerce, and other fields. Four or five years of schooling no longer suffice as training for skilled or highly skilled employment. This economic-technological fact argues for extending the period of compulsory schooling.

The second factor is a psychological one. As the research cited in the last chapter suggests, it is difficult to predict at the age of ten or eleven a student's longtime abilities and interests (i.e., whether he is "made" for a career requiring a good deal of abstraction, such as law or engineering science, or whether he is "destined" for work with his hands, such as carpentry).

Third is a democratic-cultural factor. Democratic social ideology has opposed any social-class favoritism. Nine or ten years of school are now mandatory. Once only a social elite were consumers of these opportunities and challenges. Now they are for the masses of Europe.

The fourth factor has proved crucial in the arguments for the comprehensive school. It can be called the socialization-enculturation factor.[1] Socialization means that the socialized person has learned to live and work with a random sample of others from his society. This qualification is not met if a young person usually associates only with members of his own social class. Enculturation points to acceptance of the values, beliefs, attitudes, and customs which make up the nonmaterial part of a culture. Proponents of the comprehensive system argue that in order for most members of a society to truly share the major values of the culture, and for socialization and enculturation to occur, a student must be allowed more than a four- or five-year school experience. Moreover, they claim it to be self-evident that socialization and enculturation require a common school experience for all pupils.

There may well be other factors producing the new era in education, but these four have provided sound arguments against those who believe in differentiating pupils at an early age. For the reasons given above, it has seemed logical to postpone the period of career determination until later in adolescence and to mix pupils of all classes together. During the 1960's these commonsensical conclusions have resulted in a strong preference for the comprehensive school in country after country. However, not all countries that can be thought of as culturally advanced have comprehensive schools. As we shall see, in West Germany there are powerful and persuasive voices raised against the *Gesamtschule*, as the Germans call their comprehensive school. Like every other West European country, Germany has wrestled with the issue of whether (and how) to differentiate pupils who are ready for some sort of secondary school. The advocates of a type of gesamtschule face real opposition. There are the well-established multilateral schools, the famous gymnasium and the powerful *Realschule*. The gymnasium is stoutly defended by those who feel that it has done outstanding work in history, ancient languages, and German language and literature, as well as in other modern languages and mathematics. Advocates of the realschule praise it for its preparation of pupils in mathematics, modern languages, and the sciences. Separate vocational and technical schools also have their proponents. Moreover, all will claim that pupils can transfer readily from one type of school to another, a claim more honored on paper than in reality. A similar problem exists in the other countries of West Europe. Nevertheless, the tide is running with those who favor the comprehensive school, and it seems likely that by the mid-seventies comprehensive schools for youth to the age of sixteen will be a commonplace, although one cannot yet predict how the schooling of older youth will be treated.

There is a precedent for the comprehensive organization of schooling. The record of the recent past in European educational philosophy shows that the concept of a school for young people of all social classes goes back to World War I and the pioneer work of French enlisted men (generally of lower-class origin) and officers, recently mustered out of the army. These men wished to get away from schools organized as they were in the French national system, where lower- and lower-middle-class youngsters were segregated from upper-class youngsters. For the lower-class pupil, schooling ended at the age of fourteen and he or she then left school, usually for a job. The others were expected to go on to secondary school and prepare for the university. Increasingly, the question was asked: Was there really so much more academic talent among upper-class young people? Did they actually form the potential for an intellectual elite or a "natural aristocracy of the mind," as the phrase went? Since in the trenches there were no social class distinctions between enlisted men and their officers, who were usually drawn from the upper classes, the soldiers naturally challenged a school system that reflected class privilege for the upper class and class prejudice for those who historically had been the drawers of water and hewers of wood.

Reguzzoni recalls the early French initiative with its "plans et projets de démocratisation de l'enseignement." [2] At the end of the war many French veterans joined together to form "Les Compagnons de l'Université Nouvelle," which roughly translates as "proponents of a new education." [3] A small group of men made up the group; among the leaders were H. Luc, Carré, and Girard, all of whom published articles supporting *l'école unique* (the comprehensive system). The movement was to have influence far beyond what could have been expected from the size of its membership. *L'école unique* very soon found a sympathetic reception in other countries, and Les Compagnons, had, perhaps unknowingly, joined forces with a social democratic ideology. The general movement, however, did not bear fruit for many years.

As it turned out, the major thrust for comprehensive education was to come in Sweden. Beginning in 1940, that country carried out extensive studies, investigations, and reforms of the public school system. On trial, so to speak, was Sweden's dual or parallel system of education, with practical schooling for the masses and academic or pre-university for the few.[4] Writing of this time, Torsten Husén has described the "main issue in Swedish school policy from 1940 to 1962" as the "problem of differentiation." He wrote: "It could briefly be stated like this: At what age should the students considered to be academically talented be separated from their nonintellectual classmates?" Most Swedish secondary-school teachers, supporting the traditional system, believed that "both categories of students would gain from an early separation. The theoretically geared would not be hampered by their slow-learning classmates, and the latter would be saved the feeling of inferiority that would be caused by the constant confrontation with their bright peers." [5]

German educators, like those in Sweden, have known for some time that the multilateral school with its early differentiation of pupils is neither democratically sound nor pragmatically effective. A thorough review of research published by Robinsohn and Thomas in the late 1960's called attention to a number of facts about the German school system. In 1966, for example, only one-fifth of the German fourteen year olds and one-seventh of the seventeen year olds attended a general education school — essentially either the five-year *Hauptschule*, the six-year realschule, or the nine-year gymnasium (all of which follow the four years of the German *Grundschule*).[6] These percentages were markedly lower than in Sweden, the USSR, or France. Selection of students for separate schools was made between the ages of ten and thirteen, with 62.7 percent of all thirteen year olds attending the hauptschule, which does not allow its graduates to enter the humanistic university.[7] Less than a fifth of the same age group were in the gymnasium, the only school in West Germany which admitted students to the humanistic university.

The annual rate of failure at the gymnasium during the second half of the 1960's was about 9 percent. While the hauptschule has a much lower rate of failure (2 percent annually), it loses 20 percent of its entering class by the time of graduation. The drop-out rates for the realschule and gymnasium were even higher. Between 1954 and 1966 the number of gymnasium graduates rose from 4 to 7.4 percent, but the doubling meant that only 7.4 percent of those who had been selected for the gymnasium were eligible for the humanistic university! [8]

In Baden-Württemberg, which may be taken as a typical province, between 1958 and 1964 fewer than two-thirds of those entering the first class of the realschule finished their secondary schooling. Of these, nearly half failed at least once during the course of their schooling. For the gymnasium, 37 percent of the group reached the secondary leaving examination (abitur), but there were only 18.3 percent who had not failed at least once.[9] The pupils who were selected for the gymnasium and were thus stamped as the most academically talented were not impressively successful.

The same conclusion can be reached by another route. If the seventh year of schooling is called the first gymnasium year (the education road is essentially decided by this time), the drop-out rate between the first year of gymnasium and the abitur is 57 percent. If more than half the students selected for academic secondary education leading to the university fail to reach abitur, thereby negating the initial prognosis, it at least should be asked whether all the students who qualified for the gymnasium were indeed qualified at the time of selection.

At one time or another, as we have said, every Western European country has had problems with differentiation. In no nation perhaps has the solution been more radical than in Sweden, where the nine-year comprehensive structure postpones differentiation until the age of fifteen or sixteen. For the first six years, young people from all social classes attend a single school with a common course of study. Only in the seventh year is any departure from the common core permitted – a choice in the number of foreign languages available. By the ninth grade, however, there are nine separate curriculum groups possible, five of which are available to about 78 percent of pupils and give access to the academic gymnasium. The OECD report admits that Sweden may be exceptional but that its example "shows possible growth once all pupils are granted access to academic education in mid-adolescence." [10] (For a fuller discussion of the Swedish reforms, see Chapter 8.)

France, too, has shown progress in moving toward a comprehensive secondary school. In the early 1970's it has in essence a semicomprehensive structure where pupils enter a number of differentiated tracks when they are twelve to thirteen years old. The results in terms of the growth of educational opportunities have been described in a recent OECD publication: "Of all European countries, France has perhaps had the largest recent increase in the number of certificated secondary leavers, giving rise to an enormous growth in higher education admission." The increases in the number of first-year university students between 1960 and 1965, the report adds, "show the growth potential in an educational system which is changing its secondary structure, and by postponing selection, putting off the moment when decisions concerning courses must be made . . ." [11]

During the latter half of the 1960's the socialist countries have even studied the possibilities of postponing differentiation *within* the comprehensive school. In 1967 the Soviets began differentiation after the seventh year of common schooling, which is a little earlier than in Sweden. In 1968 as many as twelve hours a week could be elected for special classes reflecting the interests and/or abilities of the pupils.[12] In East Germany the Law on the Unified Socialistic Educational System, passed in February 1965 (after discussion ranging back to 1959), allowed for differentiation in mathematics and science to keep pace with the technical development and the need for highly trained manpower.[13] The 1965 law also discussed in detail recent pedagogical-psychological research.

In educational systems where differentiation is postponed until mid-adolescence – about the age when compulsory schooling ends, as in France, Norway, and Sweden – there has been a rapid increase in the percentage entering upper secondary education.[14] An OECD report indicates that in these countries this rapid increase is due largely to the fact that "decisions to enter are made in mid-adolescence and the entire age-group, in principle, is still eligible for admission to academic type courses."

In countries such as West Germany, the Netherlands, and Austria, where the bulk of the secondary-school population is enrolled in a multilateral system, potential candidates for higher education are a distinct group by the time they are eleven to thirteen years old. Only as the group succeeds in "surviving" — with few flunking out or giving up after repeating grades — can it hope to have a good showing in admissions to higher education. But as the OECD document *Development of Secondary Education* points out, "there are obvious limitations to improvements in the survival rate. In most systems of secondary education the percentage of repeaters and drop-outs is remarkably stable and is perhaps to some extent inevitable." [15]

The conclusions, then, about delaying differentiation and approaching a comprehensive school system are obvious. More and more European nations are attempting to convert their organization of education.

Secondary-School Guidance

Europe does not offer anything comparable to the programs dealing with emotional problems which are an integral part of personnel work in the schools of Canada and the United States.[16] And there are no trends in this area upon which to speculate, since the area itself does not exist.[17] Personality development has been an unimportant part of European education. Our attention will thus be focused on academic guidance, except for a brief look at Belgium's unique *Service Psycho-Medical*. The "psycho" part of the service really has little to do with mental hygiene, but rather includes tests and measures, neither of which have been highly developed. There has been some work done in psychosomatic medicine — that is, diagnosis and treatment of symptoms whose causes may not be organic (such as headache, nausea, and stomach or back pains which may relate to anxiety about school examinations). This kind of service, however, is by no means routine or systematic. Individual parents may consult with clinical psychologists or psychiatrists on their own initiative or at the suggestion of the school, but the arrangement is thoroughly unofficial.

Such emotional help is rare. Moreover, continuous academic guidance of individual pupils is rare in Europe. Even the career masters of Great

Britain are no more than a blend of academic and vocational counselors. They have been taught to look upon a career as something which calls for a certain level of performance in given subjects. Their professional vocabulary does not include the all-round development of an individual, which is evaluated by the staff in boarding schools and by parents and others in community schools. This is the case all over Europe.

Perhaps the establishment of certain elective classes, as Russia and Sweden have done, shows the beginning of a perception of the student as an individual. But this is a hazardous guess. More often European guidance workers, sometimes with the aid of teachers, act rather like agents trying to match pupils and courses of study in increasingly atomized curriculums.

There has been little use in Europe of standardized inventories like the Strong Interest Inventory, which is familiar to guidance counselors in Canada and the United States. In the absence of such instruments, there has been a much greater reliance on the opinion of teachers. Indeed, confidence in the teacher may have led European educators to play down the importance of personality inventories and other assessments of interests and abilities. There is a clearly defined trend toward supplementing observation with tests, toward a greater use of valid and reliable psychological instruments along with professionals who can interpret and administer the tests and inventories. At the outset of the 1970's, however, the mainstay of guidance is still observation by the teacher. The Belgian program of guidance is impressive because of its active, though still small, program of psychological testing. But the French program is more typical.[18]

The French *cycle d'observation*, which is applied to the four years of lower secondary education, has gained dominance. Although the lower division of the secondary school is supposed to provide time for orientation, some differentiation of pupils by French primary school teachers has already taken place. (The degree to which French primary school teachers are trained for this responsibility cannot be reported but presumably it is very little.) In lower secondary school, pupils try out one of three curriculums. At the end of the lower secondary school the cycle d'observation comes to its conclusion with the orientation council (*conseil d'orientation*), which includes teachers, acting as a review board for pupil promotion and categorizing.

Can the conseil d'orientation, as it convenes to determine a pupil's future course, do more than guess at what he has been like? Both in the four

109

years of the lower division of secondary education and in the first year of the lycée, students are never observed performing outside a previously selected, one-track course of study. That is, even in the secondary schools (*collèges d'enseignement secondaire*), pupils are divided among three sections: (1) classical and modern languages (the latter including natural science), leading to the upper division lycées; (2) a "modern course" (for those not expected to succeed in the literary or scientific sections of the second level), which may lead to technical and professional sections of the second level; (3) a "practical" section, including a two-year transitional period followed by a two-year terminal program.

On the basis of a year of study and reflection, the conseil meets to pronounce judgment on whether each pupil has a chance to succeed in the upper secondary program which he has chosen. It is probable that in the highly stratified European social structure the conseil d'orientation almost automatically directs the "best" pupils to the literary and scientific sections of the lycée, which prepares for the university faculties of letters, law, and science.

When the conseil directs pupils to a technical curriculum in upper secondary education, there are several alternatives. Slightly different three-year curriculums lead to the *Baccalauréat de Technicien Economique* or the *Baccalauréat de Technicien Industriel*. Some pupils enter two-year schools heading for the *Brevet d'Enseignement Professionnel* in industrial, commercial, and administrative sections. Finally, there are one-year schools leading to the *Certificat de Formation Professionnelle*, as well as apprenticeship training and its *Certificat d'Aptitude Professionnelle*. Clearly a certificat has been of less weight than a brevet and a brevet has been less than a baccalauréat. But are all the baccalauréats of equal prestige? This query has some relevance because social class membership, and the attitudes, language, and other habits associated with it, may influence the recommendations of the conseil d'orientation. Certainly the conseil d'orientation has a formidable challenge and a difficult task to perform.

Although the French upper secondary school has about four times the curriculum categories of the lower school, French higher education (*enseignements superieurs*) offers even more alternatives, for in addition to the university faculties, there are the famous *grandes écoles*, higher education in specialized fields of engineering, economics, and so on. The complexity of these programs requires that guidance must do a good deal of traffic control. Therefore, a *conseil des professeurs* operates in the lycée and similar schools to review the curriculum which pupils have followed during their first year of the lycée. (Students in nonacademic or manual education have no conseil des professeurs.) It is impossible to know whether the conseil des professeurs, which really has no parallel in other European countries, is more or less adequate than the conseil d'orientation (though it has far less to do), but it has not been adapted with the same enthusiasm as the conseil d'orientation. The conseil des professeurs meets when a pupil is only a year away from baccalauréat. Some European educators criticize the conseil for meeting rather late in the game and for proceeding largely without the benefit of standardized tests or personality inventories.

Perhaps the conseil des professeurs is better understood as a body that judges whether the correct decision has been made by the conseil d'orientation or whether the student should be reassigned to another curriculum. Again, on what basis are and should these judgments be made? Europeans of course wish to know as much as possible about the potentialities of their pupils, but how can such potentiality be judged objectively when the very first judgment has been passed by the conseil d'orientation after pupils have already been grouped into sections?

Europe's foremost expert on vocational guidance, Maurice Reuchlin, has commented on the handicap necessarily imposed by one of the recommendations that the conseil can make: the transfer of students from one type of school to another. One objective of the sweeping reforms since 1958 has been to permit pupils to move from one type of school and curriculum to another in order to increase the flow into more advanced schooling (technical schooling included). This objective benefits both the pool of manpower and the social status of technical schooling. It also provides more educational opportunity for youngsters from the lower class and pays at least a gesture of recognition to the different aptitudes and interests which pupils have. However, as Reuchlin writes, educators must now work with a "horizontal structure superimposed on an already existing vertical structure," and "under such conditions the effectiveness of the horizontal structure is limited. When it is possible for a child to continue his studies in the school which he is already attending it is much more difficult to persuade him to change his course, however desirable this may be in other respects. The child himself and his family are resistant to change: friendships have been established, practical arrangements have been made as regards transport and meals, the child wants to reach the senior forms in his own school which seem to him truly magnificent because they are the only ones he knows: all this militates against change. As for the heads and the staff, they may be ready to transfer to another school pupils whom they do not think likely to succeed in their own, but they find it more difficult to part with the brightest and hand them over to a school which will provide longer, more academic courses." [19] All these problems inhibit the effectiveness of guidance and suggest an inadequate realization of the students' abilities.

It is impossible to determine the extent to which Europe will finally accept professionally prepared guidance workers who can encourage the full maturation of a student's talents. The lower secondary school, rather than the primary school, is increasingly seen as the time to determine the curriculum in which a student is likely to succeed at the upper secondary level.

Table 11 illustrates the degree to which guidance periods, such as the *cycle d'observation*, have been used. In West Germany, for example, the guidance period (*Förderstufe*)[20] for fifth and sixth grades has not been introduced in all länder. As of 1966 only Hesse had the förderstufe, and less than 7 percent of the eligible age group was covered.[21] If the Structural Plan for the Educational System does become the general policy governing education in West Germany, one more country will have adopted the French model of guidance nationwide.

The "projected" programs of guidance remain projected. This is note-

Table 11. Countries with Established or Projected
Guidance Period Programs, 1963[a]

Country	Program	Age Covered
Belgium	Established	12–15
Denmark	Established	12–14
France	Established	11–13
Germany (FR)	Projected	10–12 [b]
Italy	Projected	11–14
Netherlands	Projected	12–13
Switzerland (Geneva Canton)	Projected	12–13
Turkey	Projected	11–14

SOURCE: Based on Jean Thomas and Joseph Majault, *Primary and Secondary Education: Modern Trends and Common Problems* (Strasbourg: CCC, 1963), pp. 27–31, and *International Yearbook of Education*, Vol. 27 (Paris: UNESCO, 1965), p. 31.

[a] Austria, Norway, Sweden, and the United Kingdom consider guidance to be a continuous process throughout school.

[b] Will include only 10–11 year olds when school-entering age drops to 5.

worthy because it suggests that European education, in the east as well as in the west, has not gone far toward mounting a professional guidance program spanning a large number of years of school. (Incidentally, by stressing the professional nature of the program we intend to distinguish formal guidance from the sensitivity of a teacher to each pupil in his or her class.) Worth at least as much note is the concentration of existing programs on a very few years. Belgium must be excepted because, despite what is indicated in Table 11 about the age group covered by the guidance program, in that country there is guidance that reaches beyond the years from twelve to fifteen. But in most countries guidance is something that happens during lower secondary schooling and aims at steering a pupil into a curriculum that matches his ability and ambition.

The French scheme of guidance has recently undergone some revision. A liberal reform of secondary-school orientation calls for continual guidance and observation of pupils rather than merely an examination at the end of the primary grades followed by a steering of pupils into a longer or shorter secondary course of study. The reform also calls for some mechanism by which parents can appeal the decision of the conseil d'orientation. The heart of the proposal significantly calls for the conseil des professeurs to act on the basis of *more* information. Certainly such reforms and an effort towards better academic guidance are needed throughout Europe.[22]

Too often European students are Platonically "typed." That is, guidance has fitted a student into one or another course of study without any real attempt to know the individual beyond his type. It would be fair to say that European guidance is oriented toward groups and not individuals. We think, however, that change is coming. There is hope that the goal of Les Compagnons (who pressed for a "single ladder" in education) will be realized in the 1970's. By prolonging the years of compulsory schooling, adolescent young people will stay together. In Sweden they will even take a common core of courses (never part of the dream of Les Compagnons). Those who forcefully advocate that democracy favors permitting individuals to have a program of study and/or work tailored to their individual needs and interests are, of course, repelled by the common core of courses which delays this choice until the age of sixteen. Yet the comprehensive school will permit the realization of the dream of socialization and enculturation. It will also increase the number of elective courses open to pupils as well as make a conscientious effort to correct any mistakes made in a pupil's program before the age of sixteen. All of Europe will soon blanket

113

mid-adolescence with observation and guidance, but we think that observation must include reliable, standardized measures of abilities and interests.

The postponement of the French-style cycle d'observation can also be predicted. In France this period already has been delayed until mid-adolescence, when the interests of pupils are supposed to be stabilized. But in countries such as West Germany the förderstufe could be postponed for two years after the primary grundschule, as Robinsohn and Thomas have recommended.[23] What now seems likely is that a two-year "orientation stage" for ten and eleven year olds will be added to German schooling directly after the primary sphere.[24]

Finally, those European countries which do not follow the French model will probably gather a corps of guidance workers who function continuously through a pupil's school life. As Table 11 indicates, Austria, Norway, Sweden, and the United Kingdom now consider guidance to be a continuous process throughout school, and they will, we predict, continue to implement their program. Concepts of academic guidance are obviously changing in Europe, along with changes in the multilalteral structure of the secondary school. The curriculum of the secondary school and its changes should also be spotlighted.

Current Trends in Curriculum

THE NEW EDUCATION

European countries without exception have continued to follow a trend in education which started at the turn of the century with the zealous promotion of the "activity method." This "research attitude," which so many European professors wish to foster among students, is more creative than memorization and is related to the application of technology to teaching (films, radio, television).

The term "place of work" sums up the educational philosophy of the New Education, which uniformly emphasizes the activities of the pupils and learning as a matter of doing. At its conception, the New Education was tried out at a few country boarding schools, such as Herman Lietz's Landerziehungsheim and Paul Geheeb's Odenwaldschule in Germany, where pupils could learn as they participated in the productive work necessary to their school and to the farming community. This philosophy of education came to be described as that of the "activity school"[25] in Europe and as "learning by doing" in the United States.

114

The New Education was the first step in the European cultural integration of schooling. If one man is to be remembered as a pioneer in what was to become a movement, it is Adolph Ferrière, who at one time taught in Lietz's Landerziehungsheim and who came to believe that the "new schools" should profit from the experiences of several other experimental schools. There was coeducation at the Odenwaldschule,[26] for example, and some degree of student self-government in all of the new schools. Students, it was felt, matured as they assumed responsibility for living together. In 1899 at Geneva, Ferrière opened the Bureau International des Ecoles Nouvelles with the purpose of disseminating information on the work of these experimental schools. The mission of the bureau received a setback with the outbreak of World War I, which demonstrated all too vividly the depth of the cleavages between European nations. In the war's aftermath, however, Ferrière and the others hoped that the New Education might help to create a brotherhood among Western Europeans.

In 1921 the Ligue Internationale pour l'Education Nouvelle assembled in Calais, France, to promote the principles of the activity school.[27] The all-European quality of the league was evident from the fact that journals reporting on pupil psychology, methodology, and curriculum in the new schools appeared in Germany, France, and England. For many years Beatrice Ensor edited *The New Era* in England. In Germany Elizabeth Rotten edited *Das Werdende Zeitalter* (the German "new era"), until it was banned by the Nazis; Dr. Rotten then moved to Geneva and joined Ferrière in the bureau.[28] In France the journal *La Nouvelle Education* was edited by Mme Guerrite and Roger Cousinet. The New Education has finally evolved into the International New Education Fellowship.

The values upheld by the new schools and the New Education were the humanistic ones that were championed so vigorously by the distinguished Europeanist Denis de Rougemont.[29] The values were humane, to be shared by all without distinction of income, birth, race, sex, or location. The dormitories at the Odenwaldschule were named for such German poets and scientists as Goethe and Fichte, prominent figures in the neohumanist thought of Germany. The goal of that school was typical of all the new schools, based as it was on the belief that "what matters in education is that a man should be able to understand life clearly and live it well, in such a way that he cannot easily be imitated." [30] The more active and involved method of learning called for in the New Education has now been accepted in all education as teachers no longer merely present material for the passive consumption of the student.[31] But this change in attitude is only one part of the whole; curriculum alterations in other areas are also worthy of scrutiny.

CURRICULUM SUBJECTS

Among the countries of Europe there is a good deal of variation in how intensively pupils study a given subject.[32] According to the report *Modernizing Our Schools*, "in the first year of elementary education, the total number of hours per week varies from a low [of] 18 (Germany, Austria, Norway), to a high [of] 30 (Spain, Luxembourg). In the final year the variations are between 23 (U.K.) and 35 (Sweden). Equally large variations can be observed in the weekly time devoted to the individual subjects. In the final year of primary school, the number of hours available for teaching of the mother tongue varies from 5 to 10 hours per week; for arithmetic, from 4–6½ hours; for science, 0–4; foreign languages, 0–5; in the majority of . . . countries no foreign language is taught in primary schools." [33]

In foreign language instruction, the European secondary-school teacher continues to be governed by a tradition which de-emphasizes the oral-aural or conversational approach. Traditionally, the pupils who have done the most profitable work in modern foreign languages are those who have traveled during vacations; European hostels and European Houses, where young people from all over Europe visit and have informal discussions, are staffed to facilitate interchange. As the population of the academic or general secondary school changes and includes more students of lower-class background, language teachers will probably have many more pupils who lack travel experience and who are unable to afford it. By contrast in East European countries the so-called Pioneer Movement for youth aged ten to fifteen sponsors language circles that do practice communication.

It is impossible to detect a trend in the proportion of time allotted to modern foreign languages because of the absence of such figures over the years. Yet certainly a new appreciation is signaled by their appearance in the upper primary grades. In the mid-sixties the number of hours devoted to a modern foreign language in secondary schools ranged from two to eleven hours a week.[34]

The relatively high amount of class time devoted to instruction in this subject is indicated by the fact that in 1965 about the same number of class periods were assigned to modern foreign languages as to mathematics, a subject which has been held in high esteem. Only Latin has been scheduled for more class time.

To move from languages to social science is to be impressed with the developments in the writing of texts for general history, geography, and civics (which, as we have seen, has been a prominent part of the education program of the Council of Europe's ccc). There is little evidence on how widely these revised texts are used, but at least scholarly work has been invested in the adequacy of their presentation. A comparable statement cannot be made about any of the other social sciences. Even in the case of economics, European secondary schools have been sporadic in their use of texts, with only a few national exceptions, such as France and Holland. Economics has had difficulty in being recognized as an independent social science, even in higher education, and has only recently been separated from the faculty of law. (Historically, economics was one of the ways to see the justice of a contract or a claim and was thus appropriate to the study of law.) Only relatively recently has it become worthwhile to include an economic understanding of agricultural topics (manpower, trade, production, and so forth) in general and even academic education. Technical and scientific studies of economics changed the status of economics. In France a pupil in upper secondary school can take a *Baccalauréat de Technicien Economique*. Before very long, economics may find an equal place in general education down to the European primary school. In general education, of course, economics would be closely associated with history and geography. It is hazardous to guess about the fate of other social sciences such as cultural anthropology, political theory, and social psychology. The East European countries, however, seem to be a special case because of the socialist stress on ideological interpretations of date. In the ussr, for example, the study of geography also includes economic geography in both the primary and secondary grades.

The study of the social sciences may have gained popularity shortly after World War II, when radicals in curriculum innovation talked of what the British call "nearer home" and what the French call the "study of the environment." These terms are adaptations of old ideas. Pestalozzi taught in the eighteenth century that children learn what is concrete and close at hand before they learn what is abstract or remote in space and time. Pestalozzi may have erred, but *l'étude de milieu* exploited his ideas. (The field trips familiar to parents in the United States have much the same background.) In primary school pupils learn about "friends and neighbors" and "helpers" of everyday life, like the postman. If this study is to be more than sentimentalism, the social sciences and the technology of applied natural science must find a firm place in the upper primary and secondary school.

Polytechnical education is also increasing and is changing the makeup of the secondary curriculum. Soviet educators use the phrase "work experience" to express a belief that all citizens need to understand materials and their use in industrial or agricultural enterprise. The East European countries have emphasized polytechnical education more than have their western neighbors. Polytechnical education has actually become the compromise between training the hand and educating the mind. The dualism of the theoretical and the practical, with all its social class connotations, was eliminated by integrating polytechnical education within general education (the study of the humanities and sciences). The essence of the move was to give the arts of production and vocational training parity of esteem with academic training. At the close of the 1960's, it has been suggested, "the problem is no longer whether the two should be combined, but rather what is the most effective way of combining work and study, at what age, level of training, and to what degree instruction should be combined with work and with what particular kind of work." [35]

Polytechnical education has objectives similar to those of the industrial arts of Canada and the United States, which have also reflected the urban scene and industry. Both industrial arts and polytechnical education have helped to fill citizens' needs for knowledge of materials and design in production. However, since there is much more to modern commercial, agricultural, extractive, and industrial processes than is found in the old polytechnical education, it seems reasonable to assume that this part of the curriculum will be overhauled during the 1970's.

Polytechnical education has been vigorously pushed in Eastern Europe not only because of the honor which socialist ideology pays to labor, but also because it provides factories with a much needed staff of skilled workers. Changes to meet the needs of the labor market have taken place both in polytechnical education and in the heavily humanistic and theoretical science courses of the traditional secondary and higher education curriculum of Europe. The youngster who once made nuts, screws, bolts, and simple machine parts in his polytechnical metals course has been replaced by the pupil who is acquainted with electronics, automation in machining,

118

and other technical processes. The "technical" in polytechnical has become more of a reality and less a bit of propagandistic wishful thinking. This trend towards a technical and scientific study has dramatically changed the European curriculum.

Changes in scientific subjects also mark the European curriculum. Scientific curriculums have traditionally meant the natural sciences and mathematics, but there is now variation within this pattern. France and the USSR have developed mathematics curriculums which reflect the role of mathematics in science and technology, and other European countries will do the same. A full panoply of scientific curriculums in the biological sciences, meteorology and astronomy, and geology and geography, however, has not yet been represented in European education. Rather, the catchall science course, similar to the one taught in the United States, is found in the lower secondary grades in a number of European schools. Scientific method appears to be gaining acceptance in the upper secondary schools, and science allied with technology probably will be accepted in the future. France, Sweden, and Yugoslavia have introduced scientific and technical general curriculums, but laboratory work involving students has not been frequent.

The traditional humanistic curriculums are a bloc made up primarily of

Table 12. Growth Indexes for Enrollments in Humanities and Science Programs in Academic General Education in Selected Countries (1955 = 100)

Country	Early 1950's	Mid 1950's	Early 1960's	Mid 1960's
Austria				
Humanities	77	100	99	110
Sciences	77	100	103	59
Belgium				
Humanities	87	100	112	145
Sciences	85	100	180	287
Italy				
Humanities	84	100	103	128
Sciences	85	100	134	224
Switzerland				
Humanities	70	100	111	148
Sciences	90	100	141	211
Turkey				
Humanities	...	100	426	524
Sciences	...	100	581	676

SOURCE: Adapted from *Development of Secondary Education* (Paris: OECD, 1969), Table 17, pp. 48–49.

119

language courses and literature. Of course, the native language and history are taught, but they are not considered as essential to the humanities. European and world history, and civics — when these are not classed as social sciences — have been included in the humanities. But the lion's share of prestige and focus has been given to classic language and literature. Which program, the scientific or the humanistic program, is the faster growing?

Table 12 shows that enrollments in the science programs of Belgium, Italy, Switzerland, and Turkey have grown more than those in the humani-

Table 13. Growth Indexes for General and Technical-Vocational Secondary Education, 1950–65 (1955 = 100)

Country	Early 1950's	Mid 1950's	Early 1960's	Mid 1960's
Austria				
General	78	100	105	117
Technical	58	100	94	100
Belgium				
General	91	100	158	181
Technical	93	100	157	214
Germany (FR)				
General	28	100	101	111
Technical	74	100	82	81
Greece				
General	...	100	130	149
Technical	...	...	...	...
Netherlands				
General	74	100	152	163
Technical	82	100	135	144
Spain				
General	66	100	147	245
Technical	102	100	125	168
Sweden				
General	85	100	128	111
Technical	74	100	255	368
United Kingdom (England and Wales)				
General	...	100	131	134
Technical	...	100	117	101
Turkey				
General	54	100	220	329
Technical	73	100	132	224
Yugoslavia [a]				
General	72	100	90	209
Technical	94	100	162	262

SOURCE: Adapted from *Development of Secondary Education* (Paris: OECD, 1969), Table 14, p. 41.

[a] Excluding upper primary.

ties; Austria, however, has experienced more growth in the humanities curriculums, with a marked decline in science enrollments between 1960 and 1965. Table 13 presents some fifteen years of growth indexes for enrollment in the secondary school. There appears to have been a drop in technical education enrollment in Germany between the academic years 1955–56 and 1965–66. For a country which wishes to have a strong competitive position in the world's economy, this decline is a cause for concern. The most remarkable gains in technical education have been registered in Sweden, Turkey, and Yugoslavia. The net gain of interest by European youth in technical curriculums in all likelihood will be sustained. These studies in curriculum and enrollment change should be supplemented with examinations of educational innovation and research.

PEDAGOGICAL INNOVATION AND RESEARCH

In education, as an OECD report has observed, "change is notoriously slow in getting accepted. Complete diffusion of successful 'innovations' in the field of education appears to take approximately fifty years after the first 'authentic introduction.' It has been estimated that approximately fifteen years elapse before 3% of the schools adapt the innovations. The rate has, however, in recent times grown considerably faster. . . . In fact, in the natural sciences, where the cleavage between what is taught in the schools and the state of advancement of the science in question has been particularly impressive, as a result of serious efforts in the past decade both in the United States and in several European countries, the gap has been considerably reduced." [36]

The fact is that professional organizations in education, centers for educational research, and centers for the preparation of educational specialists have easy access to findings and data of all types and they rapidly distribute research findings to the teacher. There are several admirable models for both coordinating and disseminating research to European teachers, among them the Max-Planck-Gesellschaft in West Berlin, a relatively new and promising institute, and the USSR Academy of Pedagogical Sciences, a research center which was founded in 1943 and is thus one of Europe's oldest.[37]

The USSR Academy is a large and complex organization with twelve institutes, a publishing branch, and a library that houses about a million Soviet and foreign pedagogical books and journals. This center has done impressive work in many areas, in the history of education, for example, and

121

in the study of language and its use and of textbooks and teaching materials. It is also outstanding in special education for the physically handicapped. Nevertheless, Western observers have seen weaknesses in the general programs of the academy. One criticism relates to inadequate research techniques. The lack of a truly scientific, statistical base of experimental research finds academy researchers, as Soviet analysts have pointed out, ill-equipped and unprepared to describe the results of research in any terms other than the imprecise language of demonstrations. "Little of what can be found in Soviet 'research' reports has any clearly stated experimental hypotheses, a description of how data were collected and treated in an attempt to prove or disprove the experimental hypotheses of the study. Much of the studies described are descriptions of a 'how-we-did-it-in-Smolensk-order.'"[38] The downgrading of tests and measurements was a feature of Russian research in the 1930's, and these techniques were only restored to respectability in 1962.

European investigators have also emphasized the moral point that research cannot be tied to a party line; it must be done in such a way that the chips fall where they may. Two aspects of the Soviet approach are invariably identified as weaknesses. In the first place, "every social, political, economic, and educational organization in the U.S.S.R. can, in the final analysis, only be a legitimizer of Party policy. . . . The Academy, within this framework, can function only as the implementer of these policies." In the second place, "basic questions that affect the national economy of a centralized political system can only be viewed in a political sense. Therefore, fundamental educational research devoid of political realities can have no place in a centralized society."[39]

The British Schools Council is a very different and (in essence) a politically free pedagogical research institute. In an atmosphere conducive to unfettered research, the council has proved its effectiveness and now has responsibility for much of the work on curriculum and examinations previously carried out by the Secondary Schools Examinations Council and the Curricular Study Group. Other research tasks are to be delegated to such groups as the National Foundation for Educational Research in England and Wales, the universities, and the Government Social Survey. The English style is not to centralize and not to dictate. As one might expect, then, the British Schools Council is to cooperate with such a prestigious body as the Standing Conference on University Entrance. Although cooperation is the hallmark of English research on education, the council is expected to look into the well-being of individual subjects and to add power to the whole enterprise of schooling. England is particularly fortunate in being able to add to this power through pedagogical research.[40]

A student's curriculum and education are, needless to say, essentially dependent on teachers, and there have been changes in the teaching profession that should be mentioned. Training for teachers is being lengthened. Primary school teachers, for example, now spend a longer time in professional preparation; pedagogical research, a modest amount of it to be sure, is being added to the training. There are also more evaluations and empirical studies on child growth and development, including (thanks to the Luria studies in Moscow and Piaget's research in Switzerland) a good deal on conditioning and cognitive development. Such sophisticated studies will probably enhance the social prestige and, consequently, the career attractiveness of primary and secondary school teaching.

Professors in Canada and in the United States often envy the degree of respect shown their European colleagues by their students, but the difference in status between American and European secondary school teachers is astronomical. The European professor is on a much loftier pedestal than his American counterpart, and the European secondary-school teacher is regarded as almost on a par with a European professor. In North America the high school teacher, lacking such adulation, is simply a teacher. In Holland, where the secondary-school teacher is a *Leraar* and the university professor a *Hoogleraar*, the difference in title suggests only that the professor teaches in higher rather than secondary education and it is not intended to imply a qualitative difference. In France the appellations make this even more clear. Both the Sorbonne professor and the French secondary-school teacher are *Professeurs*. The French elementary-school teacher, however, is only an *Instituteur*, just as the Dutch elementary-school teacher is *Onderwijzer*. In France, Holland, and elsewhere in Europe strong colleague relationships exist between secondary and higher education staff. Not only does the prestige of the secondary-school teacher approach that of the professor, but his academic qualifications do too. In Europe, where institutions of higher education have been in short supply, many secondary-school teachers could have taught in the universities had there been places for them. The secondary-school teacher is very much at home in his subject matter, and he often writes not only textbooks but scholarly works. His proficiency makes any extension of pedagogical training even more impressive. Further training would supplement the ordinary academic program consisting of techniques of teaching (known as didactics) and theory of education (pedagogy or pedagogical theory), which includes history, philosophy, and psychology of education. In design this combined program is not much different from the Master in the Art of Teaching (MAT), or fifth-year program, in the United States.

But the European program for preparation of teachers may be changing. In the past, didactics has been viewed as comprising techniques that were no more difficult to learn than the skills needed for the middle-level professions — skills that were distinctly less taxing and required much less training than, say, those of a physician. Didactics, then, was something learned at a secondary level and associated with the craft skills of primary teachers. But as the preparation of primary-school teaching moved from secondary school to higher education and thereby upgraded the image of teaching as a whole, Europe has seen the entry of didactics into higher education. Though it is not yet on a par with the techniques of the historically learned professions in the university, didactics now appears at least to be in the same league.

Didactics is gaining higher status and so too is the elementary-school teacher. The Robbins report on higher education in Great Britain recommends that all primary-school teachers be prepared in university departments of education rather than in the three-year institutes that are found in England and most of the continent. While the Robbins report is not primarily concerned with raising the status of teachers, it has sought to make their preparation more adequate. An increase in status is a likely by-product. The Robbins committee further recommends that departments of education be converted into the more complex collection of departments of a school of education: "We consider that they are an essential element in Schools of Education. We recommend therefore that each University Department of Education should either merge with or become a part of the School of Education of its university." [41]

The Majault report, the best guide to teacher training in Europe, is quite explicit about other recent developments in professional preparation of teachers.[42] The report alludes to the new European venture in introducing secondary teachers to more than just how-to courses: "the secondary school teacher no longer needs to acquire knowledge which he already possesses, but to discover how to teach his pupils, or in other words, *to learn to impart knowledge*." In surveying the preparation of primary teachers, Majault does not mention the inclusion of primary teacher training in universities, but he does remark that a "higher standard of entry" has tended to be "general in all countries." [43] This means that a teacher beginning primary education training in Europe will be about eighteen years old and will have successfully completed secondary education — he will have passed the baccalauréat or its equivalent. In addition most countries will expect a candidate for primary teaching to sit for an entrance examination, which probably would not be required for a university graduate expecting to teach in a secondary school.[44]

The Majault report affirms that there is more communication and a greater sense of a common goal between teachers of academic or general courses in secondary schools and teachers of vocational and technical courses; such progress is due to the increase in the *general* education content of obligatory education.[45] Specific practical innovations have supplemented these general changes. For example, several series of brief courses, some for only one or two weeks, are being arranged to help keep teachers up to date. The 1967 Swedish legislation on the professional preparation of teachers provides for a variety of short courses. In Czechoslovakia there is an effort to use teachers' reactions to new materials and methods. A similar effort is made in the USSR, where prizes are given for suggestions from teachers. In Great Britain, the inspectors of the ministry, fulfilling their primary duty, bring research findings to teachers. All of these steps are promising for the improvement of curriculum and of teaching.

In summary, European secondary education exhibits a movement towards comprehensive school organization and a postponement of differentiation. More effective and continuous academic guidance is also a goal of most European educational systems. A "learning by doing" attitude is now prevalent in secondary curriculum. Also to be noticed in the curriculum is the growth of modern language courses; the probable growth of the social sciences, especially economics; the addition of polytechnical courses; and the alliance of science and technology. Pedagogical research will also help to alter the secondary curriculum, as will the upgrading of teacher training programs and the inclusion of didactics in higher education. European secondary curriculum, then, is being refocused, and this refocus is yet another sign of European harmonization. The teacher is increasingly encouraged to learn better *how* to teach, and the student is being encouraged to respond more actively to an updated curriculum.

CHAPTER SEVEN

Training
for Occupations

Vocational-technical training in Europe is experiencing a remarkable growth in status, popularity, and reform. The cause of this educational change is to be found in changes in the European economic world — in industry, trade, commerce, and business. Frank Bowles, who has written about these economic alterations, pinpoints three changes which have had important educational implications:

1. A sharp rise in urban population resulting from the increase in the size of the industrial labor force and its concentration in industrial centers. This, in turn, has resulted in new concentration of markets and new patterns of consumption. It has also resulted in new patterns of communal living which, in turn, have made possible a concentration of educational activity.

2. The rationalization of industrial production following upon increased size of industrial plants and increased concentrations of industrial labor. These factors have eroded the foundations of small enterprise in many fields and forced industrial concentrations to the levels of medium and even larger enterprise.

3. A rising demand for technical personnel resulting directly from the rationalization of industrial production, as a direct product of facilities. In particular, there has emerged a demand for the type of senior technician capable of assuming supervisory and management responsibilities which in smaller enterprises were dealt with directly by the proprietor in his role as manager.[1]

Bowles also notes that the efficient and rational use of land- and farm-related labor has had educational implications. A reduction in the agricultural population, for example, has further contributed to urbanization and "has made possible a concentration of educational activities which was simply not possible in sparsely populated rural areas." Furthermore the technological changes in farming have brought "pressure on agricultural education to add a professional level to the vocational and technical levels at which it has been offered until recently." [2]

These new concentrations of markets, new patterns of consumption, larger urban centers of education, and greater needs for technical skills have forced a renewed emphasis on vocational education.

What type of vocational education will now suffice? It is safe to assume that apprenticeship — learning on the job — will be a thing of the past in Europe.[3] Machinery has become so complex and expensive that no one school can possibly provide training for every individual position. Employers prefer, therefore, that employees be trained in a more general way, making them more flexible and adaptable to training in a specific skill by the hiring firm. This method of training, already existent in the United States, will no doubt become the trend in Europe as well. Science simply does not turn back the clock; more innovation in technology is certain to be the case.[4] It would seem to follow that European pedagogy will respond, though with national differences in timing.[5] In training for the service occupations — and a society becoming affluent always increases them — inferior programs teaching the skills of hairdressing and so forth are not enough. The limitations of such inferior programs are apparent.

The lowest grade of vocational training (this form of training hardly merits being called technical) probably has been on-the-job training, or apprenticeship in the repetitive jobs of a factory, such as grinding, polishing, and cutting, jobs which disappear with automation or even semi-automation. The successful apprentice learns certain skills, but he is inflexible because he lacks training in a whole family of vocations, or because he lacks enough general training to make him a skilled worker at the jobs offering some on-the-job training. The worker with one or two years of vocational training is no more economically flexible, and his chances for acquiring new techniques have been slim.

Often training methods have had the same content for generation after generation; the quickening tempo of change has obviously outdated many of the programs. Training youngsters in this archaic fashion has not helped them to be re-employable. They have a trade or craft, but the skill does not involve a competence that is likely to survive the inevitable changes in a highly technological society. The craftsman has become unemployed at a time when help-wanted advertisements and employment offices have listed openings. The most desirable jobs probably call for "senior technicians" (Bowles's term for someone able to assume supervisory or managerial tasks). Mechanization has forced apprenticeship programs to change. How is more adequate vocational training being organized?

The Reconstruction of Vocational Training

The best available information on reforms in vocational training in various countries appears in the 1965 *International Yearbook of Education*.[6] In France, for example, a new structure of agricultural training was defined, pending the full effects of prolonged compulsory schooling. "This compulsory vocational training is for young people who have reached school leaving age and are to take up agriculture without any further study." Also proposed was better preparation of young people for middle-level jobs in commerce, business, industry, and so forth. However, as the report notes, the "strengthening of the short upper secondary course is in no way intended to turn pupils with ability away from the long course, but rather to provide a more general education alongside an essentially vocational training." [7]

The following are samples of vocational-technical programs from six other countries:

Belgium. New specialized programs: (a) Graduate certificate in speech therapy; (b) Certificate of candidate-translator, graduate translator, and graduate interpreter, at the 3rd level of higher technical education; (c) Certificate of laureate in higher industrial studies; (d) Certificate in scenic arts and broadcasting techniques.

Italy. Technical education being reorganized. Bill has been approved establishing 5-year course technical institute to train administrative secretaries and foreign language correspondents. Courses in dietetics and for community leaders have been set up in the vocational institutes for girls. The diploma from state vocational schools will qualify one for admission to the Civil Service exams.

Netherlands. As of April 1965, 14-year old boys cannot work more than 8 hours a day, 32 hours a week. They must attend general educational or vocational training classes one whole or 2 half days a week, or receive at least 8 hours tuition per week. New (the third) school for advanced technology, but of a university character, opened in Entschede.

Norway. Gradual change in technical school courses from 2 to 3 years

128

continues; majority now have 3-year courses. In some cases, matriculation exams now required.

Spain. Vast reorganization of technical education in law of 29 April 1964.

United Kingdom. Several colleges of advanced technology now have university status.[8]

More specific reconstructions of vocational preparation will be discussed later. But first a definition of terms is needed. In this book "vocational" and "technical" are used interchangeably. In North America and Europe an academic program is usually called "education" and a technical program "training." But after this initial agreement come subtleties in the uses of terms. For example, in North America "vocational" often, but certainly not always, has meant preparation for low-level occupations, and "technical" has been used for middle-level occupations. The term "professional" has been reserved for such high-level occupations as medicine, dentistry, the law, the ministry, and so on. On the continent, however, Europeans often call "professional" what has been termed "vocational" in Canada and the United States. In Western Europe "vocational" usually connotes a school whose graduates are qualified for a low level of occupation, such as semiskilled workers. Excited debates in European education have focused on training versus education, on whether education should be arranged as it has been in the past or whether it should be modified to permit more accommodation of technical abilities. The trend is clearly toward greater accommodation.

Many reforms, some of which have sought to reduce social class privilege, have occurred in the structure of European education since 1940. In Great Britain the Butler Act of 1944 made a variety of secondary education options available to almost all young people. This act attempted to insure that no pupil was barred from an academic or technical school because his family could not afford the fees or lived too far away. Under a rubric of providing education for all in accordance with ability and interests, technical schools and "modern" schools (for those who did not do well on the 11-plus examinations) were authorized. Yet many academically able children were not sent to these schools for lack of family interest.

Undoubtedly one motivation for the legislation was to increase the pool of talent in the schools. Manpower economists had been critical of what seemed to be restrictionist practices. In their opinion young people aged twelve to eighteen from the lower social class were not adequately represented in such schools as the lycée or the gymnasium in relation to their percentage in the total population. This ratio, according to manpower economists, had the effect of holding down the number of technicians and professionals. However, it is not enough to give the lower social class access to academic schools which are normally attended by the social elite. These schools have always had the lion's share of social prestige, but creating more academic schools — even giving access to lower-class students — does not increase the social prestige of the technical schools and universities except when the civilization becomes more technically oriented.

If formal education shows an appropriate response to the changes that have been taking place in technology, some interesting things may happen. For one thing, the social status of secondary vocational schools will increase because the term "vocational" suggests training for a single skill, and all that belongs to the world of yesterday. There is no doubt now that technical secondary and higher education, whose graduates possess skills and mobility well above the apprenticeship level, will flourish. When technical education finally has won its place in the curriculum, it will look very much like a part of academic secondary and higher education. The overlap will include the social sciences, modern languages, natural sciences, and mathematics.[9] There is every reason to hope for accommodation between social classes and between academic and technical studies in the future, and for an end to the class-prejudiced distinction between academic and technical-scientific emphases in education. Some of this special education begins after the period of obligatory schooling, but the lower stages of technical-scientific education should diverge somewhat to include non-scientific studies as well. And each side must move to more demanding and fundamental study, even to research, which adds new knowledge and art forms. At the same time the area of general education also must exist separately — the whole show is not in technical education — and the higher levels of general education must borrow from the sciences, technology, and the arts. But all of these are statements of preference.

Adequate Training for Occupational Categories

A list of occupational categories developed by Herbert Parnes aids the forecasting of manpower needs and the routing of students into different kinds of education and training.

Class A: All occupations for which a university education or an advanced teachers' college degree, or its equivalent, would normally be required.

Class B: Occupations for which two or three years of education beyond the secondary level . . . may be required.

Class C: Occupations for which a secondary school education (either technical or academic) or its equivalent, would normally be required.

Class D: All occupations not included in Class A, B, or C. Furthermore, Class A occupations should be sub-divided into those that normally require scientific or technical education and those that require general academic education.[10]

This manpower classification is helpful with the qualification that the formal education necessary for Class C occupations should be divided into the incomplete or short form of secondary school [11] and the complete secondary school. Two examples of the short form of secondary education are the German realschule and the French four-year Moderne (*type court*).[12] The short or "middle" form of instruction has given the lower-class youngster an education more advanced than the German *Berufsschule* or *Berufsfachschule* (part-time and full-time vocational schools), which terminate in a vocation highly liable to obsolescence.[13]

The French reforms in vocational education, extending from 1959 to 1966, have resulted in an entire spectrum of vocational education following both primary education and a portion of the incomplete secondary school (*enseignement secondaire*) or any one-year school of vocational training whose graduates receive the *Certificat de Formation Professionnelle*.

Apprentissage and even one-year vocational training are dead-end types of preparation which often lead to unemployment. A 1966 report on French education by the Institut Pédagogique National of the national Ministry of Education did not even mention apprentissage, although it existed at the time. On one-year vocational training the report said: "In the industrial and commercial sections, alongside the two-year training of qualified professionals [i.e., skilled workers], it has appeared necessary to provide a more specialized vocational training to last one year. This training could be for adolescents, who, at the end of compulsory schooling, enter active life without any vocational preparation and also for those who do not have sufficient capacities to engage, with any real chance of success, in preparation for the diploma of vocational studies." [14]

The two-year French vocational course is a step toward more adequate occupational preparation. This course has been an interesting departure from traditional programs. There are three sections, sometimes but not necessarily in the same school. The industrial and commercial sections provide technical training which corresponds to groups of trades and no longer to an individual specialty.[15] The administrative section was "conceived in relation to the realities of life and social activity and will be rounded out by the acquisition of indispensable working instruments such as writing, living foreign languages, documentation techniques, etc. . . ." [16] If a two-year course is realistic training for the objectives established, its effectiveness will be proved by the employability of its graduates.

Class D includes the "unskilled" occupations such as farming, fishing, hunting, and logging. The necessary skills have not been taught in school, though they may be learned through informal apprenticeship. There is a great deal of overlap between the groups of jobs classified as C and D, and there is often no easy way to distinguish them. Because no vocational training has been needed for unskilled workers, whose jobs are fading away with the increased mechanization of work, all European nations face common problems of finding employment for them.

The manpower in Class C occupations are "skilled," as the term is used by manpower economists; they are clerical workers and such skilled manual workers as railway engine drivers and firemen, postmen, weavers, tailors and dressmakers, milliners, shoemakers, metal rolling mill operators, precision-instrument makers, and others. Some sales workers, service and recreation workers, and athletes have also been classified in C.[17]

Class C occupations seem to be adequately provided for by schools such as the French two-year schools leading to the B.E.P. (*Brevet d'Enseignement Professionnel*) with their industrial, commercial, and administrative sections. The German *Fachschulen* (technical schools) matriculate pupils who are at least eighteen years of age and have had two or three years of a berufsschule (part-time vocation) or a school closely akin.[18]

Class B occupations are those which require about two or three years of education beyond the secondary level. Typical Class B occupations have been those of technicians in science and engineering, draughtsmen, surveyors, medical and dental technicians, nurses, transport and communications workers (e.g., deck officers, engineer officers, pilots of ships and aircraft, traffic control workers), nonworking foremen, primary and nursery school teachers (until they move to Class A with attendance at a university), and insurance and securities salesmen.[19] The "senior technician" capable of managerial or supervisory responsibilities probably would be classified in Class B.

The French two-year university institutes of technology (I.U.T.), which have been operating only since 1965, are among the clearest examples of educational institutions for the purpose of training the "senior technician." In contrast with the greater attention to basic science of the university faculty of science, the French Ministry of Education reports that "these new higher educational institutions will ensure, by means of an appropriate pedagogy and with the collaboration of members of the different professions, a scientific and technical training of a concrete character, well adapted to modern realities and preparing directly for the functions of technical cadres in production, applied research and services." [20] No part or stage of French technological curriculums has been closed to further reform and many alternatives are available to students.

The I.U.T.'s receive many lycée graduates in technical economics and in industrial techniques, although some of these graduates enter the university faculties of letters or science. Without such further education, however, it is difficult to imagine for what occupations these pupils had been adequately prepared, since there is so little mathematics and natural science in the technical and industrial classes of the lycée. These three-year courses in the lycée leading to the *Baccalauréat de Technicien Economique* and the *Baccalauréat de Technicien Industriel* appear to ready pupils for the Class C occupations, but no more than this can be said with reasonable certainty.

In the French educational structure, a pupil steps into higher education when he has left secondary education and taken the baccalauréat or an equivalent examination or diploma. All subsequent areas and stages of training are considered to be higher education. The German organization has been an outstanding alternative to the French. The *Hohëre Fachschule* (advanced technical school) prepares pupils for Class B and Class A occupations such as the senior technicians needed in commerce and social work.[21] Graduates of the hohëre fachschule and an equivalent institution, the three-year *Ingenieurschule* (college of engineering)[22] have been much in demand for Class B occupations. Yet are these pupils in higher education or not? A guide to European school systems published by the CCC describes the ingenieurschule as a "college" and the hohëre fachschule as an advanced technical school, immediately below university level but having some characteristics of higher education. It seems only sensible to accept as a part of higher education any formal education that follows the European full or complete secondary education.

The Swedish Reform of Vocational Training

During the 1960's Sweden has reshaped its upper secondary school, the gymnasium. In the past, after obligatory education (or the lower secondary or girls' school) the only choice for further education lay between the essentially theoretical gymnasiums and the practical, applied studies of vocational schools.[23] In 1966 the gymnasium had three separate courses of study, the familiar tripartite division of general academic, technical, and commercial, with further reforms still in progress. It is quite likely that there will be some form of consolidation of upper-level secondary schooling.[24] Perhaps the gymnasium, the new two-year *fackskola*, and the vocational schools will be grouped on common campuses, as they are in Holland, or maybe a consolidated school (a "*gymnasieskola*") will be formed as recommended in 1966 by the Vocational School Committee.

There were a number of reasons for the Swedish reforms. One was an increasing demand for complete upper secondary schooling. Another was the economic need for graduates of upper secondary schools.[25] However, there were not enough openings in the academic technical gymnasiums, and perhaps 25 percent of the eligible students were turned away.

Swedish academic gymnasiums, as in all of Western Europe, have had the highest social status of secondary schools. Nevertheless, pupils applying for the gymnasium did not make a rush for the academic course.[26] In 1966, for example, 40 percent of the students applying for admission to the commercial and technical courses could not be accepted; the comparable figure for the academic gymnasiums was only 20 percent. "Attendance at other schools whose pupils are mainly in the 16–19 age group, particularly the *vocational schools*, has also greatly expanded in recent years. In 1955 total enrollment in the vocational schools was less than 20,000, while the present [1966] figure is about 75,000 in fulltime courses only . . . It is difficult to give an exact indication of the proportion of the total age group which attends vocational schools . . . At present, however, it is estimated that about 23 per cent of the 16–19 age group are enrolled in a vocational school . . . The boom in the 'demand' from applicants rejected at the 'gymnasium' has focused attention on this part of upper-secondary schooling in recent years." [27]

The commercial and technical wings of the Swedish gymnasiums, then, were more desired by pupils than the academic wing. Combined with this was the demand for instruction in vocational schools of various sorts catering to the sixteen to nineteen age group, although a part of that demand was created by pupils who could not find a place in the commercial or technical curriculums of the gymnasiums. All of this seems to indicate that technical vocational instruction is perceived by Swedish pupils and their parents as highly desirable.

Perhaps this desire and demand is realistic. In a way it complements the widely diffused discussion among lay and professional groups that had earlier paved the way for the Swedish comprehensive school. Part of the argument for the comprehensive school was that all vocational choice should be postponed until students were fifteen years old and had some information on occupations. (After a period of counseling, technical study is allowed in the last year of the comprehensive school.)

Perhaps there had been enough public discussion to establish the respectability, and thus desirability, of technical study in the upper secondary school — after the obligatory period of comprehensive schooling. This, however, does not mean that there has been an adequate statement of what the three separate parts of Swedish secondary technical schooling might accomplish. Nor does it mean that pupils have found their way to the technical school where they can be most successful for themselves and the economy. Until technical education has been more carefully studied and reported on in Sweden, answers to these questions can only be tentative.

Have these most recent Swedish reforms of vocational education [28] actually represented a pattern that truly departed from the traditional social-class-oriented structure? A report on the reforms prepared for the OECD in 1966 says that, "on paper," the latest reconstruction has a traditional look. Old wine may have been placed in new bottles when the three-year gymnasium was reformed with five main curriculums "for liberal arts, for social sciences, for economics, for natural sciences, and for technical studies. The curricula, for liberal arts, for social sciences and for natural sciences, taken together, correspond roughly to the present general academic 'gymnasium,' even though the contents differ in many respects. Similarly, the economic and technical curricula correspond to the present commercial 'gymnasium' and technical 'gymnasium' respectively." [29]

The same query could be asked about the two-year fackskola, which was established by the Swedish Parliament in 1964 as a "specialized professional school" with three main curriculums, which branch out into special courses after a year: social, economic and technical. In 1966 the fackskola enrolled about 10 percent of the 16 year olds.[30]

The new "social course" might be examined for a clue to the nature of the fackskola reforms. As described in *Educational Policy and Planning in Sweden*, the "social course [or curriculum] has as a major purpose the preparation of students for 'social' occupations, including a large number of pedagogical occupations. In this course of study there are four branches, the *natural sciences*, the *social sciences*, the *linguistic* and the *domestic economy* branch. The last mentioned branch is a novelty. It aims at the training of personnel who will be able to give advice and information on consumers' problems and assist in the quality inspection of foodstuffs, textiles and housefurnishing requisites." Other occupations for which the social curriculum prepares are "those in the 'domestic economy' sector and certain intermediate-level posts in agriculture, forestry and industry. The social science branch is considered to be suitable preparation for intermediate-level posts in public administration and for several service occupations. Specialization in the arts, which is possible in the social science branch, may be provided by municipalities who wish to do so. Finally, this branch with its wide general scope, provides a general education which will equip students to go on to higher theoretical studies."

Turning to the economic course of the fackskola, the OECD reports comments that this curriculum "gives a broad general education, similar to that provided by the social course. It is also intended as preparation for intermediate-level posts in the so-called 'assistant careers' [Class B and C occupations]; it provides a good general training for office work, leading to occupations in wide sectors of the economy, both public and private. It also offers suitable basic education to students who will enter advertising, public relations and hostess activities of various kinds."

The third and final curriculum of the fackskola is the technical course, which "provides more specialized education than the two others. The path to gainful employment may, therefore, seem shorter for a student following this curriculum. It should be observed, however, that students in the technical course must perform a year's practical work, usually between the first and the second year of study. A student with a leaving certificate from the technical course should be well-qualified to start work at once in posts at the same level as those taken formerly by the so-called 'technical-institute engineers.' . . . This education should also be suitable for many posts in agriculture, forestry, the merchant navy, communications and defense."

"The new applied chemistry branch [of the technical course] will qualify students in the technical course for many posts in such industries as cellulose, drugs, foodstuffs, metallurgy, plastics, etc., as well as in scientific institutions, the health services and so on. Some students will probably move on to higher theoretical studies. Thus a student may, after completing the technical course of the 'fackskola,' enter the third form of the four-year technical course of the 'gymnasium.' " [31]

"The fackskola is to provide pre-vocational training aiming at middle-level posts in certain sectors of the economy, without completely foreclosing the possibility of training and education. The goal-directed education provided by the 'fackskola' is intended to prepare all students to enter work immediately and advance to posts at the intermediate level, e.g., as assistants to executives, as supervisors of small departments, or as wholly or partly independent entrepreneurs, posts which themselves provide prospects of advancement."

The vocational school system has been at the bottom of the hierarchy of technical education in Sweden just as it has been throughout Western Europe. Will its reconstruction change both the content of courses and the present overrepresentation in the vocational system of the lower social class? [32]

There will probably be changes in the activities and subject matter of the vocational school courses, which enroll about 20 percent of the sixteen year olds. The 1966 OECD report states that "in the past few years, questions concerning vocational training have assumed greater importance than ever before. Industry and commerce urgently require vocationally trained personnel who, at present, cannot be found in sufficient numbers. The number of applications for admission to vocational schools is very high. The interest in vocational training is, of course, primarily due to the structural transformation in progress in industry and commerce. The processes of production have become so complicated that industry needs skilled personnel to a much greater extent than ever before." [33]

In reference to apprenticeship the report notes that "in Sweden traditional apprenticeship training still exists to a certain degree with the State contributing to the employer for his expenses. The apprenticeship system is chiefly found within specialized skilled crafts and the building and construction industry. In the entire country there are, at present, no more than about 5,000 apprentices whose training to a limited extent is being subsidized by the State." [34]

There was no comment on the economic soundness of apprenticeship training, but 5,000 apprentices is a small number when compared with 75,000 pupils in vocational schools. As of 1966, half of the later were in "workshop schools" (*verkstadsskola*) and "incorporated workshop schools" with about 7,700 in "special central workshop schools" and boarding schools which are located in rural areas for youth who otherwise would not have access to that form of vocational school. [35]

In some of the workshop schools and certainly in the incorporated workshop schools, industries, with state subsidy, provide the practical training, and theoretical study is left to the schools. The economic soundness of this arrangement will depend upon whether industry's management looks ahead and welcomes innovation. Otherwise, the program is practical enough in training but only for the short run. The same can be said for any other of Sweden's vocational schools. [36]

In our opinion, the Swedish reconstruction of education has not been merely a matter of finding new names for yesterday's schools and their subject matter, but nevertheless the entire path of professional preparation of teachers will have to be remade, and new schools and teaching aids will have to be created. To make light of these needs is to invite disillusionment. [37] The degree to which Swedish school reconstruction has been or will continue to be informed by open-minded leaders of agriculture, industry, commerce, business, and other fields cannot be asserted with confidence. Here, if anywhere, the proof will be in the outcome. Either the technical graduates of Swedish secondary schools will do well economically and be judged by society as citizens and as human beings, or they will not. For example, in a country whose industry is international, educational policy is vulnerable to criticism if there should fail to be a growth of foreign language instruction. Or in a country where less than 10 percent of the working population is employed in agriculture, any preparation of a large force of agricultural workers would cause one to wonder about the planning. The public discussions that have marked all changes proposed for Swedish education have been vigorous, and these debates will continue to bring questions of adequacy to the public forum.

Beginning in 1965, Sweden has also moved to increase its educational facilities for Class A manpower. In that year the parliament agreed to a primarily quantitative expansion of university education, which would

138

enable some 87,000 students to attain higher education by 1970, compared to slightly over 60,000 in 1964.[38] Limited national resources have dictated that highly qualified manpower be divided between what are termed the "free faculties" — theology, law, liberal arts, social and natural sciences, and liberal sciences (economics excepted) — and the "blockaded faculties" — such as medicine, economics and engineering — where entry has been truly restricted by a *numerus clausus*. The selection procedure allows the "blockaded faculties" to admit only a specified number of students, whereas the "free faculties" have to accept anyone who is eligible.

Since technical instruction, particularly secondary technical schooling, is notably more expensive than academic schooling, one might predict that the "poorer" the country, the less technical education it will have. At the level of higher education a parallel situation holds. The largest enrollment will be in the faculty of law, not in engineering or science curriculums. Graduates of law, customarily middle- and upper-class young people, have been in control of government and education. Because of their academic background, these officials have tended to join the academic faculty in perpetuating a type of education that is anything but vocational and technical.

The European sense of social status has meant that greater prestige attaches to persons or courses in a full or complete secondary school which is preparatory for a university. It is impossible to say how long Europeans will feel the university to be the most prestigious form of higher education. Inextricably bound up with this feeling has been another: that the oldest, most venerable tradition of the university is that of arts and letters. Science, in this philosophy of higher education, is a relative newcomer, and the technical studies have not even arrived. An assumption which has been rarely articulated, but tacitly held, is that the university should be attended by those from the upper-middle and upper social classes. For quite a long time, only a reform-minded minority held that this was too restricted a view of the elite. Even fewer reformers held that the European faculties of letters really were not at home with, and perhaps were even hostile to, technology.

In the last chapter we noted that the more types of schools there are, the greater is the need for guidance of choice among many curriculums. This is not to minimize the very real needs of students in comprehensive schools; nevertheless, a highly differentiated secondary-school system poses special problems of guidance. A complex organization of secondary schools like the German one, for example, offers the student a bewildering array of choices:

1. After nine years of primary schooling, combining a four-year grundschule and a five-year hauptschule, a pupil can enter a two-year berufsfachschule (full-time vocational school) at the age of fifteen. The berufsfachschule is terminal, and no further schooling has been open to its graduates.

2. Or, after the four-year grundschule the pupil, then aged ten, might transfer either to a realschule (shorter general course) or to a gymnasium, a choice which requires more than a flip of the coin. However, the opportunities for transfer to a six-year realschule or to a gymnasium are not limited to the age of ten. There are other transfer points when a pupil is twelve or thirteen.

The gymnasium is presently a nine-year school which pupils enter at the age of ten; however, it is possible for older students to enter a school which prepares in three years for transfer to the gymnasium, from which they will graduate in another three years. This preparatory school also provides schooling for students who do *not* transfer to the gymnasium.

3. A pupil who graduates from the gymnasium and passes his abitur can enter any institution of higher learning, including a university or one of the fachschulen (technical schools) or the ingenieurschule (engineering school).

The "guidance" of students according to social class origin has been rejected on all sides in Germany, and one may assume that pupils are guided in their selection of curriculums solely by their inherent capabilities, even though this assumption cannot be tested.

The reconstruction of all levels of education has been carried out, certainly in Western Europe, by middle-class men and women but on behalf of the lower class. This was clearly the case in the effort to increase the social status of secondary and higher technical education, including technical universities, and to increase the possibility of a pupil's transferring from one school to another.

Buttressing the effort to build the social status of technical education were two factors. One was the trend toward more highly technical agriculture, commerce, industry, and defense, a trend which has created a market for highly skilled manpower. All of Europe has felt this trend and it has heightened the need for the "equivalence" of diplomas and training all over Europe, at least all over Western Europe (see Chapter 1). The other force that helped to advance technical education was the greater application of science to the spectrum of man's needs. This application has reduced the dominance of academic education and has encouraged academics to review the educational structure, particularly in light of social-class representation. In the past this appraisal had not been necessary; it was taken for granted that academic education, especially in the classic languages of Greek and Latin, was the best education for the best pupils. The evolution of natural science into an intellectually significant subject has been a threat to this assumption, as has been the role modern languages have played in literature and science.

The old idea of the nontechnical academic secondary school faded as the idea of what is technical underwent a transformation. Mathematics, natural and social science, and modern languages all have technical sides. All are applicable to commerce and many other fields. And the handwork — the menial and manual work associated with the servant, the lower class, and the peasant — has been slowly vanishing.

The evolution of technical education (especially on the secondary level) and the great pedagogical reforms in Western Europe since the mid-1940's have been aimed at creating a balance of prestige between academic and general courses. In the United States there is already this poised equilibrium. In Eastern Europe, on the other hand, the equality has been destroyed for some time, for academic subjects are far less important than science and technology. Western Europe will probably maintain a delicate balance between the academic and the technical.

CHAPTER EIGHT

A Contrast
in European School Reform
West Germany and Sweden

By closely examining the fate of school reform in Germany and Sweden, we will be able to summarize themes which have threaded through this book. The first part of the chapter describes the two decades of "non-reform" in West Germany and the reasons for this lethargy, which persisted to 1970. The second part is devoted to educational reconstruction in Sweden; some of the Swedish reforms will be familiar to the reader by now.

Any fair comparison of Germany and Sweden must at the beginning acknowledge the great cultural and political differences between the two nations. Unlike West Germany, Sweden is a relatively small country which enjoys cultural homogeneity, which was virtually untouched by the last two world wars, and which has the advantage of political centralization. In contrast the German länder possess a political autonomy similar to that of the Swiss cantons, the Canadian provinces, or the several American states. The existence of this autonomy not only tempers a reader's probable impatience with Germany but it also encourages realistic thinking about European harmonization of education. It would be sheer naïveté to expect all European educators to subscribe to similar educational philosophies. Many German (and other European) educators still believe that pupils differ in their natures and that separate multilateral schools are the only way to recognize these differences. Such thinking rejects any alteration in course content for the purpose of educating greater numbers of students. On the other hand, most Swedes are keenly interested in educa-

142

tion and they have supported relatively dramatic educational reforms, especially the democratic comprehensive school. Their entire educational system is a laboratory.

Two Decades of Nonreform in West German Education

It was very difficult for the Germans to accomplish much during the era of educational reform which characterized other European nations after World War II. The country had been tremendously shaken by Nazism and the disruptions of the wartime and postwar experiences. "The conservatism which prevailed in post-war Germany," Robinsohn and Kuhlmann point out, was a "product of the overwhelming desire to recapture material well-being and social stability and a distrust of 'new beginnings' and experiments. Most of the leading university scholars rejected proposed reforms of the German secondary school and recommended retaining the traditional nine-year *Gymnasium*." [1]

The German system of secondary education was typical of the postwar European structure; it was differentiated and required that students pass a selective examination at the age of ten and a secondary-school leaving examination, the abitur, before admission to the university.[2] More than three-quarters of the pupils ended their general education at age eleven or twelve, after four years in the grundschule or five years in the hauptschule, both branches of the volksschule. These youngsters then went on to two- or three-year vocational schools, which were not thought of as secondary schools though they were post-primary.

Looking back at the accomplishments of the prewar secondary schools, one finds little reason to doubt that their graduates were very satisfactory workers and craftsmen. Only a minority of prophets predicted that scientifically inspired technology would create new industries, new office practices, and a strange hunger for all sorts of technicians. The old-style graduates of the vocational schools seemed adequate enough, and there was no apparent need for a new brand, the technician. Only a few people argued for prolonging general education, perhaps to nine years. And few argued that there should be more youngsters in advanced vocational schools (beyond the level of the berufsfachschule or berufsschule).

Twenty or even ten years ago it would have been quite visionary to speak about schools that prepared more pupils for advanced schooling. The class structure of German society meant that pupils from lower-class homes more often than not stopped their general education at about the age of eleven and went off to a two- or three-year vocational school. There was very little selection of suitable schools on the basis of tests — a German equivalent to the famous British 11-plus examination was not usual. It was taken for granted that the class structure reflected inborn differences in abilities. (Recent changes have made it somewhat easier for pupils to transfer among many types of curriculums and schools. This freedom has been a major objective of the six-year general secondary school (realschule), but this school does not grant admission to the German university. Only graduation from the gymnasium, which few students of lower-class origin attend, qualifies a student for admission to a German university.)

German technical schools were few, and they were not well attended.[3] Children from upper-class homes left the volksschule after four years and entered the nine-year gymnasium. In modern times the gymnasium, and similar European secondary schools, has evolved a three-part curriculum. The oldest wing is occupied by Greek and Latin; more recently divisions specializing in modern languages and in mathematics and science have been added. In some countries these three sections have been subdivided; in France, for example, a technical wing was added to the curriculum of the lycée. The most recent innovations in German pedagogy, however, have not added technical studies to the gymnasium. A place was made for mathematics and science at the turn of the century, although these subjects were seen by some as a most materialistic departure from classical humanism, but the technology of industry, commerce, business, and agriculture have not been added to the curriculum of the gymnasium.

Immediately after World War II the Allied Control Commission urged the adoption of pedagogical reforms. In a directive to the provincial ministers of education, the commission defined the concept of "democratizing" education and proposed the following criteria: "equality of educational opportunity; free tuition and teaching materials; an additional ninth year of obligatory schooling; education for international understanding; educational guidance; health supervision; academic training for all teachers; democratic school administration." [4] Although the reforms were accepted in principle during the early postwar period, the Germans thereafter dropped them as soon as possible. Changes imposed by the occupying power were doomed to be rejected when occupation was abandoned. Today only one of the recommendations, that all teachers be given academic training, has taken on life and in some of the länder teachers of primary grades are required to attend a university rather than a separate pedagogical seminary.

There were other indications that change was needed. During the 1960's Germans were warned of an impending teacher shortage and of educational disaster that might soon follow.[5] Manpower economists conducted surveys of the needs of industry for different types of manpower, drawing conclusions that were identical with those in other European nations. Nevertheless, German education was not significantly altered.

Technical training has been especially poor. About two-thirds of the 14 to 15 year olds today have had no more than a limited general education plus some training in either full- or part-time vocational schools such as the comparatively new full-time coeducational schools (berufsfachschulen) and the part-time schools (berufsaufbauschulen or berufsschulen), where pupils study when they are not at work. But this part-time vocational schooling is inadequate for the needs of modern German industry and business, and the general education of the part- or full-time vocational schools no longer suffices.

The "middle school" (realschule) has been unfairly relied on to train for positions of "intermediate responsibility" (*mittlere Führung*). This reliance has been caused partly by the technological revolution that we have so often mentioned. If the world of work still separated itself into the three conventional divisions of professional, middle-level, and semi- or unskilled occupations, unreconstructed secondary education would *almost* function. (There still would be the task of increasing the representation of the lower economic and social classes in schools preparing for the top positions.) But technology has complicated this division and demanded more specialized and advanced skills. And the German schools have not adequately accommodated these needs.[6]

The full secondary school (gymnasium) is also disappointing. Ten percent of the 10 to 14 year olds attend, and in 1953 only 3.3 percent of the average age group graduated.[7] Reformers argue that half the pupils in this age group should be encouraged to continue in higher education.

The reconstructionists of European secondary education have striven to increase the ease of transfer within a vertical system of secondary schools, but this aspiration apparently has not succeeded in Germany. Robinsohn and Kuhlmann reported in 1967 that there were "few if any possibilities of transfer from one main tier to the other. Only a very limited number of continuation schools (*Aufbauschulen*), and these mainly in

145

rural regions, offer a six-year course for later secondary school graduation. However, a third type of school existed in some länder after the war
and has steadily grown in importance — the Middle School (*Mittel-
schule*), now generally called *Realschule*. In 1953, 5 per cent of the 10 to
14 age group were at *Mittel-* or *Realschulen*; 6.1 per cent of the 17 year
olds reached 'intermediate graduation.' This diploma is also offered — evidently as a substitute — by the academic secondary schools and by continuation classes at elementary schools." [8]

Whether the realschule has continued to gain in importance is question-
able. The enrollment of 5 percent of the 10 to 14 year olds is an unimpres-
sive figure, even for 1953. In the late 1960's the important questions still
were whether the flow of young people into the full secondary schools was
satisfactory and whether the technical curriculums could be accommodated in these secondary schools.

Robinsohn and Kuhlmann have reported a rate of academic failure in
Germany which is alarming: "In each of the years 1955 to 1957, 3 to 4
per cent of elementary school pupils and middle school pupils had to repeat their grades. In the secondary grades the figure was 6 per cent and it
is at present about 9 per cent. According to a calculation of the *Wissen-
schaftsrat* [Directorate of Schools], only one-third of those studying in
grade three of the secondary school in 1950 eventually were graduated.
Analyses of selected age groups have shown that less than 20 per cent of
secondary school graduates reach graduation without repeating one of
more classes." [9]

There has recently been some improvement, however. More pupils are
graduating from secondary school; 6.9 percent of the relevant age group
took the secondary school leaving examination in 1965, an increase of almost 50 percent over 1950. But 6.9 percent of the relevant age group is
still a small percentage of graduates.[10] Although Robinsohn and Kuhlmann were more encouraged by these increases than I am, they nevertheless asked: "But are these developments educational reform, or are they
rather examples of a process which comparative education often has demonstrated — that quantitative as well as qualitative deficiencies of an educational system are usually met by modifying the existing structure before
undertaking more radical reform?" [11]

The tenor of the Robinsohn-Kuhlmann conclusion is justified; the reform measures advocated by many German educators failed to effect real
structural modification. Neither did two proposed reform plans, the *Rah-*

146

menplan and the *Bremer Plan*, find their way into public policy.[12] The Rahmenplan, published in 1959, was the work of a committee established by the federal government and by the länder. The Rahmenplan was not endorsed by the universities nor by any important elements of the scholarly establishment. When the committee proposed that German education needed to be reconstructed, though not at all drastically, the proposal was rejected.[13] The Bremer Plan, sponsored in 1960 by the German Teachers Union and differing only slightly from the Rahmenplan, was politically no more successful. Both plans had been put together only after years of work — the Rahmenplan required six years for completion and the Bremer Plan eight.

BARRIERS TO REFORM

What blocked educational innovation? In Germany the degree of sovereignty exercised by the länder, by teachers and parents, and by tradition has created a force which protects the *ancien régime* in pedagogy.[14] Leaders in commerce and industry have not pressed for plans to increase the prestige of technical education, though they might have been expected to do so, and interpretation of their motivation would be hazardous. One can say only that perhaps the defenders of the status quo have not been aware of educational reform.

In the main the churches have resisted innovation. Clergymen have been prepared in the gymnasium and they wish to preserve what they feel to be a superior form of education.[15] The pedagogical views of the churches have been most influential in the rural areas of Germany. The clergy have defended the small one- and two-grade village schools, which make up about half of all German schools and enroll about 14 percent of the primary school pupils.

Opposition to reform has also been related to a biological assessment of the pool of ability. The views of K. V. Müller, a distinguished social theorist, on the sociology of education cannot be discounted. Müller believes that ability is determined by heredity and that "any socio-political measures employed to change 'the natural correspondence of school selection and social selection' " are futile. For at least a decade the secondary school masters, the conservative political parties, organized industry and commerce, and a number of ministries have relied heavily on Müller's "expertise." [16] They assumed that no more than 5 to 10 percent of the population could benefit from higher education and that any plans which tampered with the process of "natural selection" would adversely affect industry and commerce.

There were few groups friendly to a broad and fundamental reform of German pedagogy prior to the last three or four years of the 1960's. Nevertheless there were some organizations with more modest objectives, like the Farmers' Association, which abandoned its commitment to the one- and two-class schools of the rural community and came to support the "introduction of central schools and orientation classes, in order to improve standards of production and organization." Representatives of the *Philologenverband* (Language Association) also changed their stand to some degree. They did not go so far as to admit that "secondary schools have a social class bias" or to agree that "enrollments should be greatly increased." Nonetheless leaders of the association were apparently "impressed by the accumulating evidence of research showing the range of untapped reserves, for example that two-thirds of the 'gifted' children of lower income groups never even attempt a secondary school education, and that this low level of aspiration must be explained by the inability to overcome language and other cultural barriers." [17]

SIGNS OF CHANGE

Confronted by mounting evidence of alarming problems in education, the two major political parties of West Germany, the Christian Democratic Union (CDU) and the Social Democratic Party (SPD), advanced rival plans of reform in the late 1960's. The CDU backed the Martin Plan while the SPD supported the Evers Plan.[18] It should be noted, however, that by 1970 both parties agreed on one essential: the value of a comprehensive form of school organization. Neither party suffered a setback because it recommended a form of the gesamtschule,[19] a clear indication that the political leaders had correctly assessed the German people's interest in the comprehensive organization of secondary and higher education.

At the heart of the CDU's Martin Plan (also called the "Climbing Plan") were two features: a two-year higher technical school and a combination of vocational-technical school and evening college. The latter would permit ambitious and able pupils to reach the technical, and even the humanistic, university.[20] Unfortunately, the success of the Martin Plan seemed to depend on great motivation on the part of pupils, motivation which is lacking in the very pupils — those from the lower classes — to whom Ber-

148

thold Martin wished to give an opportunity which they lacked in the old vertical structure of German education.

The SPD, which traditionally has taken more risks than the CDU, proposed in the Evers Plan to create a true gesamtschule, designed to get a larger number of youth from working-class backgrounds into advanced secondary and higher education, to reduce social class discrimination based on ignorance, and to allow for greater inter-school transfer from a theoretical to a practical emphasis.

The Evers Plan differed in essence from the Martin Plan by lodging all institutions for vocational instruction within the comprehensive school. But it is not with secondary education that Senator Karl-Heinz Evers staked out his chief innovation. The senator's comprehensive university (*Gesamthochschule*) offered the most radical change in European higher education that has yet been introduced into discussion. In effect it took the topic of comprehensive schooling to a third stage, that of higher education, and proposed a structure similar to the universities and colleges of Canada and the United States. That is, a student could terminate his academic career after the first two of the three- or four-year course and receive a "first degree." Alternatively he could choose to continue his education for another year or even two. It was hoped that the provision of these alternatives would lessen aborted university careers.

Although neither of these two plans were political successes, they did clear the air, and paved the way for the famous *Strukturplan für das Bildungswesen* (Structural Plan for the Educational System). The time is apparently ripe for educational change in West Germany, and it seems likely that schooling there will be altered in the direction of the organization now in effect in France. In 1970 the Structural Plan was presented by the Educational Commission of the German Educational Council to Federal Minister Hans Leussink, who described it as the "most progressive, all-embracing general plan for the educational system which we have ever had." [21]

Advocates of the comprehensive school may be somewhat discouraged by the Structural Plan's continual emphasis on giving pupils a chance to specialize. But they will doubtless be pleased by the plan's liberal emphasis on achievement, even though within specialized programs. As in France, pupils beginning their secondary schooling will be offered a rather large selection of courses so that their bent may be determined. A sympathetic outsider can only hope that this bent will reveal itself, for unless

149

there is a professional guidance program, success in this area seems somewhat unlikely.

The Structural Plan not only greatly enlarges the range of choices but also challenges the shibboleth of examinations. *Education in Germany* makes the point succinctly: "Ability and the attitude of a pupil are more important than knowing facts. . . . The problem of selection by means of examination and learning controls cannot be solved in present-day educational institutions simply by 'examination' but only by ensuring that the 'examination' takes place within the educational courses which provide for the best possible individual advancement of the pupil." [22]

The principal elements of the plan consist of five spheres and stages.

1. Elementary sphere (conventionally designated as preschool), for 3 to 4 year olds.

2. Primary sphere, for 5 to 9 year olds.

3. Orientation stage, for 10 and 11 year olds. The orientation stage is very similar to that initiated by the French. It is supposed to make it easier for the pupil "to recognize his own learning possibilities and fields of interest in order to prepare the later choice of a suitable main course of instruction." [23] The schedule of studies is the same for all pupils; there is no specialization.

4. Secondary Stage I (usually called lower-secondary education by Europeans), for the 12 to 15 year olds. It is the chief aim of this stage to conclude an "up-to-date basic education common to all pupils." [24] At the same time the special interests of pupils should have manifested themselves both in classroom performance and in test results. The pedagogical language in which the plan is summarized should not disguise the simple fact of differentiation, though it is differentiation based on the success pupils experience in one of several types of programs. Although a "common basis of subjects and learning aims" is to be maintained in the first two years of Secondary Stage I, nevertheless, "structural differentiations according to achievement classes (streaming) and/or achievement groups (setting)" will be undertaken "where the possibilities of internal differentiation as a means of individual advancement are no longer sufficient." And, as an article in *Education in Germany* points out, "in addition to this comes the external differentiation according to fields of interest." [25] This two-year trial period is to be followed by the final two years of Secondary Stage I, during which pupils will concentrate more in their specialties. Although compulsory education ends at this point, individual pupils will be

150

carefully counseled with an eye to encouraging them to enter Secondary Stage II for the two or three additional years of voluntary study. Actually the duration of Secondary Stage I has not been finally determined. It may span the fifth to the tenth school year or only the seventh to the tenth, but in any case it leads to the degree Abitur I. It is hoped that by 1990 all young people will complete a ten-year course of study and receive the Abitur I.[26]

5. Secondary Stage II (usually called upper secondary education by Europeans), for 16 to 19 year olds or older. Some of the programs will require two years to complete, others will demand a full three years. The chief aim of this stage is to amalgamate academic and technical-professional courses, a dramatic departure from convention and one which will certainly boost the status of teacher training and all other professional-technical study.

Roughly parallel with these professional-technical schools will be a reconstructed version of the traditional gymnasiums. The final two or three years of these schools, together with so-called "higher technical colleges," will form a "compound system." [27] The schools of the compound system and the other schools of the Secondary Stage II lead to the Abitur II. According to the plan, those holding the Abitur II may attend a university or go to a technical university or prepare to teach in one of the primary or secondary schools.

Doubtless the Structural Plan will be modified in the give-and-take of political debate. This modification is to be expected and must not be allowed to shadow a truly significant change in West German education. What began on the "downbeat" of two decades of nonreform in West German education has ended on the "upbeat" of success in innovation.

Two Decades of Reform in Sweden

No European reconstruction of education has been better known or more widely heralded than the Swedish.[28] The Butler Act of 1944 put England in the lead chronologically, but the first Swedish legislation came soon after the end of World War II. The Swedish Comprehensive School Committee was appointed in 1946 and two years later presented its first recommendation, which laid the necessary groundwork for the education acts of 1950 and 1962 and the establishment of the nine-year comprehensive school. In 1966 educators in Sweden were able to state their objectives clearly in a report prepared for discussion with OECD education experts.[29]

Five objectives were listed. The first objective was concerned with the individual and his development and proposed that attention be paid to every stage of a person's life, from preschool education to adult education. In an equalitarian spirit, the first objective also pressed for equal esteem for all curriculums.[30]

The second objective was more social: "The school should aim at safeguarding and strengthening the democratic system." The cause of European integration was enhanced by this objective, for, as the Swedish Minister of Education put it, the schools should "develop those characteristics of the pupils which constitute the foundation for, and strengthen the democratic principles of co-operation and tolerance between sexes, races and nations . . ." In the same spirit Swedish educators felt that the objective of strengthening the democratic system meant not only that there should be a common core of subjects in the comprehensive and upper secondary school but also that there should be students habituated in cooperation and understanding of alternative social systems. Certainly the idea that "critical and independent thinking should be encouraged and excessive stress on absorption of factual data should be avoided" is endorsed by such attitudes.

The third objective, that educational policy should contribute to general economic development (e.g., by producing the required types and amounts of qualified manpower), has been fundamental to any balance between individual and social good. Vocational counselors should interpret to students the manpower forecasts, uncertain as they may be. But no pupil will be denied entrance into a curriculum whose graduates may not be in needed occupations: "The satisfaction of total demand for school places is . . . not subject to any restrictions imposed by estimated manpower requirements (although it clearly is affected by restrictions arising from the availability of resources . . .)"[31]

The fourth objective called for an educational system that was flexible and adaptive to change. Flexibility is necessary, said the report, to enable the system to respond to the "changing structure of demand for education by the individual members of the society as well as the equally dynamic requirements of the economy; to provide sufficient breadth in the content or educational offering and to allow for changes in students' school careers. It should be possible for individuals to alter their educational decisions either during the normal school career or later (adult education), thus eliminating 'dead ends' in the system."

The desideratum is freedom both for students and for planners. It was hoped that changes would be the result of reflection, of weighing alternatives, of thinking about probable results. A world of wise selection among competing options was imagined. The fifth and final objective, a fundamental condition for the implementation of the other four, was the prudent allocation of resources: "The educational system should make efficient use of limited human and real resources." All five of these objectives were realized in the creation of the comprehensive school system.

THE RATIONALE OF THE SWEDISH COMPREHENSIVE SCHOOL

The pre-reform Swedish educational system was typical of multilateral schools in Western Europe. Graduates from the lower secondary *realskola* who were considered the brightest were steered to the general gymnasium, the next brightest to the technical gymnasium, and the least bright to the commercial gymnasium. Such separation and selection was consistent with an adapted version of the Platonic philosophy. The largest percentage of pupils continued in schools that offered some general education and, depending on the occupations for which they prepared, one or more years of study. Higher education was not for these pupils.

The comprehensive school has changed things. The early occupational choice, if it can be called a choice, is postponed until the eighth grade of the comprehensive school, when the adolescent is fifteen or sixteen years old. More important, the comprehensive school has been successful in encouraging pupils to stay on in school. In 1965, for example, 78 percent of the pupils who graduated from the comprehensive school opted for a combination of courses that would take them to the gymnasium. In 1959 only 19 percent entered the gymnasium, and about 70 percent graduated. (Sweden has had a fivefold increase in the number of students in higher education in the twenty years from 1950 to 1970.) [32]

The establishment of the comprehensive school in Sweden was a victory for both social democratic ideology and educational psychology — the ideology was critical of the Western European social class structure and the data from educational psychology supported that ideology. Instead of accepting the social mode of differentiating pupils, Swedish supporters of the comprehensive school successfully opposed it with research data. Indeed, the first publication of truly comparative studies of academic achievement, including samples of pupils from the United States, was prepared by the Swedish educator Torsten Husén. Before this publication, opinions were merely conjecture, often founded on a very limited range of experience and necessarily confined to national scenes.[33]

To put the Swedish educational reforms in some perspective, we should recall that the first steps were taken during World War II, when the Swedish Minister of Education appointed the School Committee of 1940. For the next twenty years a very great deal of research and political spadework was done. No one was more assiduous nor more effective in setting the comprehensive school of Sweden on a solid foundation of investigation than Torsten Husén, director of the Institute of Educational Research at the University of Stockholm. Writing in 1961, Husén had the Swedish situation in mind particularly when he said: "The great dilemma with which most countries in Europe have been faced when extending compulsory schooling and changing school organisation, has been the connection and/ or integration of the common elementary school with the university-preparing academic type of school. The attempts to create a unified or a comprehensive school organisation have come up against historic and social forces according to which the two school types are designed for different social classes and therefore each has a different amount of prestige." [34]

Husén writes with three social classes in mind. Class 1 is populated by those conventionally labeled aristocrats, the wealthy and the upper levels of the professional, managerial, and other groups that we have referred to earlier. Discussing the lowest class, Husén observes: "A large body of research has shown that students from social class 3 (consisting for the most part of working class families) . . . are greatly underrepresented in the secondary academic school. This is the case in all countries of Europe, as well as in the United States. In France, for example, until recently only one-eighth of the student population comes from working class homes, who form two-thirds of the nation's families. When Premier Khrushchev announced the new educational reform in a speech before the Supreme Soviet, he said that 60 per cent of the enrollment in Moscow's upper-level schools was recruited from the intelligentsia and bureaucracy, and only 40 per cent from the homes of manual workers and farmers." [35]

When there is a policy of limited access to schools preparing for higher education, it is most important, Husén wrote, that the screening be efficient. The academic failure of those admitted is one index of inefficient screening, and the underrepresentation of a social class in these schools

154

and in the universities themselves is another. A third index is overrepresentation of a social class. He cites the British report *Early Leaving*: "The most striking datum is that failures were about five times more common for pupils in social class 3 among the *top third of entrance examination scores* than for pupils coming from homes which by and large correspond to social class 1." Husén further noted that of the upper quarter of pupils who received the upper third of school marks "non-applicants from social class 3 exceed those from 1 by between two and three times." [36] There were similar results when the reports measured ability and not achievement.

Other research supported the Swedish comprehensive plan. John Elmgren discovered that the "so-called practical and theoretical aptitudes were positively correlated. Furthermore, according to the factor analyses, 'practical' aptitude did not seem to be 'as simple and unitary in its structure as general intelligence' (the latter being apparently equated with 'theoretical' aptitude)." [37]

The School Committee of 1940 concluded in its 1948 report that the "earlier conception of 'theoretical' and 'practical' aptitudes as being in a compensatory way related to each other was not valid. That finding certainly did not support a parallel school structure; an early differentiation by the transfer of the 'academics' to a selective secondary school was not justified. In the first place, since the 'greatest comprehensiveness' of abilities was to be found in pupils of high general ability, an early transfer would imply that the practical vocations would not then get their share of people of high general ability and would thereby suffer a great loss of prestige. This would then in the long run widen gaps between the social classes." [38]

Other research favored the comprehensive structure. The findings of Kjell Härnqvist were reported to the OECD in the early 1960s. [39] Härnqvist found that any student was likely to have great differences in ability between one school subject and another ("profile variations"). One of the chief justifications of differentiating pupils had been that men fell naturally into two main groups, one predisposed to theory and the other to hand-minded tasks. Instead, Härnqvist showed, the range of ability in any one pupil was about 60 percent as large as the range of differences in ability between two groups of pupils.

Härnqvist's findings were important in another way. He had evidence that as children grow, their interests become more specific. A further rea-

155

son for postponing differentiation, then, was to limit choices based on premature expressions of interest. Interests, and with them abilities, were liable to change. Härnqvist recommended that to avoid frequent failures, division on the basis of broad interests should come rather late. His data indicated that pupils should be permitted to do advanced work in areas where they had strength and to take less difficult courses where they lacked the requisite ability. The comprehensive organization of courses offered this alternative to differentiation in curriculum early in adolescence.

By 1960 Swedish psychologists and others concerned with the progress of pupils also recommended that early differentiation be abolished and that classes be mixed. Their research had determined that mixing did not lower the achievement of the very able students. On the other hand, the students of less ability were found to have higher levels of achievement than they had had in classes where they were presumably grouped homogeneously.[40]

Much research criticized early differentiation. The findings of J. Orring, for example, bore out what was concluded on the basis of Härnqvist's research. Out of a group of 8,500 pupils "who in 1951 entered the various streams of the 'realskola' (which provided an early organizational differentiation according to marks) more than half the boys in most branches and almost half the girls, either repeated one or several years or simply dropped out, the two phenomena occurring with equal frequency. For the most part, only those with very high primary school marks completed the school in the normally prescribed time period. The findings were particularly striking in the practical 'realskola.' Apparently this kind of differentiation had proved unsatisfactory." [41]

As a final sample of Swedish educational research on ability grouping, we may take a study made by N. E. Svensson. Svensson wanted to discover whether various types of schools or curriculums made a difference in scholastic achievement. Among other comparisons, the achievement of pupils in a comprehensive school was compared with those in a realskola. The latter pupils performed somewhat better at an early age but were not consistent as they grew older. Svensson's conclusions were:

1. Achievements of pupils in selective (i.e., "realskola") classes did not correlate in any way with the type of previous schooling. A slight tendency towards superiority on the part of pupils in early-differentiated classes, observed in the first phase of the study, disappeared in grades 8 and 9.

2. The type of school in which the classes were located (at that time,

the classes could be part of lower secondary, primary or experimental comprehensive schools) had no bearing on achievement of pupils in the long run.

3. With regard to pupils in non-selective classes (i.e., the lower secondary parts of the "folkskola"), the time at which differentiation began appeared to have no demonstrable effect on achievement.[42]

With the weight of this and past research, the opposition was defeated and Sweden passed the School Law of 1962.

OTHER SWEDISH REFORMS

The creation of the comprehensive system is certainly a landmark in Swedish and European education. But reform in Sweden has not stopped at that point. There has been consideration of the reduction of class size in order to give pupils more individualized instruction. It has been estimated that reducing the average size of classes in the compulsory school would require approximately two thousand additional teachers and about as many additional classrooms.[43] The maximum size for the lower department of the comprehensive school (grades 1 to 3) is set at twenty-five students and for grades 4 to 9 at thirty.

But smaller classes constitute only one element of rationalization within the educational process. (Rationalization means thoughtful application of time in teaching methods to maximize one's effort.) A teacher training committee was appointed in 1960 to increase the "productivity" of the teachers.[44] Reporting in 1965, the committee recommended that teaching methods and supervised student teaching, as well as any probationary teaching, should be the responsibility of the teachers' colleges. The academic subjects of the teachers were, as before, to be included in the province of the universities.

Class teachers in Sweden have traditionally been prepared in the equivalent of the American teachers' college. The subject teachers have enrolled in the universities as they do throughout Europe. In July 1968 the Swedish Ministry of Education made plans to replace most of the primary teacher training colleges with specialized colleges of education. Professional preparation of teachers is to be considered part of higher education. Teachers of the first six grades of the comprehensive school are to be graduates of upper secondary schools and will study at the teachers' colleges for two and a half to three years. These requirements are similar to the ones for primary-school teachers in Great Britain and they will most

157

likely become common throughout Europe. In the future, it appears that European teachers' colleges will concentrate on courses in teaching methods — on pedagogics and didactics. Research, on the other hand, will be done in the universities which are now the hosts of such educational research institutes as the one led by Torsten Husén at the University of Stockholm.

Unmistakably, the trend in Europe is to separate courses about teaching from the research which generates ideas about the teaching-learning process. How-to-do techniques will be forthcoming from experienced teachers, as well as from the teachers' colleges, but none of this will be thought of as fundamental research. This trend seems most unfortunate, because it will make the methods courses, as they are called in the United States, matters of learning technique. Instructors will be expected to pass along to their students the applications of research which they themselves have not done. Students will not be expected to adopt a research point of view — that is, a critical point of view, one which asks whether a technique squares with the literature on human learning, and so on. It appears that European educators are once again divorcing theory from practice, after having fought successfully against that distinction (in education *versus* training, for example). Again, the teachers' colleges — and therefore the technical aspects of teaching and school administration — are by implication relegated to second-class citizenship in the academic world. That is, secondary-school teachers will be asked to study methods, the applied science of teaching, at a teachers' college, but they will study their subject matter, the theoretical materials, at universities. This decision is lamentable.

But the Swedish secondary-school teacher's mastery of subject matter has not been diluted; the teacher in the upper grades of the secondary school is to be a university graduate. His load has been made heavier than the ordinary university student's since he is required to take professional courses in pedagogy in addition to the full requirements of his academic major. The Swedish teacher is thus well-qualified, but his education might be even better if the study of teaching methods was not segregated from the university. Sweden is typically European in maintaining this separation, yet in many other ways Sweden is atypically distinguished. Its creation of a comprehensive school system, its gathering of pertinent research on differentiation, its involvement of an informed public are all praiseworthy. So, too, is its policy of "rolling reform."

The Swedish pedagogical reforms of the 1960's were undertaken in response to data and recommendations from ad hoc committees appointed to scrutinize particular problems. These ad hoc committees have typically been chaired by prominent officials or political figures and their members have included members of Parliament, representatives of the trade unions and other public interest groups, and civil servants from the ministries or the central administration. By contrast, rolling reform means a continuous study, and those who work with it are technical experts in educational planning who have specialized in the use of the mass media, closed circuit television, independent study using "programmed learning," financial aid to university students, or some other aspect.[45]

As one might expect, rolling reform places a premium on planning and research. In July 1965 all Swedish ministries were reorganized, and a planning and budgetary secretariat was made a part of each ministry. The Ministry of Education already had such a unit, its forecasting and planning group. The P-group, as it has been known, was expanded after July 1965. The planning and budget secretariat of the Ministry of Education which coordinates all planning within the ministry has been a major part of the rolling reform. So too has the National Board of Education, one of whose five departments deals primarily with fiscal matters.[46] The division for educational research and development of the National Board of Education has been charged with "rationalizing" instruction with respect to curriculums, teaching aids, and methods of instruction.[47] The division's work has been supplemented by pedagogical research institutes such as the well-known School of Education at the University of Stockholm.[48] A portion of rolling reform must necessarily be these quantitative (or fiscal) and qualitative reforms, including provision for more staff, facilities, and students in higher education.[49] Sweden's rolling reform is admirable and has drawn attention from all parts of Europe.

Sweden's educational system in the 1970's includes four essential parts:

1. Children enter the nine-year compulsory comprehensive school when they are seven years old. The curriculum is common to all pupils for eight years, and the ninth year is a trial year to determine upper secondary specialization. On the basis of that trial, and if the guidance has been adequate, pupils pass on to a specialized type of upper secondary school.[50]

2. Sweden has offered three types of secondary schooling since a reconstruction in 1964 lumped the three gymnasiums (commercial, technical, and academic) into one to provide equal status as well as shared facilities

for the curriculums. The three secondary schools are the gymnasium, the fackskola, and the vocational school, and each has several alternative specialized courses. In the first year, however, a core of courses is required for all pupils. (These upper secondary schools are to be located so that no Swedish pupil or adult, however remote his residence, is without upper secondary schooling.)[51]

3. The university system offers both highly selective "blockaded faculties" and "free faculties"; the latter are open to all students who attend a vocational school, a fackskola, or the technical and commercial branches of the consolidated gymnasium. There is also a variety of "professional" schools for social work, teacher education, art, music, and so on.[52] Sweden has a generous system of student grants and loans in higher education which allow for out-of-pocket expenses. But this aid does not replace the income a student must forgo when he elects to matriculate in higher education rather than to enter the labor market.

By 1975 or earlier the Swedish government (in contrast with the West German government) plans to give eleven or twelve years of schooling to at least 80 percent of its youth. And even the preschool segment has had some attention; in 1962 a Family Committee was appointed.[53]

4. Sweden, and the other Scandinavian countries, have made provision for adult education. Institutions and programs are financed out of the public treasury in the belief that all individuals have a right to education, which they may have missed, and that the economy needs the highest levels of skills.[54]

Adult education is seen as the best mechanism for retraining that part of the labor force which has held jobs made obsolete by technological changes. Since the least qualified are the most prone to unemployment, adult education and retraining can be a partial safeguard against manpower wastage.[55] The relation of education to the economy has been carefully studied by Swedish educators and planners.

EDUCATIONAL PLANNING AND THE ECONOMY

Most European educators are of one mind about the economic return produced by a nation's investment in education. American economists laud the handsome reward paid to an economy for diversion of resources to education, and Europeans have heeded this praise. The economist T. W. Schultz has claimed that the return on investment in education in the United States (during a time of dramatic educational expansion and democratization of access) was between 9 and 14 percent.[56] Thus those educators not moved by appeals to democratic social ideology are moved by appeals to the economy.

Moreover, all of Europe, including Sweden, as we shall see, struggles with the question articulated by Jean Floud: "given that in a modern economy the quality and efficiency of the working population very largely depend on the educational system, how can we secure a qualified, fluid and economically distributed labour force? The skill of labour at various levels reflects the nature, scale and organisation of educational provision, which also exercises a decisive influence on vocational choice and movement. How should we envisage the contribution of the educational system to the task of adjusting the supply and the demand for trained labour?" [57] This question lies at the heart of a new OECD organization, the Mediterranean Regional Project, comprised of poor countries (Greece, Italy, Portugal, Spain, Turkey, and Yugoslavia) who are trying to relate education to economic growth and social advancement.[58]

In an attempt to adjust labor supply and demand, Swedish and other European educators make use of manpower requirement forecasts.[59] Occupational needs can be moderately well forecast in the public sector of the economy — public schools and universities, railroads, roads, public institutions, and welfare and administration. But in the private sector, especially when a substantial fraction of business is dependent on foreign markets, forecast is chancy. The uncertainty increases when highly qualified manpower is involved. This does not hold for clearly specialized fields such as law, dentistry, or medicine — all specialties for which most countries can demonstrate either great demand or real shortage of supply. The prescription for the proper training of a politician or an official in foreign or national service, however, must be somewhat cautious. Swedish planning has been typical of educational planning throughout Western Europe, yet it is also unusually flexible.

In summary, Sweden is remarkable for its innovative planning and its great concern with education. Like other European countries, it is spending more and more money on education. Between 1950–51 and 1962–63, the Swedish GNP more than doubled and expenditure on education increased four times.[60] (This estimate is probably conservative, because it has been next to impossible to know how much the private sector spends in training, which is part of education. Nor are military expenditures on training usually considered as part of public financing of education.) In

1966 about 6 percent of the GNP went to educational research.[61] This percentage will probably increase, although it would not be justified to think that all educational innovation has increased costs.

Sweden, then, is an educational laboratory. Its postponement of differentiation is emulated in most European countries. This reform has removed examinations at the end of primary education or at the terminus of lower secondary education. These examinations, many researchers claim, are premature, unjust, and thwart individual development and social and economic good. Freedom of movement from one curriculum to another has been achieved in Sweden. Vocational-technical training is increasing in status. More and more students, especially lower class students are being attracted to secondary schooling and higher education. Everywhere in Europe, especially in Sweden, ad hoc reform promises to give way to rolling reform. And everywhere, but particularly in Sweden, pedagogical research and planning are gaining popularity. The great demand for more education unites both East and West Europe, but some countries, like Sweden, are outstanding in their responses to this demand and their encouragement of it. The comprehensive system is the most impressive innovation and, as we have noted in Chapter 6, it is being copied, in different degrees, by other nations.

In general, European education, then, is converting to the comprehensive school structure. The fullest realization of a student's ability is the guideline. More educational planning and research, as we have seen, are being used. Training for occupations is improving, and the prestige of vocational-technical training is increasing. Demands for enrollment, especially from the lower class, tightly press both secondary and higher education. Reconstruction of both systems is taking place. These general trends, along with the formal educational organizations and communication between East and West Europe which were discussed in the first two chapters, are contributing to a remarkable harmonization of European education.

It is well, nevertheless, to be realistic. The educational leaders of Europe, as well as the political leaders whom they advise, know that their national systems of education have some distance to go before attaining their goals. Nevertheless, it seems likely that they will achieve notable success in solving their common problems. At the same time, however, there will be new challenges in the next decade. In the 1960's the main aim was to win equality of opportunity, greater opportunity, and relevance in curriculum; in the 1970's European educators will be concerned with the economic and political issues of "accountability," "cost-benefit analysis," "management and systems analysis," and "phasing" — all problems that haunt educators on this side of the ocean. Typical questions will be, Who is accountable for an educational program and for innovation? How is the superiority of one curriculum arrangement (or organizational pattern or administrative approach) to be demonstrated? What proportion of the national budget, or of relatively scarce resources, should go to education and what priorities can be established? Are there relatively more effective models for educational planning?

All these problems are common to many countries in Europe. And the very fact that no single nation has a monopoly on them will further contribute to the gradual development of a European education.

BIBLIOGRAPHIC NOTE AND NOTES

Bibliographic Note

Most of the titles that have been used in this book are listed in the footnotes; an extended list of references is available through the National Auxiliary Publication Service. It seems important, however, to call attention to certain journals and series and to agencies which have important publications. Anyone with a serious interest in comparative international education should be aware of *Comparative Education Review*, the journal of the Comparative-International Education Association in the United States, and of *Comparative Education*, the British publication. There are in addition some excellent studies published by the United States Department of Health, Education, and Welfare. Typical is Randolph L. Brahman's monograph *Education in the Hungarian People's Republic* (Department of Health Education and Welfare Publication OE-14140; Washington, D.C.: GPO, 1970).

Anyone interested in research and teaching at the university level on the harmonization of European practice should consult the series *University Studies on European Integration*, published by the European Community Institute for University Studies in Brussels (51, rue Belliard, Brussels 4, Belgium).

Useful for a grasp of European educational movements are the publications of the Council of Europe and its Council for Cultural Co-operation (Strasbourg, France), which has issued an *Information Bulletin*. Many of the council's publications are distributed in the United States by the Manhattan Publishing Company (225 Lafayette Street, New York, N.Y. 10012). Less well known are the publications of the Organization

NOTE: For an extended bibliography on change and harmonization in European education, order NAPS document 01637 from ASIS, National Auxiliary Publications Service, CCM Information Corporation, 909 Third Avenue, New York, N.Y. 10022, remitting $2.00 for microfiche or $5.00 for photocopies.

for Economic Cooperation and Development, but they are well worth having and can be secured from Paris (2, rue André-Pascal, Parks XVIe). Easily available too are *Education in Germany* (Inter Nationes, 532 Bad Godesberg, Kennedy Allee 91–103, Federal Republic of Germany) and *Education in France* (Cultural Services of the French Embassy, 972 Fifth Avenue, New York, N.Y. 10021). The reader who wishes to inquire into educational issues that are of pan-European significance should consult the journal *Paedogogica Europaea*, which appears annually and features articles in English. On this side of the Atlantic is the invaluable *Western European Education*. There are also the publications of leading educational centers, an example of which is the journal *Soviet Education*, available from the USSR Academy of Pedagogical Sciences.

The *International Journal of Educational Science*, the *International Review of Education*, and *The World Year Book of Education* are invaluable sources of essays on educational topics of international scope, as is the publications list of UNESCO, which has its headquarters in Paris. UNESCO supports important documentation centers in Europe and most European nations host their own, often associated with their ministries of education. A helpful volume in this connection is Joseph Majault's *Education Documentation Centers in Western Europe* (Paris: UNESCO, 1963). The nations of Central and Eastern Europe have similar centers. One of the very great depositories of information on education is in Geneva, Switzerland, in the headquarters of the International Bureau of Education; at Geneva too are the offices of the International Schools Association and the International Schools Baccalauréat. Devoted to higher education are the publications of the Paris-based International Association of Universities. There are a number of reports on higher education in individual countries but none as adequate as *Higher Education*, issued in England in 1963 by the Committee on Higher Education under the chairmanship of Lord Robbins.

For the student of European educational research the publications of outstanding research centers are essential. Among these centers are West Germany's Deutsches Institut für Internationale Pädagogische Forschung, headed by Dr. Walter Schulze, and the Institut für Bildungsforschung in Der Max-Planck-Gesellschaft, directed by Dr. Saul B. Robinsohn; East Germany's Deutsches Pädagogisches Zentralinstitut, under the direction of Dr. Kienitz; the Department of Education and Psychological Studies led by Torsten Husén in Stockholm, Sweden; and the well-known British Department of Education and Science Research and Intelligence Branch. UNESCO underwrites its own Institutes for Education; the best known one is in Hamburg, Germany, and publishes the *International Review of Education.*

The College of Europe's journal, *Agenor*, offers evidence on the extent to which Europe can reach harmonization in education. The more specialized student will wish to consult the *Bilan des Activités Culturelles au Service de la Culture* of the Centre Europeén de la Culture in Geneva. There is, unfortunately, much less material available on educational harmonization than on educational change. This is regrettable because harmonization is a less well-known concept, certainly in Canada and the United States. The same cannot be said for Europeans, although their interest in the subject has not yet been matched by publication.

Notes

CHAPTER 1. *Communication and Coordination: Part I*

1. For a recent account, see "Educational and Cultural Activities of the Council of Europe (1949–1969)," *Western European Education*, Vol. 2, No. 1 (Spring 1970), pp. 8–41.

2. C. H. Dand and J. A. Harrison, *Educational and Cultural Films: Experiments in European Co-production*, in the series Education in Europe, Section IV — Film and Television, No. 5, ed. S. I. Van Nooten (Strasbourg: Council of Europe, Council for Cultural Co-operation [hereafter designated as ccc], 1965).

3. *Information Bulletin* (Strasbourg: ccc, Documentation Centre for Education in Europe, August 1968). The best overall statement of the council's objectives can be found in Council for Cultural Co-operation and Cultural Fund of the Council of Europe, *Annual Report, 1965* (Strasbourg: Council of Europe, 1966). For details of the European Cultural Convention, see *European Treaty Series*, No. 18 (Strasbourg: Council of Europe, n.d.). On policy, machinery, directives, methods, and program, see a brochure titled *Council for Cultural Co-operation of the Council of Europe.*

4. Laurent Capdecomme, "France: The Expansion of the Universities, Planning for Higher Education, and Reforms and Innovations in the University Field," in *Reform and Expansion of Higher Education in Europe: National Reports, 1962–1967* (Strasbourg: ccc, 1967), p. 113.

5. M. Gorosch, B. Pottier, and D. C. Riddy, *Modern Languages and the World of Today* (Strasbourg: ccc, 1967).

6. *Information Bulletin*, pp. 7f.

7. *Education in Germany*, 1969, No. 1, pp. 18ff. (Bonn–Bad Godesberg: Inter Nationes.)

8. The organization is based on a treaty signed January 22, 1963, by de Gaulle and Adenauer. Article 50 of the Treaty of Rome creating the eec explicitly encourages the exchange of young workers within the community. While this is not a function of the schools, which are not mentioned in the treaty, it is an important activity and a charge accepted by the organization represented by the Office Franco-Allemand pour la Jeunesse.

9. The European Schools are official educational institutions set up by the governments of the six eec member states and have the legal status of public institutions in these countries. They are governed by intergovernmental agreements signed in Luxembourg in 1957. The governing provisions apply to the existent schools at Luxembourg City; Brussels and Mol, Belgium; Varese, Italy; Karlsruhe, Germany; and Bergen, Netherlands. They apply also "to any further schools which the signatory governments may unanimously decide to found for the children of the European

communities staff to be educated together." See the bulletin *Schola Europaea* (Brussels: Service des Publications des Communautés Européennes, n.d.), pp. 1f.

10. For a careful and complete review of the European Schools, see H. Hans Merten, *Rapport: fait au nom de la commission de la recherche et de la culture sur les écoles européennes et leur développement,* Documents de Séance, No. 8, Parlement Européen (March 7, 1966).

11. *Schola Europaea,* p. 3.

12. K. Voss, "The European Schools," in *Forward in Europe* (Strasbourg: Council of Europe, Directorate of Information, 1967), p. 8. See also *Schola Europaea,* pp. 6, 15: "Every day, each pupil studies either German or French as a second language. Beginning the second year of the secondary section (the secondary school is seven years long), this second language will be used in the teaching of certain subjects. Pupils whose mother tongue is German will study French; those whose mother tongue is French will study German; the other linguistic groups can choose either of these two languages as a second language. This second language (German or French) is taught by the direct method, that is to say that conversation and comprehension are given the most importance. Particularly by means of games the children are given a sound grasp of this working language, which they use from their third year at school onwards in periods known as 'European hours.' All pupils of these same classes, regardless of their nationality or mother tongue, are grouped together during these European hours for singing, drawing, handicraft and physical training. The two languages are used alternately. . . . In order to provide for better understanding among pupils of several different nationalities and to allow them access to the roots of each other's national cultures, opportunities for contact and exchange between the pupils had to be increased in the European School, and modern language teaching, particularly as regards a second, or working language, had to be extended. This is done by teaching certain subjects in the working language. Pupils are grouped for these 'joint lessons' in such a way that those whose mother tongue is French or German attend the lessons given in their second language. Italian and Dutch pupils may choose to attend those lessons in whichever of the two working languages at which they are most proficient. All pupils, whatever linguistic section they may belong to, will thus be obliged to attend a certain number of lessons in one of the working languages, which will help to improve their practical knowledge of this language. Where pupils whose mother tongue is Italian or Dutch are concerned, and who may therefore choose their working language, the school rules that they should, in principle, keep to the same working language during all their time at school. Pupils of any one class, whatever their nationality or mother tongue, join together for physical training and the arts, and in these lessons any language may be used."

13. *Information Bulletin,* p. 7.

14. Freedom of establishment originally meant the licensing of a general practitioner in medicine by country X when the applicant has been schooled in country Y.

15. *Education in Germany,* 1969, No. 1, p. 20.

16. John Vaizey, "A Note on Comparative Statistics," in *Ability and Educational Opportunity,* ed. A. H. Halsey (Paris: OECD, 1961), p. 183.

17. *Education in France,* No. 38, January 1969, p. 6 (New York: Cultural Services of the French Embassy).

18. Jean Murat, "The Problem of the Equivalence of Degrees and Diplomas," in *The World Year Book of Education: Education and International Life,* ed. George Z. F. Bereday and Joseph Lauwerys (London: Evans Brothers, 1964), p. 339.

19. *Education in Germany,* 1969, No. 1, p. 18.

20. The Commission of the EEC in its *Ninth General Report* (Brussels, 1960, p. 286) noted that the EEC had organized and financed a number of seminars and arranged one-week visits to its headquarters by more than 200 professors and advanced students.

21. W. Hanle and A. Scharmann, *The Teaching of Physics at University Level,* in

the series Education in Europe, Section I – Higher Education in Europe, No. 5 (Strasbourg: CCC, 1967).

22. *Information Bulletin*, p. 67.

23. W. D. Halls and Doreen Humphreys, *Mathematics*, in the series Education in Europe, Section II – European Curriculum Studies (in the Academic Secondary School), No. 1 (Strasbourg: CCC, 1968). This study is an example of the searching inquiry that needs to be undertaken for each of the fields in secondary curriculum.

24. In their introduction, Halls and Humphreys explain that the pupils studied were in the most specialized mathematics curriculums. The goal of the tests was to determine the effect of harmonization on the most advanced secondary-school students.

25. Halls and Humphreys, *Mathematics*, p. 10.

26. *Ibid.*, p. 10.

27. *Ibid.*, pp. 12, 13.

28. *Ibid.*, p. 26.

29. *Ibid.*, p. 35.

30. Ministère de l'Education Nationale, *Les Mathématiques*, Brochure No. 69 (Institut Pédagogique National, 1964), p. 6.

31. *Education in Germany*, 1969, No. 1, p. 20.

32. "Regulations of the European Baccalaureate," *Schola Europaea*, p. 1. The French spelling, *baccalauréat*, has been used throughout Europe but the International Schools Examination Syndicate, Geneva, which sponsors the International Schools and the International Baccalaureate, has been making the English-American spelling popular. The ISES refers to a "university entrance examination"; this anglicization of *baccalauréat* allows the examination to be thought of in the United States as equivalent to the traditional College Entrance Examination. The European Schools have followed the practice of anglicization in the English language version of their bulletin.

The bulletin *Schola Europaea* devotes a section to the European baccalaureate. The formality of the phrasing and the use of italic type (in the original) signifies how much importance is attached to the subject by parents and educators: "1. Successfully completed studies at the school and all diplomas and certificates sanctioning these studies are valid in the countries of the contracting parties, in accordance with the table of qualification equivalents appended hereafter and under the conditions laid down by the Board of Governors in article 8, subject to agreement of the competent national authorities. 2. Upon completion of their secondary studies, pupils of the school may sit for the European Baccalaureate examination, the conditions of which have been laid down in a separate agreement which will be joined to the Statute. All holders of the European Baccalaureate: (a) are granted the same exemptions and advantages in their own country as holders of that country's school-leaving certificate; (b) may apply for admission to any university in the six countries of the contracting parties, and will be granted the same rights as natives of any of these six countries holding equivalent qualifications. For the purpose of the present agreement, the term 'university' covers: (a) universities, (b) all institutions considered to be of an equivalent nature by the authorities of the contracting country in whose territories these institutions may be situated."

33. Both European and International Baccalaureates have been under study at the Capital Research Centre under the direction of W. D. Halls.

34. International Baccalaureate Office, *Semi-Annual Bulletin*, No. 1 (November 1968), p. 15 (Geneva: International Schools Examination Syndicate). A long list of universities in the United States have joined the University of Sophia and universities in Australia, India, and New Zealand in accepting the International Baccalaureate.

35. The cooperating schools include the International School of Geneva; Atlantic College, South Wales; Copenhagen International High School and the Søberg Gym-

172

nasium, Denmark; John F. Kennedy School, Berlin; Frankfort's International School; and "associated schools" which enter "volunteer candidates for examinations in different subjects to provide material for educational research and for comparison with the results of national examinations." The list of associated schools includes the Lycée International, Saint-Germain-en-Laye, and the Lycée de Sèvres of France; Switzerland's Collège de Genève and Ecole Nouvelle de Chailly/Lausanne; and Grännaskolan in Sweden.

The general scheme of the International Baccalaureate has covered six branches, the first two of which have had to do with language. Which modern European languages truly are working languages is very difficult to determine, as is, apparently, a pupil's native language. The IBO *Semi-Annual Bulletin*, No. 1 (November 1968), p. 4, defines "Language A," the first branch of the examination, as the "language of instruction, which in an international school is not necessarily the candidate's native tongue (though special arrangements may be made, if necessary, to gave this a place in the examination)." We think the working languages that will be regarded as essential during the 1970's will be first English and French — the two official languages of the OECD and the Council of Europe — and then Russian. "Language B" is defined as a "second language, which is usually, but not necessarily a foreign language."

Examination branches 3–6 are described in the *Bulletin* as the Study of Man (including a course on the theory of knowledge and one of the following: history, geography, philosophy, economics, psychology, social anthropology; an experimental science; mathematics; and a sixth subject, which may be fine arts, a third language, a second subject from the Study of Man, a second experimental science, or a special subject submitted by the school. A number of special arrangements are also permitted.

36. The research center which Halls directed has worked closely with the organization known as the International Educational Achievement and the Oxford Council of Europe Study for the Evaluation of Curriculum and Examinations.

37. International Baccalaureate Office, *Semi-Annual Bulletin*, No. 1, p. 2.

38. Eugene Egger, *Les examens de fin d'Etude secondaires superieures et l'Accession aux etudes universitaires* (Geneva: Privately printed, 1966).

39. The utility of secondary-school leaving examinations has been called into question by the research of Gerhard Brinkmann on the abitur. See "Berufsausbildung und Einkommen," in *Beiträge zur Verhaltensforschung* (Berlin: Duncker and Humboldt, 1967), and "Success at School, at University, and in Professional Life," *Education in Germany*, 1969, No. 2. Brinkmann's study sought to relate performance on the abitur to success for a group of 1,000 economics and management students taking their final university examinations (the "diploma" candidates) in 1965. Some of his findings, as reported in *Education in Germany*, pp. 5f, were: "Of those who were awarded a bare pass in the Abitur 57.6% . . . passed with 'good' or 'satisfactory.' In other words, a 'bare pass' in the Abitur is a far from reliable indication of how well a student will do at university.

"The middle grade on the Abitur scale is . . . the least reliable indication of all. Here the diploma examination results range from 'excellent' to failure.

"The best grades in the Abitur present a different picture: here nearly 60% who scored 'good' or 'very good' in the Abitur passed the diploma examination with the same grade.

"Looking at the matter from the opposite viewpoint, however, it is not possible to predict which students will pass the diploma with the grading 'good' or 'very good.' Those who passed the Abitur with the grading 'good' represent only a fifth (20.6%) of all the diploma candidates who passed the examination with the grading 'good' or 'very good.'

"At best, the Abitur gradings can predict future performance in university examinations with little more than 20% accuracy."

Doubtless, this thorough study has led to one of the most recent and interesting departures from the standard leaving examination, the projected Abitur I and Abitur II. For details, see *Zur Neugestaltung der Abschlüsse im Sekundarschulwesen* (Bonn–Bad Godesberg: Geschäftstelle des Deutschen Bildungsrates, 1969). Abitur I, which would be awarded during the 9th and 10th years of school when pupils are about 15, will indicate a pupil's performance in subjects close to his field of special interest. (The present elementary school final certificate only indicates a pupil's standing in a universally required program of studies.) The Abitur II, to be awarded at the end of 12 or 13 years of schooling when most students are 18 or 19, will indicate a pupil's achievement in one or more specialties or subjects related to a core interest in social or natural science or some branch of the humanities.

40. Jean Maquet, "Ces Faux Elèves Révolutionnent l'Université," *Paris Match*, November 26, 1966, pp. 53f; Raymond Aron, "Que Valent les Etudes Françaises?" *L'Express*, October 31–November 5, 1966, p. 78.

41. Michel Debeauvais and others, "France," in *Access to Higher Education*, ed. Frank Bowles (Paris: UNESCO and International Association of Universities, 1965), 2:107. See also Guy Herzlich, "Le Baccalauréat 1969," *Le Monde*, May 13, 1969, p. 12.

42. Aldo Agazzi, *The Educational Aspects of Examinations,* in the series Education in Europe, Section II – General and Technical Education, No. 10 (Strasbourg: CCC, 1967).

43. Egger, *Les examens,* pp. 16f.

44. The reports of the conferences were published by the Secrétariat, Bruges.

45. In the series Education in Europe, Section II – General and Technical Education, No. 9 (Strasbourg: CCC, 1968).

46. Leyden: A. W. Sythoff, 1960. The two chief sources for a chronicle of history textbook revision are Otto-Ernst Schüddekopf, *20 Jahre Schulbuch Revision in Westeuropa* (Braunschweig: Albert Limbach Verlag, 1966), and the compendious volume by Schüddekopf and others, *History Teaching and Textbook Revision,* in the series Education in Europe, Section II – General and Technical Education, No. 9. (Strasbourg: CCC, 1967). The latter is especially valuable. See also E. H. Dance, *History the Betrayer* (London: Hutchinson, 1960), and Georg Eckert, "International Textbook Revision," in *The World Year Book of Education: Education and International Life,* 1964, pp. 319ff.

47. The propriety of pride in one's nation is granted by both Bruley and Dance, but with the plea that there be a balance of achievement. See *A History,* pp. 53ff.

48. *Ibid.,* pp. 46f.

49. For the locations and themes of the conferences, see *ibid.,* pp. 14ff.

50. *Enseignement de l'Histoire dans une Perspective Européenne* (Association Européenne des Enseignements, 1966).

51. Schüddekopf, *History Teaching,* p. 168. See also Robert Multhoff, "The Work of the Brunswick International Schoolbook Institute in Revising History Textbooks," *Western European Education,* Vol. 2, No. 1 (Spring 1970), pp. 71–85.

52. Resolution (65) 17, adopted by the Council of Europe ministers' deputies, recommended the establishment of "national centres or other bodies to be responsible for: (i) propagation of knowledge of their country through the dissemination of brochures, carefully selected anthologies or other material illustrative of national life and history: (ii) dissemination in the country of information on other countries; (iii) propagation of teaching materials (films, photographs, slides, reading-lists, maps, and so forth); (iv) facilitating the organization of 'refresher courses' for teachers of history and geography; (v) supplying, on request, opinions on the accuracy of information on the country to be found in textbooks . . . " Schüddekopf, *History Teaching,* p. 223.

53. *Ibid.,* p. 235.

54. *Ibid.,* p. 164.

55. *Ibid.,* pp. 170ff.

56. *Ibid.*, pp. 171, 172.

57. *Ibid.*, p. 172.

58. See *Die zwei Entwicklungswege unserer Nation und ihre Widerspiegelung im Schulbuch* ("The Two Roads of Development of Our Nation and Their Reflection in Textbooks"), published by the Deutsches Pädogogisches Zentralinstitut in East Berlin in 1963. Similar approaches, according to Schüddekopf, are made in the study "School Textbooks in the German Federal Republic," published in 1961–62 in Poland by the Zachodnia Agencja Prasowa (Western Press Agency).

59. Schüddekopf, *History Teaching*, p. 160. For another clue to the development of Communist ideology, see the East German journal *Vergleichende Pädagogik,* Vol. 1, No. 2 (1965).

60. The resolution is of sufficient historic importance, and so well defines civics, that it is worthwhile quoting its central provisions:

"A. To recommend that Governments, signatory or acceding to the European Cultural Convention: (1) draw up, with the above considerations in mind, a syllabus which can serve as a model for possible school curricula; (2) do everything within their power to ensure that all disciplines concerned — for instance history, geography, literature, modern languages — contribute to the creation of a European consciousness; (3) with a view to rendering the European aspect of civics teaching more interesting and consequently more effective, encourage the teaching profession to go beyond a purely static description of European institutions, explaining their function in the light of the vital interdependence of the European peoples and of Europe's place in the world, and by attempting to bring out the dynamic aspects of the European integration process and the concessions, indeed sacrifices, that it entails, and the political and cultural difficulties, even tensions, it may create; (4) promote methods of encouraging older pupils to take an active part in the study of current events and problems; (5) make, or stimulate the making of, up-to-date documentation especially devised for educational purposes available to both teachers and pupils; (6) include in the general professional training course a preparation for the teaching of civics in a European context; (7) bear in mind that refresher courses are an excellent means of ensuring the up-to-dateness of teaching methods and material; (8) encourage collaboration between family and school in order to ensure the harmonious development of a civic consciousness among the young; (9) encourage the fullest use of broadcasting, television and other audio-visual aids in civic education . . ."

61. In the series Education in Europe, Section II — General and Technical Education, No. 6 (Strasbourg: CCC, 1966).

62. The CCC met in 1963 and published *Civics and European Education at the Primary and Secondary Level.* Teachers (and pupils?) have available to them bibliographical help in *Books Dealing with Europe — a Bibliography for Teachers* (Strasbourg: CCC, 1965). A major publication in civics commissioned by the CCC is *Civics and European Education in Primary and Secondary Instruction* (Strasbourg, 1963), prepared by Denis de Rougemont. De Rougemont's Service d'Information de la Campagne d'Education Civique Européenne is attached to the Centre Européen de la Culture, Geneva. See also below, note 18 of Chapter 2.

63. Jotterand, *Introducing Europe,* p. 7.

64. *Ibid.*, p. 11.

65. *Ibid.*, p. 12.

66. Bertrand Schwartz, "L'Education à la Responsabilité Civique: Expériences pédagogiques," in *L'Europe de Demain et Ses Responsables* (Bruges: College of Europe, 1966), p. 5. The translation is my own.

67. Denis de Rougemont, "Douze Langues, Une Littérature," *Les Amis de Sèvres,* September 1967, p. 11. The translation is my own.

68. The author was in residence at the center for a fortnight in March 1956, and is grateful for his opportunity to sit in on classes, on the Conseil d'Orientation, and

on the lectures on education attended by the staff of teachers, and above all for his visits with the distinguished director of the center, Mme E. Hatinguais. Mme Hatinguais has since been succeeded at Sèvres by Jacques Quignard, whom the author visited in 1966 and who has continued to maintain the center at the front rank of European educational evolution.

69. EAT's first meeting was at Paris in 1956 and its second in Luxembourg in 1961. The 1961 meeting was attended by delegates from national sections in Austria, Belgium, France, Italy, Luxembourg, the Netherlands, West Germany, and Switzerland. After 1961 sections were formed in Eire, Greece, and the United Kingdom.

CHAPTER 2. *Communication and Coordination: Part II*

1. See reports in *University Studies on European Integration* (Brussels: European Community Institute for University Studies, 1954–). Until 1967 this journal was called *University Research and Studies on European Integration*. See also European Economic Community, Commission's *Eighth General Report* (June 1965), Sec. 268.

2. The institute's president has been responsible for raising the bulk of its supporting funds. The directors of the institute (*le Conseil*), who are the prime movers of the EEC, are Louis Armand, Pietro Campilli, Dino Del Bo, André Donner, Paride Formentini, Walter Hallstein, Etienne Hirsch, Jean Monnet, Jean Rey, and Max Kohnstamm, president.

3. *Nouvelles Universitaires* is published in Paris by the Bureau d'Information des Communautés Européennes.

4. *University Studies on European Integration*, No. 3, 1966, pp. x, xvi; *University Studies on European Integration: Tuition, 1969–1970*, p. vii.

5. H. Lesguillons, "Memorandum on the Development of Teaching and Research on Europe in the Community Member States and Switzerland," p. 26f. Prepared for the United States Mission to the European Communities and loaned to the author.

6. *University Studies on European Integration*, No. 3, 1966, p. xiv.

7. For example, L'Institut d'Etudes Européennes (Brussels); European Studies Institute (Saarbrucken); Centre Européen Universitaire, Nancy; Institut Européen des Hautes Etudes Internationales, Nice; Centre Universitaire des Hautes Etudes Européennes, Strasbourg; Institut d'Etudes Européennes, Turin; Centre International d'Etudes et de Recherches Européennes, Luxembourg; Europa Instituut, Amsterdam; Institut Universitaire d'Etudes Européennes, Geneva; Center for Contemporary European Studies, University of Sussex, Brighton.

8. "Plan Europe 2000," *Western European Education*, Vol. 2, No. 1 (Spring 1970) pp. 42–70.

9. H. Lesguillons, "Memorandum," p. 10.

10. See *ibid.*, pp. 12ff.

11. *Ibid.*, p. 17.

12. *Ibid.*, pp. 26f.

13. *University Studies on European Integration*, No. 3, 1966, p. xiv; *Formation des Cadres Européens* (Geneva: Centre Européen de la Culture, 1964).

14. For an account of the liaison maintained by the EEC with private organizations (as the German Arbeitskreis für Europakunde or the French Europe-Université and the Italian Societa Italiana per le Organizazione Internationale), and the financial assistance given by the EEC for courses on European questions and other activities, see Sec. 261–62 of the EEC, *Ninth General Report*, pp. 286ff.

15. Bruges: De Tempel, 1965.

16. "*The Economic Section* comprises courses on the theory and on specific problems of economic integration, the effects of integration on international trade and economic growth. Selected problems of integration are the subject of special studies

each year. Additionally there are complementary courses on applied economics and exercises in econometrics.

"*The Legal Section* comprises courses on the positive law of the European Communities, the relationship between Community law and national law, the jurisprudence of the Court of Justice, and legal personality of the European Communities in international law and the external relations of the Community. Particular emphasis is laid on the problems of the competition in the Common Market and the European Coal and Steel Community.

"*The Political Science Section* comprises courses on the present state and future possibilities of European political integration, problems of Atlantic cooperation, the attitudes of the major political parties towards European integration, the role of pressure groups at the European level and particular questions concerning the European organizations. Additionally there are complementary courses in political sociology and political theory and a special course on nationalism." (Catalogue of the College.)

The Alumni Association of the College of Europe, with the aid of the European Cultural Foundation, began publishing a quarterly journal, *Agenor*, in 1967. According to the masthead, it is directed toward "the new generation which must build and lead the united Europe of tomorrow." Articles in French and English cover such topics as education, politics, the emergence of community in Europe, and human rights. Its scope reaches to southern and eastern Europe.

17. A prolific author whose early publications included *Disarmament* (1929), *Don Quixote* (1934), *Englishmen, Frenchmen, Spaniards* (1929), Salvador de Madariaga had an international reputation. His name attached to any enterprise having to do with European civilization would have carried weight with European intellectuals.

18. De Rougemont was part of a university group which favored European integration of a "federalist" type even before the end of World War I. See David P. Calleo, *Europe's Future: The Grand Alternatives* (New York: Horizon Press, 1965), Chap. 2. In Switzerland in 1948, de Rougemont published a pioneering work, *Europe at Stake*. Other early "federalists," many of whom were part of the French resistance, included René Courtin of the University of Montpellier and François de Menthon, M. Villey, and Pierre-Henri Teitgen. See H. Lesguillons, unpublished "Memorandum," p. 5.

19. *Le Collège d'Europe à Bruges: Ses Origines* (Langemark, Belgium: Vonksteen, n.d.), pp. 7f.

20. *Ibid.*, p. 9.

21. De Madariaga occupied the chair of Spanish studies at Oxford; his inaugural lecture was published as *Aims and Methods of a Chair of Spanish Studies* (Clarendon Press, 1929).

22. *Le Collège*, p. 10.

23. For more details see *Le Collège*, pp. 10ff.

24. For details of what was probably the first publicized memorandum, see *Le Collège*, pp. 18f.

25. *Ibid.*, p. 13.

26. *Ibid.*, p. 23.

27. On April 21–22, 1949, some members of the group met in Bruges. *Ibid.*, p. 26.

28. *Ibid.*, pp. 28, 29.

29. *Ibid.*, pp. 33ff.

30. A detailed report on the original curricular organization for the College of Europe is given in *ibid.*, pp. 41ff.

31. There were three students from Germany (not yet partitioned), an Austrian, four Belgians, a Bulgarian, a Spaniard, three Frenchmen, a Greek, and a student from Holland, along with two Hungarians and Poles. These advanced university

students had been specializing in jurisprudence, philology, history, sociology, political science and administration, and architecture. *Ibid.*, pp. 38f.

32. *Ibid.*, pp. 58ff. In addition to Hoste's commission on guiding the development or creation of specifically European institutions, there was to be a commission on a plan for a European education and one charged with evolving ideas on how to reduce the barriers to the free circulation of workers and inventions.

33. *Ibid.*, p. 60.

34. Randolph L. Braham, *Education in the Rumanian People's Republic* (Washington, D.C.: GPO, 1963; Superintendent of Documents Catalog No. FS5.214: 14087), pp. 49, 51.

35. See, for example, the East German journal *Vergleichende Pädagogik*, Vol. 3, No. 4 (1967).

36. On the shortage of satisfactory textbooks in Poland, for example, see Gusta Singer, *Teacher Education in a Communist State: Poland 1956–1961* (New York: Bookman Associates, 1965), pp. 129–36.

37. *Ibid.*, pp. 132ff.

38. *Ibid.*, pp. 185f.

39. *Ibid.*, p. 135.

40. Peter John Georgeoff, *The Social Education of Bulgarian Youth* (Minneapolis: University of Minnesota Press, 1968), pp. 39.

41. *Ibid.*

42. *Ibid.*, p. 40.

43. *Ibid.*, p. 43.

44. *Ibid.*, p. 12.

45. *Ibid.*, p. 13.

46. *Ibid.*

47. Braham, *Education in the Rumanian People's Republic*, p. 13.

48. *Ibid.*, p. 51.

49. *Ibid.*, p. 54.

50. *Ibid.*, p. 55.

51. Seymour M. Rosen, *Significant Aspects of Soviet Education* (Washington, D.C.: GPO, 1965; Superintendent of Documents Catalog No. FS 5.214:14112).

52. *Education and Training in the German Democratic Republic* (German Democratic Republic, 1966), pp. 24f.

53. *Investment in Education: Ireland*, in the series Education Investment and Planning (Paris: OECD, Directorate for Scientific Affairs, n.d.), p. 390.

54. *Schola Europaea* (Brussels: Services des Publications des Communautés Européennes, n.d.), p. 8.

55. For the quotations, see Richard Eder in *New York Times* (International Edition), March 22, 1967; unsigned article, *ibid.*, April 4, 1967.

56. William B. Tudhope, *The North Euboean Foundation: A Report on Education in the Area of the Foundation* (Prokopion, Euboea, Greece, 1965), p. 33. Tudhope writes as a friendly critic and Englishman who, as his report states, went to school in the classics.

CHAPTER 3. *The Demand for Secondary Schooling*

1. Joseph Featherstone, "Schools for Children," *New Republic*, August 1967, p. 17.

2. *Policy Conference on Economic Growth and Investment in Education* — Vol. 1, *Summary Reports and Conclusions: Keynote Speeches*; Vol. 2, *Targets for Education in Europe in 1970*; Vol. 3, *The Challenge of Aid to Newly Developing Countries*; Vol. 4, *The Planning of Education in Relation to Economic Growth*; Vol. 5, *International Flows of Students* (Paris: OECD, 1962).

3. According to an editor's note, Vol. 2, *Targets for Education in Europe in 1970*, was based on a paper prepared by Ingvar Svennilson in association with Friedrich Edding, Higher Institute for International Educational Research of Frankfurt, and Lionel Elvin, director of the Institute of Education of London University.

4. *Targets for Education*, pp. 31ff.

5. *Ibid.*

6. *Ibid.*, p. 32.

7. *Ibid.*

8. *Ibid.*, p. 34.

9. *Ibid.*, p. 35.

10. *Ibid.*

11. *Ibid.*, p. 45. See also *Reform and Expansion of Higher Education in Europe: National Reports, 1962–1967* (Strasbourg: CCC, 1967).

12. *Targets for Education*, pp. 48ff, 53ff.

13. *Ibid.*, p. 54.

14. *Ibid.*, pp. 54f.

15. See Herbert C. Rudman, *The School and the State in the USSR* (New York: Macmillan, 1967), Chap. 2.

16. *Ibid.*, pp. 40f.

17. *Targets for Education*, p. 56.

18. Alfred Rosier, "The Explosion in World Population," in the aptly subtitled *World Year Book of Education: The Education Explosion*, ed. George Z. F. Bereday and Joseph L. Lauwerys (London: Evans Brothers, 1965), p. 83.

19. See Arnold M. Rose, *Migrants in Europe: Problems of Acceptance and Adjustment* (Minneapolis: University of Minnesota Press, 1969).

20. *Development of Secondary Education: Trends and Implications* (Paris: OECD, 1969), pp. 32f. The report makes the following generalization about the enrollment rate: "Over the 20-year period 1955 to 1975, virtually all 14 year olds are expected to be in school, two out of three 15 and 16 year olds, one in two 17 year olds, and more than a third of the 18 year old age-group. The increases will be greatest for ages with lowest initial enrolments; the enrolment rate for the 18 year olds will double between 1965 and 1975; for the 17 year olds between 1955 and 1975, whereas for the 16 year olds it will increase by half over the whole period" (p. 33).

21. OECD reports on its member countries have been guardedly optimistic on the degree of expenditure, but the following comment on educational expenditure projected for 1963–75 justifies an optimistic forecast. "In most . . . countries, expenditure is expected to double (if needs are met); in most Mediterranean countries it will even treble (Italy, Spain, Greece, Portugal). . . . The annual percentage increase in total educational expenditure from the early sixties to the mid 1970's is 8.7 for Turkey, 10.6 for Greece, 11.4 for Portugal, 12.6 for Spain, and 12.8 for Yugoslavia. Greece and Turkey anticipate spending roughly 350 per cent more on education in 1974 than in 1961, Yugoslavia 480 per cent, and Spain 470 per cent. Except for Greece, these countries expect between a fifth and a quarter of all public expenditure to go to education by the mid-seventies. All six countries envisage at least the trebling of educational expenditure at constant prices" (pp. 151f).

22. See *Early Leaving*, Report of the Central Advisory Council for Education – England (London: Ministry of Education, HMSO, 1954); Jean Floud, "Social Class Factors in Educational Achievement," in *Ability and Educational Opportunity*, ed. A. H. Halsey (Paris: OECD, 1961), pp. 91–109. English research on impairment of educational opportunity is closely related to studies of early school leaving. It is excellent research and shows, among other things, the availability of educational statistics in England. See John Westergaard and Alan Little, "Educational Opportunity and Social Selection in England and Wales: Trends and Policy Implications," in *Social Objectives in Educational Planning* (Paris: OECD, 1967).

23. For an excellent study on rates of failure and retention, see Rose Knight,

"Trends in University Entry: An Intercountry Comparison," in *Social Objectives in Educational Planning*, pp. 154ff, 169ff.

24. Alan Little and Denis Kallen, "Western European Secondary School Systems and Higher Education: A Warning for Comparative Education," *Comparative Education*, Vol. 4 (March 1968), pp. 145ff. See also *Development of Secondary Education*, pp. 137f, where it is noted that in Austria between 1950 and 1955 the survival rate "changed from one out of three admissions to eight out of ten." The authors observe, however, that "part of this higher 'survival rate' is due to an increase in the number of later transfers to general from other types of secondary schools. Many more pupils from the non-academic general course (*Hauptschule*) are transferring to the new *Musisch-pädagogisches Realgymnasium* for example" (p. 138).

25. Little and Kallen, "Western European Secondary School Systems," pp. 145ff. "If anything there was a slight decline in the percentage enrolled although the significance of this can be offset by the gradual increase in comprehensive schools over the period (from 0.7 per cent in 1953 to 5.5 per cent in 1962) where grammar type courses etc. are offered."

26. Deutscher Bildungsrat, *Empfehlungen der Bildungskommission: Strukturplan für das Bildungswesen* (Bonn: Bundesdruckerei, 1970).

27. *Education in Germany*, 1970, No. 4, p. 5.

28. *Modernizing Our Schools: Curriculum Improvement and Educational Development* (Paris: OECD, 1966), p. 28.

CHAPTER 4. *Higher Education: Demand and Reconstruction*

1. Frank Bowles, "Education in the New Europe," in *A New Europe?*, ed. Stephen R. Graubard (Boston: Houghton Mifflin, 1964), pp. 442ff.

2. See Fabio L. Cavazza, "The European School System: Problems and Trends," *ibid.*, pp. 471ff.

3. *Ibid.*

4. *Ibid.*, p. 473.

5. Z. Ratuszniak, "Higher Education in Poland," in *Reform and Development of Higher Education in Europe*, Educational Studies and Documents No. 49 (Paris: UNESCO, 1964), p. 86.

6. *Ibid.*

7. *Reform and Expansion of Higher Education in Europe: National Reports, 1962–1967* (Strasbourg: CCC, 1967), p. 57.

8. The committee "comprises senior officials from the various departments concerned in the Ministries of Education, Finance, Internal Affairs and Construction, and also includes representatives of higher education, local government, trade unions, employers' organizations, and associations of parents of pupils or students." Laurent Capdecomme, "The Expansion of the Universities, Planning for Higher Education, and Reforms and Innovations in the University Field," *ibid.*, p. 103.

9. *Ibid.*, p. 104.

10. *Ibid.*, p. 90.

11. *Ibid.*, pp. 151f.

12. Murray Yanowitch and Norton Dodge, "Social Class and Education: Soviet Findings and Reactions," *Comparative Education Review*, Vol. 12, No. 3 (October 1968), pp. 256ff.

13. *Ibid.*, p. 258.

14. The greater prestige of technical and scientific study in the countries of Eastern Europe is a matter not of argument but of educational history. Since the sixteenth century, science has had difficulty winning a place in the higher reaches of education. Until well after World War II technology had no place in the secondary school of Western Europe and, as we have said, technological studies simply were

not thought proper in the university curriculum. In contrast, each socialist country has an academy of science at the apex of its education.

15. Gusta Singer, *Teacher Education in a Communist State: Poland 1956–1961* (New York: Bookman Associates, 1965), p. 34.

16. *Ibid.*

17. *Ibid.*, p. 37. On expectations for a steadily high demand, see also *Higher Education*, Report of the Committee on Higher Education under the Chairmanship of Lord Robbins, 1961–63 (London: HMSO, 1963); Rose Knight, "Trends in University Entry," in *Social Objectives in Educational Planning* (Paris: OECD, 1967); L. Capdecomme, *Higher Education in France*, in the series Reform and Development of Higher Education in Europe (Paris: UNESCO, 1964); and A. J. Piekaar, *Higher Education in the Netherlands*, in the series Reform and Development for Higher Education in Europe: Human Resources Development (Paris: OECD, Directorate for Scientific Affairs, 1964).

There would be little disagreement among European commentators that the strongest economic factor has not been a general affluence and decrease in the family's need for a juvenile's income. The more powerful influence has been the "rapidly rising demand for higher-qualified personnel, particularly in science and technology which has resulted in increased opportunities and salaries for graduates. The expectation of higher regard due to higher education has given added impetus and substance to the aspirations of parents and their offspring." Rose Knight, "Trends in University Entry," p. 199.

Enlarging opportunities in higher education, especially education in basic, engineering, and other applied science, will require substantial allocation of funds. For a recent study bearing specially on the United States, but with implications for other countries, see *Reviews of National Science Policy: United States* (Paris: OECD, 1968), Chap. 10.

18. Alan Little and Denis Kallen, "Western European Secondary School Systems and Higher Education," *Comparative Education*, Vol. 4 (March 1968), p. 140.

19. *Ibid.*

20. See Saul B. Robinsohn and Helga Thomas, *Differenzierung im Sekundarschulwesen* (Stuttgart: Ernst Klett Verlag, 1968), pp. 51ff. For information on this subject the author is also indebted to Professors T. Dams of the Institut für Entwicklungspolitik der Universität Freiburg and E. Lemberg, Deutsches Institut für Internationale Pädagogische Forschung, Frankfurt.

21. *Ibid.*, p. 52.

22. *Ibid.*, p. 51. However, the point appears to be uncertain. "According to the average figures for the Federal Republic [excluding Bavaria, Berlin, and Hamburg], more than one third (35.8%) of children in the 4th year of classes of the primary schools in 1967 changed over to a modern secondary school (Realschule) or a grammar school (Gymnasium). . . . If the figures for each state are taken separately, the city-state of Bremen heads the list with 46.7% and the Rhine Palatinate comes last with 24%." *Education in Germany*, 1968, No. 11, p. 16.

23. Robinsohn and Thomas, *Differenzierung*, p. 51.

24. *Ibid.*, p. 49.

25. *Ibid.*

26. Little and Kallen, "Western European Secondary School Systems," p. 141.

27. Ralf Dahrendorf, "Recent Changes in the Class Structure of European Societies," in Graubard, *A New Europe?*, pp. 298ff.

28. *Ibid.*, pp. 294f.

29. In this discussion of the influence of social class upon education, it is not assumed that social class has been the only important determinant of educational opportunity. For a thoughtful review of some of the many sources of power, see Arnold M. Rose, *Power Structure* (New York: Oxford University Press, 1967).

30. Dahrendorf, "Recent Changes in the Class Structure," pp. 298ff.

31. C. Arnold Anderson, "Sociological Perspectives on the Educational Explosion," in *The World Year Book of Education: The Education Explosion*, ed. George Z. F. Bereday and Joseph A. Lauwerys (London: Evans Brothers, 1969), p. 191.

32. "Higher Education in the Federal Republic of Germany: Problems and Trends," in *Reform and Expansion*, p. 77.

33. *Education in Germany*, 1970, No. 4, p. 7.

34. Yanowitch and Dodge write that it was only in the early 1960's that "studies of the educational aspirations and career plans of Soviet students have begun to appear with increasing frequency in Soviet scholarly publications." See their "Social Class and Education," p. 248. The first of these studies was N. I. Krylov, "On the Inclinations of Senior Students Toward Future Professions," *Izvestiia Akademii pedagogicheskikh nauk RSFSR* (Vypusk 123, 1962), pp. 14–46. In *The Career Plans of Youth*, ed. M. N. Rutkevich, trans. Murray Yanowitch (New York: International Arts and Sciences Press, 1969), p. v, Yanowitch dates the Soviet recognition of sociology from 1960: One of the consequences "has been the emergence of empirical social research in a variety of areas: patterns of leisure time, attitudes toward work, occupational prestige, problems of marriage and family life, and educational and career plans of youth."

35. See Singer, *Teacher Education*, p. 39.

36. The Philosophy Department and the Sociological Laboratory of the Urals State University at Sverdlovsk, USSR, has prepared *The Career Plans of Youth*, cited in n. 34 above, reporting the results of studies in the educational and career aspirations of young people, their access to advanced education, and the extent of social mobility within the USSR.

37. Yanowitch and Dodge, "Social Class and Education," p. 248.

38. *Ibid.*, pp. 248f.

39. *Ibid.*, p. 249.

40. *Ibid.*

41. "In the period 1959–1964 some young people who would normally enter the 9th grade of a full-time secondary school were induced to begin work combined with parttime (evening) study leading to completion of a secondary education. This was prompted by preferential admission to higher educational institutions (*VUZy*) given to applicants with work experience. Modification of this policy in 1965 means that very few youth planning to enter *VUZy* now go directly from 8th grade to full-time employment." *Ibid.*, p. 252, n.7.

42. *Ibid.*, pp. 251f.

43. *Ibid.*, p. 252.

44. *Ibid.*

45. *Ibid.*, pp. 253f.

46. *Ibid.*, pp. 254f.

47. *Ibid.*, p. 254.

48. *Career Plans of Youth*, p. vi.

49. Robert H. Beck, "Soviet Education as Training for Life," in *The Soviet Union: Paradox and Change*, ed. Robert T. Holt and John Turner (New York: Holt, Rinehart, and Winston, 1962), p. 139.

50. *Career Plans of Youth*, p. vi.

51. Debeauvais and others, "France," in *Access to Higher Education*, ed. Frank Bowles (Paris: UNESCO and International Association of Universities, 1965), Vol. 2, Appendix, p. 165.

52. Vocational instruction of two or three years at most sufficed. Cavazza, "The European School System," in Graubard, *A New Europe?*, p. 478.

53. *Ibid.*, p. 477.

54. Mario Reguzzoni, *La Réforme de L'Enseignement dans la Communauté Economique Européenne* (Paris: Aubier-Montaigne, 1966), pp. 206ff. See also Ursula Springer, *Curriculum Reform in French, West German and Italian Schools: A Study*

of Developments at the Middle School Level (New York: Teachers College Press, 1969). The author is indebted to Professor Springer, Brooklyn College of the City University of New York, for information on the *scuola media*.

55. Chap. 4 of Reguzzoni's book has the title "La Création d'une 'Ecole Moyenne Unique' en Italie."

56. *Reform and Expansion*, p. 154.

57. *Ibid.*, p. 90.

58. It may seem that student participation complements the policy of worker participation in the profits made by a French industry, but the author fails to see the parallel. It was not de Gaulle's policy to allow workers to share in the setting of industrial policies in production, marketing, and so forth — many of which call for a high level of technical competence.

59. With some abstentions but no nays, the French Assembly voted to approve the Orientation of Higher Education Act (law no. 68–978, enacted November 7, 1968, and published in the *Journal Officiel de la République Française*, November 11–13). For an English translation, see *Education in France*, No. 38 (January 1969), pp. 5–18 (New York: Cultural Services of the French Embassy). The French know the law as *la loi Faure*, Edgar Faure having been minister of education when it was passed. The incorporation of students in the governance of the French university was not greeted with unanimous enthusiasm. So well-known a figure as Jean-Paul Sartre called the act a deception, hoodwinking students who might think that the structure of French higher education actually was to be altered. See his "La jeunesse piégée," *Le Nouvel Observateur*, No. 227, March 17–23, 1969, pp. 8–10, 13, 15, and Faure's response, No. 229, March 31–April 6, 1969, pp. 20–25.

60. Title III, "Administrate Autonomy and Participation," Article 14, in part reads: "Student representatives are selected from a list of students by simple majority vote. . . . Provisions will be made to insure the regularity of the vote and the representativeness of those elected, particularly by prohibiting voting registration in two or more education and research units and by requiring a quorum of at least 60% of the enrolled students. If the number of voters is less than 60% of the enrolled students, the number of representatives is determined in proportion with the number of voters in relation to this figure. . . . Elections for student delegates take place, inasmuch as possible, by distinct electoral colleges and by years or cycles of study. . . . The right to vote is reserved to those students who have satisfied the normal academic requirements for the preceding year. The percentage of first year student representatives cannot exceed one-fifth of all the student representatives when the unit requires more than two years. . . . Foreign students regularly enrolled in an institution of higher education have the right to vote. But only those foreign students from countries with which France has reciprocal agreements can be elected." *Education in France*, p. 10.

61. Raoul F. Kneucker, "Austria: Report on the Development, Organisation, Innovations and Reforms in Higher Education," in *Reform and Expansion*, p. 18.

62. *Ibid.*, p. 18, n.4.

63. *Ibid.*, p. 18.

64. "Denmark: The Development of the Universities," in *Reform and Expansion*, p. 60.

65. The draft was published in *Information Bulletin* (Strasbourg: ccc, 1968), pp. 34–43.

66. *Ibid.*, p. 36.

67. The draft was published in *Information Bulletin*, pp. 43–50.

68. *Ibid.*, p. 50.

69. *Ibid.*, p. 51.

70. When Europeans discuss the reconstruction of higher education, they often have American colleges and universities in mind. Admiration for the American example seems to have been general among the young, and not so young, Turks. For

example, when the French responded to the 1968 student riots in Paris by opening an Experimental University Center for 9,000 students in the Bois de Vincennes, the rector was a former dean at the Sorbonne, Raymond Las Vergnas, a specialist in English literature, and his assistant was Pierre Dommergue, a professor of American studies. Even the jargon reflected the American liberal arts influence. Las Vergnas was quoted as saying: "We want to give a pluridisciplinary education — that is, one opening on modern life and including political economy, law, arts, even journalism. We want to train multidimensional men, good men of the end of the 20th century." *New York Times*, February 27, 1969, p. 39.

71. *Khrushchev and the Central Committee Speak on Education*, ed. George S. Counts (Pittsburgh: University of Pittsburgh Press, 1959); George Z. F. Bereday and Richard V. Rapacz, "Khrushchev's Proposals for Soviet Education," *Teachers College Record*, Vol. 60 (December 1958), pp. 131–149.

72. *Reform and Expansion*, pp. 101ff.

73. *Ibid.*, p. 104.

74. "Ireland," in *Reform and Expansion*, p. 147.

75. *Education in France*, p. 5.

76. "Italy: The Development of the Universities, the Organisation of Higher Education, and the Reforms and Innovations in the University Field," in *Reform and Expansion*, p. 155.

77. *Ibid.*, p. 158.

78. *Ibid.*, p. 81.

79. *Ibid.*

80. *Ibid.*

81. Debeauvais and others, "France," in *Access to Higher Education*, Vol. 2; Frederic Gaussen, "La Vie de la Région Parisienne," *Le Monde*, November 23, 1966, p. 11.

82. See, for example, *Minnesota's Stake in the Future: Higher Education, 1965–1970*, Report of the Governor's Committee on Higher Education (Minneapolis: Governor's Committee on Higher Education, 1956).

CHAPTER 5. *The Extent of Abilities*

1. Torsten Husén, "The Effect of School Structure Upon Utilization of Ability: The Case of Sweden and Some International Comparisons," in *Social Objectives in Educational Planning* (Paris: OECD, 1967), pp. 53ff. There is little question that the graduates of selective and multilateral secondary schools have higher achievement scores than graduates of comprehensive secondary schools, at least of the American comprehensive high school. See *ibid.*, p. 53, and Torsten Husén, ed., *International Study of Achievement in Mathematics: A Comparison of Twelve Countries*, 2 vols. (New York: Wiley, 1967).

A. H. Halsey felt that the most striking single point of agreement arrived at by the OECD conferees in 1961 was the "ready abandonment of the metaphor of the 'pool of ability' as scientifically misleading and, from the point of view of policy, irrelevant." Halsey, "Review of the Conference," in *Ability and Educational Opportunity* (Paris: OECD, 1961), p. 23. The metaphor was rejected on the grounds that it suggested "the idea of genetic qualities in a population which sets limits to the amount of human energy and intelligence that could be liberated by a programme of education." Instead, wrote Halsey, discussion at the conference "yielded a conception of ability, not as a unitary capacity, but as a whole range of human skills and excellencies, literate, numerate and manual. Thus refinement or differentiation of the measures used, a widening of the curriculum of school or, indeed, any change in the demands that a society puts on its members will reveal new abilities among them. Not one ability but many abilities are to be sought in a programme designed to mobilize talent." Moreover, "it became clear that intelligence and other human capacities have to be seen less as the property of individuals and more as social or cultural products. It is not only that different societies, according to their values and their culture, will recognize and reward different kinds of abilities, but, what is of crucial significance in the present context, *a process of economic and social development is a process of creating ability.* This investment in education as a means to satisfy the manpower requirements of economic growth is not a simple one way process. Increased resources make it possible to mobilize new reserves of talent. And so it was that the Conference was led to the conclusion that the higher the national income per head enjoyed by a country, the greater the amount of human ability which can in practice be made available for mobilization" (pp. 24f).

2. Freely adapted from the argument of Aristotle, *Politics*, Book IV, Chapter 12, especially the contrast of the few, an elite, and the multitude. Schopenhauer too draws a distinction between the "bestiality of the many" and the "wisdom" of the few. See Arthur Schopenhauer, *Religion: A Dialogue and Other Essays*, trans. T. Bailey Saunders (New York: Macmillan, 1891), pp. 23–24.

3. Torsten Husén, "Educational Structure and the Development of Ability," in *Ability and Educational Opportunity*, p. 121. A hard-edged differentiation between the practical and theoretical increasingly is being supplanted by training for technological employment, which blends practical and theoretical.

4. Plato held his view to be necessary because it was correct. Presumably this justified the lie about the noble and base metals that is the meat of the "old Phoenician tale" Socrates related to Glaucon. See *The Works of Plato*, tr. Benjamin Jowett, Vol. 2, *The Republic*, Book III, pp. 128f.

5. *Ibid.*, Book V, p. 212.

6. Husén, in *Ability and Educational Opportunity*, pp. 121f.

7. *Ibid.*, p. 123.

8. *Ibid.*, p. 125.

9. *Ibid.*, pp. 126f.

10. *Ibid.*

11. Floud, "Social Class Factors in Educational Achivement," *ibid.*, pp. 102ff.

12. *Ibid.*, pp. 102f. See also Husén, *ibid.*, p. 132; Saul B. Robinsohn and Helga Thomas, *Differenzierung im Sekundarschulwesen* (Stuttgart: Ernst Klett Verlag, 1968), pp. 41ff. The deleterious effect of cultural deprivation and comparative disadvantage has been very closely studied in the United States in recent years. European research on the topic has not as yet been as noticeable. However, the OECD has promoted the literature of the United States and has shown its relevance to studies on the tapping of abilities; see, for example, Selma Mushkin, "Education Policies for the Culturally Disadvantaged Child," in *Social Objectives and Educational Planning.*

13. Social class as used herein connotes that minimum of values, aspirations, and way of life in general that might be thought to belong to (1) those whose poverty and unemployment leads to the ascription "lower class" (*le prolétariat* or *die unteren Stände*); or (2) the "working class" (or manual workers, the lowest class recognized in most British sociological writing), *la classe ouvrière, la petite bourgeoisie* or *die arbeitenden Klassen*; or (3) the middle class (*der Mittelstand, la bourgeoisie*) or upper middle class (*la haute bourgeoisie* and not designated in German); or (4) the upper class (*la haute société* or *die höheren Stände*). For additional comment on nomenclature see Ralf Dahrendorf, "Recent Changes in the Class Structure," in *A New Europe?*, ed. Stephen R. Graubard (Boston: Houghton Mifflin, 1964), pp. 302ff. For an interesting description of the French "power elite," if not upper class, see Alfred Grosser, "The French Power Elite," *Encounter*, Vol. 30 (June 1968), pp. 51–56.

The OECD conferees whose reports are cited below treated the concept "social class" as a composite variable made up of different aspects of status: income, parental education, parental occupation. See C. Arnold Anderson, "Sociological Factors in the Demand for Education," in *Social Objectives in Educational Planning*, p. 33.

14. *Higher Education*, Report of the Committee on Higher Education under the Chairmanship of Lord Robbins 1961–63, Appendix I, "The Demand for Places in Higher Education" (London: HMSO, 1963), p. 81.

15. Floud, in *Ability and Educational Opportunity*, p. 99.

16. *Ibid.*, p. 94.

17. *Ibid.*

18. *Ibid.*, pp. 94f.

19. *Ibid.*, p. 106.

20. That 34 percent of the group were classified as children of "skilled manual" parents tells a good deal about the middle-class aspirations and probably all-round identification of this group in Great Britain. Generalizations on the identification of skilled workers throughout Europe are not made.

21. *Ability and Educational Opportunity*, p. 127.

22. *Ibid.*, p. 129.

23. Torsten Husén, "The Relation Between Selectivity and Social Class in Secondary Education," *International Journal of Educational Science*, Vol. 1 (1966), pp. 17f. See also Pierre Laderrière, "Regional Inequalities of Opportunity in French Education and the Measures Designed to Reduce Them," in *Social Objectives in Educational Planning*.

24. Halsey, in *Ability and Educational Opportunity*, p. 33.

25. Halsey was here reflecting a discussion that had turned on the distorting effect of values dominant in the ascendant subculture, i.e., a set within the culture of the upper classes. Halsey's summary of the discussion may be of interest because it seems to mirror what has been an influential body of thought in Europe. The discussion began, Halsey reports, with the argument that "since school marks are a cultural product, their use in identifying and quantifying reserves of ability meant that recognition and estimates are a function of the current values of the society in which measurement takes place. Professor Husén took this argument further and insisted that all of the four main methods of assessing ability (school marks, attainment tests, intelligence tests and teachers' estimates) contained elements of social evaluation of one sort or another. School marks and attainment tests are affected by the pupils' motivation, intelligence tests are not culture-free and teachers are not immune from selective perception. For this basic reason and the further reason that social values, educational curricula and methods, popular motivation, etc., are all subject to change, Professors [P.] de Wolff and [K.] Härnqvist [who have done pioneering research on the measure of intelligence and the distribution of ability] emphasized the relatively short-run character of estimates of reserves of ability, as well as their tentative nature in that they normally assume constant conditions of education and social structure." *Ibid.*, p. 27.

26. *Ibid.*, p. 33.

27. Dael Wolfle, "National Resources of Ability," *ibid.*, p. 52.

28. *Ibid.*

29. *Higher Education*, Appendix I, p. 84. On the reserves of pupils qualified for the university in Great Britain and other European countries, see also Rose Knight, "Trends in University Entry," in *Social Objectives in Educational Planning*, pp. 167ff.

30. *Higher Education*, p. 54. For a careful study of the utilization of ability by British educational institutions, see John Westergaard and Alan Little, "Educational Opportunity and Social Selection in England and Wales," in *Social Objectives in Educational Planning*.

31. For a technical treatment of estimation of reserves of ability, see the appendix to P. de Wolff and K. Härnqvist, "Reserves of Ability: Size and Distribution," in *Ability and Educational Opportunity*.

32. Torsten Husén, "Responsiveness and Resistance in the Educational System to Changing Needs of Society: Some Swedish Experiences," *International Review of Education*, Vol. 15, no. 4 (1969), p. 482.

33. But see the sobering essay by Walter Schultze, "Die Begabtenförderung in ihrer Abhängigkeit vom Schulaufbau," *Die Deutsche Schule*, Vol. 2 (February 1967), pp. 61–77; published in translation as "The Encouragement of Ability, Insofar as It Depends on School Structure," in "Comprehensive School or Vertical School Structure?" *Education in Germany* (Bonn–Bad Godesberg: Inter Nationes), p. 2.

34. Nicholas Lloyd, in *Sunday Times* (London), September 24, 1967, p. 9. The arguments for comprehensive and multilateral organization have benefited from very little comparative research on optimal patterns of organization. In 1967 the British government commissioned the National Foundation for Educational Research to do a massive study on comprehensive schools; this study aims at learning what is being asked of comprehensive schools, rather than comparing alternative patterns. However, the 1967 report on London's 77 comprehensive schools by the Inner London Education Authority does show that pupils thought to be of lower ability are performing beyond what was expected of them when they were separated from the academically promising. Lloyd's article cites the ILEA report on a sample of 11 year olds admitted in 1960, of whom "only 1,648 were 'grammar designated.' Even so, five years later when 11,431 of the total intake took their O-levels, 7,613 passed (2,160 in three or more subjects)." Lloyd also cites the generalization of Husén's *International Study of Achievement in Mathematics*, comparing pupils from Australia, France, Holland, Germany, Israel, Japan, Scotland, Sweden, and the U.S.: "From 5,450 schools, 133,000 pupils, all matched for age and picked sociologically, were given mathematical tests devised to be fair to each nationality. The broad conclusion drawn was that more does not mean worse."

Experience in the United States was particularly revealing and led (inevitably) to the conclusion that a good deal of ability is untapped by a school system that creams off the academically most able at age 10 or 11: "Although 18 percent of the 17- and 18-year-olds in America take mathematics and science compared with 4 or 5 percent in England and Germany, their top 4 percent compared favorably with other European groups."

Lloyd also concluded that creaming of the most able is joined with a subtle lesson to the others that they lack talent: "perhaps the most damning evidence against the selective system is that the high standards of the elite seem to be bought at the price of low accomplishment of the rest. Comprehensive countries in the IEA tests came off best when their lower ability groups were compared with our lowest secondary modern children, and their equivalent in the selective system." Thus, three-quarters of 11 year olds did *unnecessarily* inferior work. That it was unnecessary has been demonstrated by the same type of pupil performing more adequately in a comprehensive school. For an earlier documentation of this point, see Robert A. Anderson, "Mathematical Student Achievement of Third Form (Ninth Grade) Students in London and St.Paul-Minneapolis Metropolitan Areas" (Ph.D. dissertation, University of Minnesota, 1964).

35. *Higher Education*, p. 51.

36. *Ibid.*, p. 79.

37. Alan Little and Denis Kallen, "Western European Secondary School Systems," *Comparative Education*, Vol. 4 (March 1968), p. 143.

38. Ratuszniak, "Higher Education in Poland," in *Reform and Development of Higher Education in Europe*, Educational Studies and Documents No. 49 (Paris: UNESCO, 1964), p. 92. Ratuszniak's figures are less informative than they might be because "intellectual" and "artisan" are not defined.

39. *Ibid.*, p. 92. Obviously the Polish Ministry of Education thinks that student welfare is important. By 1980 it "plans to raise the percentage of students accom-

modated in student hostels to 70% of the total, an increase warranted by the larger number of students who will be coming from towns and villages at a distance from the university centers. Great efforts are also being made in the case of university canteen services. A scholarship scheme has been worked out and it is clear that, if the present proportion of grant-aided students — 55.9% — is to be maintained, the scholarship appropriations will have to be increased considerably."

40. The report makes use of the following categories of "standard of training": very high or high qualifications (with the corresponding vocational category of administrative and commercial personnel and engineers); technical experts and administrators (administrative and commercial personnel and technical experts and draughtsmen); works supervisors (work supervisors and clerical staff); trained personnel (clerical staff and trained workers); untrained personnel (skilled and unskilled workers). Michel Debeauvais and others, "France," in *Access to Higher Education*, ed. Frank Bowles (Paris: UNESCO and International Association of Universities, 1965), p. 124.

41. *Ibid.*, p. 112.

42. *Ibid.*, pp. 112f.

43. *Ibid.*, pp. 94f.

44. *Ibid.*, p. 94.

45. Fabio L. Cavazza, "The European School System," in Graubard, *A New Europe?*

46. *Investment in Education: Ireland*, in the series Education Investment and Planning (Paris: OECD Directorate for Scientific Affairs, n.d.), pp. 148ff.

47. Reguzzoni, *La Réforme de l'Enseignement dans la Communauté Economique Européenne* (Paris: Aubier-Montaigne, 1966).

48. Laderrière, "Regional Inequalities of Opportunity in French Education," and Westergaard and Little, "Educational Opportunity and Social Selection," both in *Social Objectives in Educational Planning*.

49. "Educational Opportunity and Social Selection," pp. 229f.

CHAPTER 6. *Secondary Education: Organization, Guidance, and Curriculum*

1. Socialization and enculturation have been described here as though social class were the only significant form of stratification, omitting such other types as sex and physical-emotional handicaps. This stand is not wholly defensible. In East European countries coeducation has been taken for granted for years, but it cannot be said that Western Europe has ignored sexual differences. However, in what Americans call "special education" — the instruction of the physically or emotionally severely handicapped — Europe has shown a common concern. The preoccupation here with social class differences has been dictated by the fact that Europeans have been far more troubled by these differences than by any others.

2. Mario Reguzzoni, *La Réforme de l'Enseignement dans la Communauté Economique Européenne* (Paris: Aubier-Montaigne, 1966), pp. 125ff.

3. The sense of *université*, as it was used by Les Compagnons, is best rendered as "teaching profession." *Membres de l'Université* has meant members of the teaching profession. Les Compagnons wished to convince teachers of primary and secondary schools — and the teachers of teachers — that *l'école unique* was morally and otherwise the preferred organization.

4. Austria, Holland, much of Germany, Spain, Portugal, Turkey, Iceland, Switzerland, Ireland, and Luxembourg all have a dualistic or a parallel system of secondary education. A more or less modified system of parallel schooling is to be found almost everywhere in Europe, including Turkey and Iceland.

Notes

5. Husén, "A Case Study in Policy-Oriented Research: The Swedish School Reforms," *School Review*, Vol. 73 (Autumn 1965), p. 218.

6. Saul B. Robinsohn and Helga Thomas, *Differenzierung im Sekundarschulwesen* (Stuttgart: Ernst Klett Verlag, 1968), p. 36.

7. *Ibid.*, p. 38. The percentage of 13 year olds attending the Realschule in 1966 was 5.2 percent, while 17.2 percent enrolled in a Gymnasium.

8. *Ibid.*, pp. 38f. The increase in the Realschule was 8.7 percent in 1954 as compared with 12.1 percent in 1966.

9. *Ibid.*, p. 39.

10. *The Development of Secondary Education: Trends and Implications* (Paris: OECD, 1969), pp. 145f.

11. *Ibid.*, pp. 144f.

12. *Education in Germany*, 1969, No. 1, pp. 8, 27f.

13. *Ibid.*, p. 29.

14. For a full examination see *Development of Secondary Education*, Chap. 3. The material here is drawn from pp. 141–42. England and Wales are complicated examples of the comprehensive organization of lower or junior secondary education; there are more than 160 independent local education authorities in Great Britain, and the Central Ministry of Education is willing to certify many schools which, because of circumstances, can make only approximations to a completely comprehensive organization. *Organisation of Secondary Education* (Circular 10.65, July 12, 1965 [London: HMSO, 1965]) describes the six principal types of comprehensive organization; minor variations are not given: "(1) The orthodox comprehensive school with an age range of 11-18; (2) a two-tier system whereby *all* pupils transfer at 11 to a junior comprehensive school and *all* go on at 13 or 14 to a senior comprehensive school; (3) a two-tier system under which *all* pupils on leaving primary school transfer to a junior comprehensive school, but at the age of 13 or 14 *some* pupils move on to a senior school while the *remainder* stay on in the same school. . . . (4) a two-tier system in which *all* pupils on leaving primary school transfer to a junior comprehensive school. At the age of 13 or 14 *all* pupils have a choice between a senior school catering for those who expect to stay at school well beyond the compulsory age, and a senior school catering for those who do not; (5) a system of middle schools which straddle the primary/secondary age ranges. Under this system pupils transfer from a primary school at the age of 8 or 9 to a comprehensive school with an age range of 8 to 12 or 9 to 13. From this middle school they move on to a comprehensive school with an age range of 12 or 13 to 18." The circular observes that types 1, 2, 5, and 6 are fully comprehensive in character but that type 1 is preferred.

15. *Ibid.*, p. 143.

16. In the United States the distinction between guidance and personnel workers goes beyond the consideration of emotional problems. The term "personnel" is preferred in the United States in order to avoid the connotation of giving guidance in an overbearing manner. For the same reason the phrase "client-centered" is often used in North America. Europeans have been less concerned to make this distinction and may not feel it necessary.

17. For an able summary of European guidance see Maurice Reuchlin, *Pupil Guidance: Facts and Problems*, in the series Education in Europe, Section II — General and Technical Education, No. 3 (Strasbourg: CCC, 1964).

18. Y. Roger, *The Observation and Guidance Period*, in the series Education in Europe (Strasbourg: CCC, 1967).

19. Reuchlin, *Pupil Guidance: Facts and Problems*, p. 76.

20. *Comparative Education Review*, Vol. 11 (October 1967), No. 3.

21. The importance of academic counseling of pupils in a comprehensive school has been recognized by the West German Education Council in *Education in Germany*, 1969, No. 7, p. 6.

22. B. Girod de l'Ain, "Libérale mais Complexe," *Le Monde*, May 28, 1969, p. 23.

23. Robinsohn and Thomas, *Differenzierung*, p. 79.

24. *Education in Germany*, 1970, No. 4, pp. 16f.

25. The best firsthand chronicles of the original New Education or new schools is in Adolph Ferrière, *The Activity School*, trans. F. Dean Moore and F. C. Wooton (New York: John Day, 1928); Stanwood Cobb, "History of the New Schools in Europe," *Progressive Education*, Vol. 1 (October-December, 1924), pp. 124–28. Earlier proponents of this kind of education were Jean Jacques Rousseau and P. E. von Fellenberg.

26. On the Odenwaldschule see Thomas Alexander and Beryle Parker, *The New Education in the German Republic* (New York: John Day, 1929), p. 201.

27. Ferrière, *Activity School*, pp. 241ff.

28. This bureau has been continuously supported by the government of Geneva. In view of the Swiss backing of the Centre Européen de la Culture in Geneva, it is apparent that the government has taken a great deal of responsibility for sustaining organizations dedicated to the advancement of European cultural integration.

29. See de Rougemont, *Vingt-Huit Siècles d'Europe* (Paris: Libraire Payot, 1964).

30. Alexander and Parker, *The New Education*, p. 200. This objective no doubt accounted for the Odenwaldschule's *Musikabende* and its *Andachten*, outdoors programs devoted to plays or singing. It inspired the *freie Abende* at Ilsenburg, as well as the *Wandervögel*, who hiked all over Europe during their vacations. This was the cultivation of an upper middle class, but it helped establish a cultural standard that has gradually become a cultural standard for many people in Europe.

31. Joseph Majault, *Teacher Training*, in the series Education in Europe, Section II – General and Technical Education, No. 4 (Strasbourg: CCC, 1965).

32. For a much more adequate presentation, including timetables of allotment to subjects, see J. Thomas and S. Majault, *Primary and Secondary Education: Modern Trends and Common Problems*, in the series Education in Europe, Section II – General and Technical Education, No. 1 (Strasbourg: CCC, 1963).

33. *Modernizing Our Schools: Curriculum Improvement and Educational Development* (OECD, 1966), p. 36 and n. 2.

34. *Ibid.*

35. Herbert C. Rudman, *The School and the State in the USSR* (New York: Macmillan, 1967), p. 225.

36. *Modernizing Our Schools*, pp. 31f. On the introduction of new thought in curriculums in the US, see Matthew B. Miles, ed., *Innovation in Education* (New York: Bureau of Publications, Teachers College, Columbia University, 1964).

37. For an excellent description of the USSR Academy of Pedagogical Sciences, see Rudman, *The School and the State*, Chap. 9.

38. *Ibid.*, p. 227.

39. *Ibid.*, p. 214.

40. On the British Council see *Modernizing Our Schools*, pp. 71f.

41. *Higher Education* (London: HMSO, 1963), p. 120.

42. Majault, *Teacher Training*, Appendix E.

43. For the quotations, see *ibid.*, p. 102.

44. *Ibid.*, p. 103.

45. *Ibid.*, p. 207.

CHAPTER 7. *Training for Occupations*

1. Frank Bowles, "Education in the New Europe," in *A New Europe?*, ed. Stephen R. Graubard (Boston: Houghton Mifflin, 1964), p. 452.

2. *Ibid.*, p. 453.

3. *Ibid.*

4. See Caroline F. Ware, K. M. Pannikar, and J. M. Romein, *The Twentieth Century*, Vol. 6 of the UNESCO-sponsored series, History of Mankind, Cultural and Scientific Development (London: George Allen and Unwin, 1966), Part I; A. A. Zvorinine, "Technical Progress and Society," in *The Evolution of Science,* ed. Guy S. Metraux and Francois Crouzet (New York: Mentor Books, 1963).

5. *Modernizing Our Schools: Curriculum Improvement and Educational Development* (OECD, 1966), pp. 30ff, 37ff, 46ff. There is European recognition of American technology in agriculture, business, and industry and a desire to increase educational attention to preparing technicians. For a contrast between American and European efforts in higher education, see "Scientific Personnel and Education," in *Reviews of National Science Policy: United States* (Paris: OECD, 1968), Chap. 2. The American development is suggested by a 500 percent increase in the number of engineers and the ten-fold increase in the number of scientists prepared in the years 1930–1964. (Table 9, page 44.)

6. "Developments in Vocational-Technical Studies during the Year 1964–65," *International Yearbook of Education*, Vol. 27 (Geneva: International Bureau of Education, 1965).

7. *Ibid.*, p. 139 and p. 136.

8. *Ibid.*, pp. 32, 193, 253, 262, 319, 379–80.

9. This leaves the ancient languages unaffected. We think that the classics have a role in the modern world, and there has been a paucity of European writing on this question. Certainly part of the value of classics lies in the literature of the ancients, who have given shape to Western culture. Perhaps philological, linguistic, and grammatical concerns have monopolized the secondary and higher study in the classics. Perhaps too the classics have been too smug, too often the bailiwick of those who looked down their noses at the lower social classes. This is a pity, because the classics contain the most elegant and systematic expressions of the values that make Europe and the Atlantic world a community. Furthermore, there is nothing in these values to exclude communication with the rest of the world, for they cut across economic and social class lines, and boundary lines and distance make no difference.

10. Herbert S. Parnes, *Forecasting Educational Needs for Economic and Social Development* (Paris: OECD, 1962), pp. 26, 77ff. According to Parnes, the four categories were suggested by Frederick A. Harbison.

11. In the USSR there is a type of school called the Incomplete Secondary School with Work Experience.

12. The German Realschule is entered at the age of 10 after four years of primary school; the French *Moderne* (*type court*) is begun at the age of 12 after six years of primary school.

13. A plan for the reorganization of West German vocational-technical training, replacing the traditional objectives and programs along lines suggested in this chapter constitutes an important portion of the proposed Structural Plan. See Deutscher Bildungsrat, *Strukturplan für das Bildungswesen* (Bonn: Bundesdruckerei, 1970), pp. 163ff.

14. Ministère de l'Education Nationale, *Le Mouvement Educatif en France pendant l'Année 1965* (Institut Pédagogique National, 1966), p. 78.

15. *Ibid.*, p. 77.

16. *Ibid.*, p. 78.

17. Parnes, *Forecasting Educational Needs*, pp. 81ff.

18. "The *Fachschule* (technical school) provides the pupil with a higher qualification than is offered by a *Berufsfachschule* or *Berufsschule*, after completion of vocational training. Its organisation and duration differ: instruction may be on a part-time or full-time basis; the length of training is between one year and two-and-a-half years. The school leaving certificate generally gives the qualifications of a foreman or technician. Among the most common types of *Fachschule* are *Technikerschule* (school for technicians), *Meisterschule* (school for master craftsmen), *Fachschule*

für Kindergärtnerinnen (school for Kindergarten teachers) and *Landwirtschafts-schule* (school of agriculture)." *School Systems: A Guide* (Strasbourg: CCC, 1965), p. 10.

19. Parnes, *Forecasting Educational Needs*, p. 78.

20. "On an experimental basis, at the beginning of the 1965 academic year, five centers, foreshadowing these new institutes, were opened at Rouen (chemistry), Paris (civil engineering and electronics), Toulouse (mechanical construction), and Nancy (applied geology). But the final structure of the university institutes of technology will be defined by an *ad hoc* pedagogic commission comprising eight sections: civil engineering; mechanical construction; electrotechnical energetics; electronics, tele-communications and automatism; chemical engineering, methodology of the laboratory, applied biology; administrative, ecnomic and financial sections common to all the specialties." Ministère de l'Education Nationale, *The Educational Movement in France* (Paris: Publication de l'Institut Pédagogique National, 1966), p. 75.

21. "The *Hohëre Fachschule* (advanced technical school, immediately below university level, having already in part characteristics of higher education) is a full-time school most often three years in length. Entrance requirements, although they vary slightly, generally are the completion of vocational training or sufficient practical experience as well as a general education of at least ten years as provided by the *Realschule* or equivalent institutions.

"The most common types of *Hohëre Fachschule* are *Hohëre Wirtschaftsfach-schule* (advanced school of economics), *Hohëre Fachschule für Sozialarbeit* (advanced school of social work) and *Fachschule* (seminar) *für Jugendleiterinnen* (advanced school for nursery school supervisors and organisers of youth work)." *School Systems: A Guide*, pp. 8f., 10.

22. "Access to the *Ingenieurschule* (college of engineering) is possible under the same conditions as those of the *Hohëre Fachschule*. The course of studies comprises three years in any one of the 17 recognized special courses (*Fachrichtungen*); graduates are entitled to be called engineers. Graduates of engineering colleges may be permitted to continue their studies at technical universities or may, with an additional examination, gain access to all forms of higher education."

23. *Educational Policy and Planning in Sweden*, in the series, Educational Investment and Planning Programme (Paris: OECD, Directorate for Scientific Affairs, 1966), p. 74.

24. "*The Technical* 'gymnasium' (Tg) provides a three-year course and leads to the degree of 'secondary-school engineer.' There is no streaming in the first year, which consequently comprises one and the same course for all pupils. Starting in the second year, this 'gymnasium' is divided into some twenty streams, to which another ten branches of specialisation are added in the third year. *The Commercial* 'gymnasium' (Cg) was a 2 year course of study until the school year 1961/62 when it became a 3 year course. In the third year, there are four branches." *Ibid.*, p. 76.

25. "The flows into the 'gymnasium' have expanded considerably during the past fifteen years. In the beginning of the 1920's, the number of new admissions to the 'gymnasia' amounted to a total of approximately 3,000 per year, or about 2.5 per cent of the corresponding age group (sixteen year olds). In the beginning of the 1950's approximately 9,000 pupils or more than 10 per cent of the age group and in the autumn of 1966, some 35,000 young people or somewhat more than a fourth of the age group are estimated to begin 'gymnasium' studies." *Ibid.*, p. 76.

26. The Swedish gymnasium has two of its five curriculums in fields that prepare for Class C occupations, a three-year curriculum for economics and a four-year technical curriculum. "The *curriculum for economics* corresponds to the present commerical 'gymnasium' . . . In the second year there is a choice between an economic and a linguistic alternative, the latter offering education and training required for qualified secretarial personnel. Furthermore in the third year, three business eco-

192

nomics alternatives are offered: a financial, a marketing and an administrative branch. The fifth programme, the technical curriculum, replaces the present technical 'gymnasium.' The differentiation is considerably less. In the third year, four alternatives are offered: machinery, building, electricity and applied chemistry. The electricity and building alternatives are each divided into two branches in the fourth year." *Ibid.*, pp. 85f.

27. *Ibid.*, p. 77.

28. See *Summary of Report by the Drafting Committee on Vocational Training*, Swedish Government Official Reports, 1966, No. 3 (Stockholm: Royal Ministry of Education, 1966).

29. *Educational Policy and Planning in Sweden*, p. 84.

30. *Ibid.*, pp. 98ff.

31. *Ibid.*, pp. 88, 89f.

32. On this question see the first report of the Vocational School Committee (1966), *ibid.*, pp. 96ff.

33. *Ibid.*, p. 91. On the vocational school and other schools of the same "level," see *ibid.*, pp. 91ff.

34. *Ibid.*, p. 92.

35. *Ibid.*

36. *Ibid.*, pp. 93f.

37. There are many references to these needs and to plans to meet them in the OECD publication, *Educational Policy and Planning in Sweden*.

38. *Ibid.*, p. 135.

CHAPTER 8. *A Contrast in European School Reform: West Germany and Sweden*

1. Saul B. Robinsohn and J. Caspar Kuhlmann, "Two Decades of Non-Reform in West German Education," *Comparative Education Review*, Vol. 11, No. 3 (October 1967), pp. 311f.

2. Walter Schultze and Christoph Führ, *Schools in the Federal Republic of Germany* (Weinheim: Verlag Julius Beltz, 1967).

3. There are now two-year technical schools, one called the *Technikerschule*, and at least eight other essentially technical schools, including the *Ingenieurschule*, which students enter at about the age of 19 after graduation from vocational school or attendance at a general education school.

4. Robinsohn and Kuhlmann, "Two Decades," p. 312.

5. See, for example, Georg Picht, *Die Deutsche Bildungskatastrophe* (Munich: Deutscher Taschenbuch Verlag, 1965). Picht did not advocate changes in the curriculum, but merely said it was not prepared to handle an increased demand for schooling.

6. This has not been true of the French lycée, as we have suggested. French secondary education has attempted to find a place for technical study, no doubt with the hope of increasing both the number of graduates of the technical section (prepared for skilled work) and the number of students who would continue into higher education.

7. Robinsohn and Kuhlmann, "Two Decades," p. 316.

8. *Ibid.*, pp. 316f.

9. *Ibid.*, p. 318.

10. *Ibid.*, p. 320. The increase in realschule graduates from 8.7 percent in 1954 to 12.4 percent in 1963 can be interpreted in the same way.

11. *Ibid.*

12. See Ursula K. Springer, "West Germany's Turn to Bildungspolitik in Educational Planning," and J. H. Van de Graff, "West German's 'Abitur' Quota and

School Reform," both in *Comparative Education Review*, Vol. 11 (February 1967). Robinsohn and Kuhlmann discuss both plans in "Two Decades," pp. 320ff.

13. The core of the proposal was to extend compulsory education by two years, to introduce a two-year period of guidance, and to promote the transfer of students within the structure.

14. As Robinsohn and Kuhlmann, put it, spokesmen for the traditional secondary schools have reacted against what they perceive as "elements antagonistic to their educational creed as well as to their social status. Emphasizing . . . the essentially scholarly character of their assignment – and, we may add, being relatively unimpressed by the methods and findings of the behavioral sciences – they hold that the different schools correspond to 'different kinds of life experience . . . to the manifold conditions and forms of the spiritual' and to different social tasks and individual interests . . . They are joined by representatives of the Realschulen, who, fearing future reintegration of their thriving institutions in a common secondary stage, resist reforms, relying on the support of organized industry and trade. The universities, as institutions, have without exception rejected reforms which aimed at changing the existing nine-grade Gymnasium structure, and parents' organizations have joined them." Robinsohn and Kuhlmann, "Two Decades," p. 324.

15. *Ibid.*, p. 325.
16. *Ibid.*, p. 325, n.54.
17. *Ibid.*, pp. 326f.
18. For specifics of the two plans see *Education in Germany* – 1968, No. 10, for the Evers Plan and 1969, No. 1, for the Martin Plan. Five years earlier a third West German party, the Free Democratic Party (FDP), though it represented only about 10 percent of the electorate, also began its support of the comprehensive secondary school and universities.
19. *Education in Germany*, 1969, No. 1, pp. 3–12.
20. As of 1969 there were few schools of the two-year higher technical school type. North-Rhine-Westphalia has begun a trial of prototype models.
21. The following description of the Structural Plan is drawn from *Education in Germany*, 1970, No. 4. For the quotation, see pp. 2f.
22. *Ibid.*, p. 12.
23. *Ibid.*, p. 16.
24. *Ibid.*, p. 18.
25. *Ibid.*
26. *Ibid.*, p. 5.
27. *Ibid.*, pp. 20f.
28. For a history see Rolland G. Paulston, *Educational Change in Sweden: Planning and Accepting the Comprehensive School Reforms* (New York: Teachers College Press, 1968).
29. The following material on the five objectives is drawn from *Educational Policy and Planning in Sweden*, in the series Educational Investment and Planning Programme (Paris: OECD, Directorate for Scientific Affairs, 1966), pp. 24–27.
30. Objective 1 reads: "All Swedes of school age (1) should enjoy an equal right to public education, without regard to income, social origin, sex or place of residence. And since all individuals are 'born equal' and are endowed with talents and personality potentials that differ but are in all cases capable of development: (a) the aim of the school system should be to meet the differentiated needs of various groups of students; and (b) no one branch of education should in itself be considered more worthy of esteem than any other, the entire school system constituting a co-ordinated whole." (*Ibid.*, pp. 24f.)
31. *Ibid.*, p. 25, but see also p. 28 and Appendix II.
32. For the figures given here, see Alan Little and Denis Kallen, "Western European Secondary School Systems and Higher Education," *Comparative Education*, Vol. 4 (March 1968), pp. 152, 148, 137 respectively.

33. "I know a student who . . ." or "the class I taught evidenced . . ." are what is meant by a too limited experience. Husén's publication is *International Study of Achievement in Mathematics: A Comparison of Twelve Countries*, 2 vols. (New York: Wiley, 1967).
34. Husén, "Educational Structure and the Development of Ability," in *Ability and Educational Opportunity* (OECD, 1961), p. 113.
35. Husén, "The Relation between Selectivity and Social Class in Secondary Education," *International Journal of Educational Science*, Vol. 1 (1966), pp. 17–27. (Reprinted by Pergamon Press, 1966.) In the United States about half of the 18–21 age group is in higher education, whereas Western Europe admits less than 10 percent. For a thorough study of admission to higher education the world over, see Frank Bowles, ed., *Access to Higher Education*, 2 vols. (Paris: UNESCO and the International Association of Universities, 1963, 1965).
36. Husén, "The Relation," pp. 20, 24. "It should be borne in mind when interpreting the results that standard tests serve the teacher as 'calibrating instruments,' whose readings give him an idea of how his class stands in relation to a nationally representative group. The level of marks is adjusted with reference to the outcome of such a comparison. This means that the tests do not affect the marking of the individual pupil in principle, but do so indirectly by virtue of the pupil's standing in the class."
37. Husén, "A Case Study in Policy-Oriented Research: The Swedish School Reforms," *School Review*, Vol. 73 (Autumn 1965), p. 214. See also his *Problems of Differentiation in Swedish Compulsory Schooling* (Stockholm: Svenska Bokforlaget, 1962), p. 58, where Husén generalizes on the measurement of the "theoretical factors" and "intelligence." The "theoretical factors," in contrast to the "practical," Husén writes, "can be defined as the ability to operate with symbols — scientists, lawyers, politicians, engineers, etc. — the masters of modern society. All the tests we use in order to measure some sort of intelligence are validated against proficiency criteria, such as success at school or success in a vocation. These criteria are mostly formalized subjective appraisals. However remote it thus appears at first glance, the instruments of intelligence testing are heavily freighted with values. In this connection, the most important aspect of intelligence is a necessary prerequisite for a successful career in general education. And since general education is a necessary prerequisite for a specialized education, good verbal ability is an important prerequisite for occupational success."
38. Hesén, "A Case Study," p. 214.
39. See particularly Kjell Härnqvist, "Indivuella Differenser och Skoldifferenser," *Ars Skolberedning II* (Stockholm: Statens Offentliga Utredninger, 1960, No. 13).
40. *Educational Policy and Planning in Sweden*, p. 36. "Corresponding results have been reported from an interesting American study concluded in 1960 in the city of New York and covering 86 classes with 2,200 pupils in ages roughly corresponding to our grades 5–7."
41. *Ibid.*, p. 37.
42. *Ibid.*
43. *Ibid.*, p. 14.
44. See *ibid.*, pp. 199ff.
45. On rolling reform see *ibid.*, Chap. 10, especially pp. 314ff.
46. *Ibid.*, pp. 201ff.
47. *Ibid.* and pp. 316ff.
48. "There are in Sweden at present seven research institutes in the psychology of education. Three of these are attached to specialized colleges of education, and four to universities. The research institutes at the colleges of education have as their primary function the performance of research directly concerned with teaching methods and other school problems. During their brief existence, they have accomplished a considerable amount of significant research and have also provided training in re-

search. At the university institutes, research is not concerned with school problems alone; other fields of enquiry have also been explored. This largely fundamental research is of course necessary as background for applied research and development work. The university institutes also play an important role in the training of research workers." *Educational Policy and Planning in Sweden*, p. 320.

49. Little and Kallen, "Western European Secondary School Systems," pp. 140f, 142ff; *Educational Policy and Planning in Sweden*, Chap. 5.

50. *Educational Policy and Planning in Sweden*, pp. 32f.

51. *Ibid.*, pp. 74ff.

52. *Ibid.*, pp. 135ff.

53. This is perhaps the least promising of Swedish reforms of education. Preschool children are looked after by the Social Welfare Authority, not the National Board of Education. This suggests a lack of consideration for the importance of preschool education. As the United States has learned, the preschool period is most important for children whose parents either are too poor to afford books, magazines, or even newspapers, or lack the motivation to do so. These children can be helped to develop an ability to profit from reading. Research repeatedly has demonstrated that children repeat the lower grades mainly because they cannot read. Inasmuch as this failure affects the estimate a child forms of himself, an estimate not easily corrected in the direction of realism, it is difficult to understand any neglect of the preschool years, particularly in a society where the development of all individuals has been highly regarded and where the economic potential of schooling has been appreciated. The latter is not exhausted by consideration for the labor mothers can contribute, if they can leave their young children with an able custodian. *Educational Policy and Planning in Sweden*, Appendix I.

54. *Ibid.*, pp. 221ff.

55. For a discussion of some of the economic aspects of education development of special concern to European educators, see Philip H. Coombs's essay in *Some Economic Aspects of Educational Development in Europe* (Paris: International Universities Bureau, 1961).

56. T. W. Schultz, "Capital Formation by Education," *Journal of Political Economy*, Vol. 67 (December 1960), No. 6. See also A. H. Halsey, "A Review of the Conference," in *Ability and Educational Opportunity*, p. 22. It is a mistake, however, to regard education as a panacea for a country's problems. There are other factors involved.

57. Jean Floud, "Social Class Factors in Educational Achievement," in *Ability and Educational Opportunity*, p. 91.

58. Behind the 1960 establishment of the MRP lies the "idea of establishing a kind of quantitative relationship between education and economic growth, in other words, the notion that it is possible broadly to ascertain the investments in education required for achieving specified economic objectives." This attempt is based on the "growing realization that education and training, as well as the volume of labour and the amount of physical capital, are an important factor in economic growth. In fact, recent economic research has shown that increases in the input of labour and of physical capital leave a substantial portion of economic growth unaccounted for, thus giving rise to the concept of 'the third factor' of production, in which education is presumed to be an important element."

It is too soon to know what impact the MRP has had, and the target date of 1975 will come too quickly. Even if that impact turns out to be less than is hoped — perhaps because the recommendations were not fully carried out — the principal idea that education is important to economic and therefore social development will not be disproved. In fact, something very like the MRP would be useful for other countries. The MRP capitalized on the ideological stand and the psychological and sociological research that had been connected with the profound reforms of education in other European countries. These reforms were necessary preconditions for the MRP.

196

For example, it was much easier for Turkey to undertake changes in education when France had provided a model on a new system of instruction at all levels of education. French education has had great prestige in both Greece and Turkey.

The MRP has been uniquely related to the study of harmonization of European education. Yugoslavia represents changes common to all Europe: the lessening of illiteracy rates, the expansion of all forms of secondary education; the raising of the status of secondary-school technical education; the enlarging of higher education, especially in the science-engineering faculties; the increasing demand for education; and the hiring of more teachers. But the commonality of problems has been less important, surely, than the commonality of reform effort. Perhaps a more political sponsorship of the MRP would have prevented cooperation between Eastern and Western Europe, but a beginning was made in the more neutral territory of economics. Whatever the reason, the MRP is a study of integration within Europe and the Atlantic community.

For an overview of the project see *An Experiment in Planning by Six Countries*, in the series Country Reports, the Mediterranean Regional Project (OECD, 1965). Separate monographs report the findings of teams operating in Portugal, Spain, Italy, Greece, Turkey, and Yugoslavia, all members of the MRP. On manpower economics as worked out in the MRP, see Herbert S. Parnes, *Forecasting Educational Needs for Economic and Social Development*, in the series Mediterranean Regional Project (Paris: OECD, 1962).

59. European nations differ in the agencies that are involved in national planning. In Sweden, as we have seen, because the committee (Royal Commissions) system has been so important (*Educational Policy and Planning in Sweden*, pp. 298ff.), the planning that has resulted from committee recommendation is not to be overlooked. More formal planning of education has been done by such a body as the National Labour Market Board (*ibid.*, pp. 307f.), which has an employment office, industrial location office, and vocational guidance service. The use of statistical theory and techniques has become very much a part of these forecasts in Sweden and elsewhere. No doubt the most specialized educational planning agency is the Swedish Educational Planning Council in the Ministry of Education. The council "advises on questions involving the objectives, the functioning and the organization of the educational system." (*Ibid.*, p. 308.)

Long-range perspectives have not had a long history in any country of Western Europe. Perhaps the first in Western Europe, certainly the first in Sweden, was drawn up in 1947, in connection with the Marshall Plan. On later Swedish long-term planning, see *ibid.*, p. 346.

60. *Ibid.*, p. 344.

61. *Ibid.*, p. 13.

INDEX

Index

Abendgymnasium, 68
Ability, 112, 144, 147, 184nl, 186n30:
  and academic elite, 87–89, 96; extent
  of, 87–90, 147–48; measurement of,
  90–91, 92, 96, 195n37; and differentiation, 90, 155, 156; and social
  classes, 91–95, 96, 185n12, 186n25;
  and leaving examinations, 94; realization of, 100, 162, 187n34
Abitur, 68, 94, 106, 140, 143, 173n39:
  Franco-German, 7; Abitur I and II,
  151, 173n39. *See also* Secondary-
  school leaving examination
Abusch, Alexander, 38
Academic curriculum, 11, 12, 102, 111,
  125,136: trends in, 114; subjects of,
  116–17, 119–21; and polytechnical
  education, 118–19
Academic elite, 87–89, 96, 139
Academic guidance, 102, 108–14, 125,
  139
Academy of Pedagogical Sciences
  (USSR), 34, 121–22
Adult education, 6, 100, 160
Agazzi, Aldo, 16
Agenor, 169, 177n16
Aristotle, 88, 89
Audric, John, 6, 7
Austria, 15, 30, 50, 53, 57–58, 80, 114,
  116, 121: school drop-outs in, 59,
  180n24; multilateral school system
  of, 70, 108; educational opportunities
  in, 77

Baccalauréat, 15, 94, 99, 110–11, 133.
  See also Secondary-school leaving
  examination
Belgium, 8, 18, 27, 28, 30, 68, 120: linguistic conflicts in, 24, 40–41; guid-

ance programs in, 108, 113; technical
  training in, 128
Berufsfachschule, 131, 140, 143, 145,
  191n18
Berufsschule, 131, 132, 143, 144, 191n18
Bowles, Frank, 63, 126, 128
Braham, Randolph, 37, 38
Bremer Plan, 147
Brinkmann, Gerhard, 173n39
British Schools Council, 122
Bruges, Belgium, 31, 32, 33
Brugmans, Henri, 30, 32, 33
Bruley, Edouard, 17, 20, 50
Bulgaria, 36–37
Bureau d'Information des Communautés
  Européennes, 29
Bureau International des Ecoles Nou-
  velles, 115
Butler Act, 129, 151

Canada, 50, 53, 108, 109, 118, 123, 129,
  149
Capdecomme, Laurent, 5, 83
Cavazza, Fabio, 63, 77, 78
Centre Européenne de la Culture, 31, 33
Civicis studies, 20, 21, 117, 175n60
Class, social: and education, 63, 69–78,
  91–95, 96, 98–100, 103, 104–5, 139,
  143–44, 148, 154–55, 181n29, 185n13
College of Europe, 24, 29, 43, 177n30:
  history of, 30–31; organization of, 32,
  33
Compagnons, Les, 105, 113, 188n3
Comparative Education Society in Europe, 24, 33–34, 35, 43
Comprehensive school system, 44, 46,
  108, 125, 149, 184nl, 189n21: and
  differentiation, 45; in Sweden, 91, 96–
  97, 105, 107, 135, 153, 154–55, 157,

Leaving examination. *See* Secondary-
school leaving examination
Leclerq, Jean, 11
Lenin, Nikolai, 37
Lesguillons, H., 26
Leussink, Hans, 149
Lietz, Herman, 114, 115
Lindsay, M., 32
Little, Alan, 59, 68, 70, 100
Luxembourg, 8, 30, 116
Lycée, 62, 110, 130, 133, 144, 193n6

Madariaga, Salvador de, 30, 31, 32, 33
Maes, L. Th., 18
Majault, Joseph, 124–25
Makarenko, A. S., 36
Marchant, E. C., 17
Martin, Berthold, 148–49
Martin Plan, 148, 149
Marx, Karl, 37
Mathematics studies, 12, 13, 23
Max-Planck-Gesellschaft, 121
Mediterranean Regional Project (MRP),
49, 161, 196n58
Moderne (*type court*), 131, 191n12
Moreau, Jean, 29
Müller, K. V., 147
Multilateral school system, 96, 97, 98,
108, 114, 142: and differentiation, 45,
105; and academic elite, 88; decline
of, 102
Murat, John, 10

National Institute of Adult Education, 5
Netherlands, 8, 27, 29, 44, 49, 55, 59–
60, 63, 108, 117, 123, 128, 134
New Education, The, 114–15, 190n25
Norway, 24, 30, 40, 42, 107–8, 114, 116,
128–29

Occupation classification, 131–33
Odenwaldschule, 114, 115, 190n30
Office Franco-Allemand pour la Jeunesse, 7
Organization for Economic Co-operation and Development (OECD), 5, 45,
46, 49, 50, 53, 56, 179n21: primary
concern of, 4; educational planning
of, 48; comments on enrollment projections, 60–61; publications of, 168–
69; official languages of, 173n35
Orring, J., 156
Ourisson, Guy, 11

Parnes, Herbert, 130

Pestalozzi, J. H., 117
Piaget, Jean, 123
Plan Europe 2000, 26
Planning, educational, 38–40, 48–50,
160–61, 162–63, 196n58, 197n59
Plato, 88, 89, 185n4
Poland, 34, 35, 63–64, 67, 72, 98–99,
178n36, 187n39
Polytechnization, 43, 125: and educa-
tion in Eastern Europe, 35, 37–38,
118–19
Population explosion: and education,
50–51, 61, 64
Portugal, 44, 49, 50, 56, 57, 161, 179n21,
197n58
Preschool education, 196n53
Primary education, 6, 7, 44–45, 56, 96,
116, 124, 125

Quignard, Jacques, 175n68

Rahmenplan, 146–47
Ratuszniak, Z., 63, 98, 99
Realschule, 104, 106, 131, 140, 144, 145,
146, 181n22, 189n7, 189n8, 191n12
Realskola, 91, 153, 156
Reguzzoni, Mario, 78, 100, 105
Retinger, Joseph, 31
Reuchlin, Maurice, 111
Robbins report, 92, 95, 98, 124
Robinsohn, Saul B., 69, 71, 105, 114,
143, 145, 146, 168
Rosen, Seymour, 38
Rosier, Y., 50, 52
Rotten, Elizabeth, 115
Rougemont, Denis de. *See* De Rouge-
mont, Denis
Rudman, Herbert, 49
Rumania, 34, 37

Sandys, Duncan, 32
Sartre, Jean-Paul, 183n59
Schüddekopf, Otto-Ernst, 18, 19
Schultz, T. W., 160
Schulze, Walter, 168
Schwartz, Bertrand, 21
Sciences, in curriculum, 119–21
Scotland, 44
Secondary education: language instruc-
tion in, 6, 116; mathematics instruc-
tion in, 12–13; demand for, 44, 45,
50, 55–56, 60, 61; definition of, 45;
expansion of, 46, 47, 50–51, 53, 56;
and educational opportunities, 46, 47;
in Great Britain, 47, 92–93, 97; en-